Beginning Web Development with Perl

From Novice to Professional

Steve Suehring

Apress®

Beginning Web Development with Perl: From Novice to Professional

Copyright © 2006 by Steve Suehring

ISBN (pbk): 1-59059-531-9

Printed and bound in the United States of America 9 8 7 6 5 4 3 2 1

Lead Editor: Ewan Buckingham
Technical Reviewer: James Lee
Editorial Board: Steve Anglin, Dan Appleman, Ewan Buckingham, Gary Cornell, Tony Davis, Jason Gilmore,
    Jonathan Hassell, Chris Mills, Dominic Shakeshaft, Jim Sumser
Project Managers: Laura Cheu, Richard Dal Porto
Copy Editors: Marilyn Smith, Nicole LeClerc
Assistant Production Director: Kari Brooks-Copony
Production Editor: Ellie Fountain
Compositor: Kinetic Publishing Services, LLC
Proofreader: Lori Bring
Indexer: Rebecca Plunkett
Cover Designer: Kurt Krames
Manufacturing Director: Tom Debolski

Distributed to the book trade worldwide by Springer-Verlag New York, Inc., 233 Spring Street, 6th Floor, New York, NY 10013. Phone 1-800-SPRINGER, fax 201-348-4505, e-mail orders-ny@springer-sbm.com, or visit http://www.springeronline.com.

For information on translations, please contact Apress directly at 2560 Ninth Street, Suite 219, Berkeley, CA 94710. Phone 510-549-5930, fax 510-549-5939, e-mail info@apress.com, or visit http://www.apress.com.

The source code for this book is available to readers at http://www.apress.com in the Source Code section.

Contents at a Glance

Naga Shannugu

PART 5 ■ ■ ■ Creating Web Templates

Contents

PART 1 ■ ■ ■ CGI Development with Perl

PART 2 ■ ■ ■ Internet Interaction with LWP and Net:: Tools

PART 3 ■■■ XML and RSS

■CHAPTER 8   Perl and RSS 153

■CHAPTER 9   XML Parsing with Perl 165

PART 4 ■ ■ ■ Performance Enhancement with mod_perl

■CHAPTER 10   Apache and mod_perl 183

PART 5 ■ ■ ■ Creating Web Templates

About the Author

STEVE SUEHRING is a technology architect with a diverse set of skills. Steve works with a wide array of technologies, from mainframe OS/390 to Microsoft Windows to several distributions of Linux. Steve has written a book on MySQL, a book on Linux firewalls, and numerous magazine articles. During his tenure as an editor for *LinuxWorld Magazine,* Steve focused on advocacy of Linux and open-source software, as well as computer security. Among the articles Steve wrote for *LinuxWorld Magazine* is a cover story featuring the WilliamsF1 team's use of Linux to design their Formula 1 car. Steve is also a Cisco Certified Network Professional (CCNP).

About the Technical Reviewer

JAMES LEE is a hacker and open-source advocate based in Illinois. He has a master's degree from Northwestern University, where he can often be seen rooting for the Wildcats during football season. The founder of Onsight (http://www.onsight.com), he has worked as a programmer, trainer, manager, writer, and open-source advocate. He is the coauthor of the recently released *Hacking Linux Exposed, Second Edition* (Osbourne/McGraw-Hill, 2002). He has also written a number of articles on Perl for *Linux Journal*. Lee enjoys hacking Perl, developing software for the Web, reading, traveling, and most of all playing with his kids, who are too young to know why Dad's favorite animals are penguins and camels.

Acknowledgments

Thanks to James Lee for the excellent technical review assistance, and thanks to the entire Apress staff. Thanks to Laura Lewin and Studio B. Many thanks to everyone who helped with this or other projects that I've worked on, not only in 2005 but throughout the years. This list is always difficult but should include Jim, John, Jer, Chris, Ron, Andy, Jay, Brian, Michael, Dan, Justin, Sarah, AJ, Denise, Rob, Tim, Greg, Jeff, Aaron, Scott, Karla, Chad, Jess, Roman, Caele, Makenna, Tony, Joe, Rebecca, Tom, Kevin, Keith, Brooke, Nick, Colin, Bob, Mary, Sue, Sandi, Amy, Chris, Emily, Mike, Sandy, Ernie, Vera, Matthew, Kyle, Eric, Erich, Erin, Heather, Nate, Brandon, Maya, Deb, Steve, Jaci, JJ, Dave, Sam, Ed, Mike, Al, Neil, Geddy, Alex, Bill, Pearl, Moff, Duff, Jason, Mark, Michelle, Tara, Al, Spencer, Pat, Nicole, Jill, and everyone else that I'm forgetting.

My hope is that by using mostly first names everyone will think that I'm thanking them personally, and I am, of course.

Introduction

This is a book about Perl, the programming language. More specifically, this is a book about some aspects of Perl interacting with the Internet. The book includes coverage of CGI through the Perl CGI.pm module, as well as much additional information. You'll explore such topics as how to send e-mail from a Perl program through Net::SMTP, how to use Net::DNS, and even how to use Net::Ping. You'll learn how to build a templated web site two different ways, one with the help of HTML::Mason and the other with the Template Toolkit. You'll learn how to consume SOAP web services, how to read and write RSS, and how to work with XML, all through Perl.

What This Book Covers

This book attempts to give readers who have learned some Perl a grasp of the concepts and considerations for programming for the Web or creating a Perl program that interacts with the network. This book is fairly Linux-centric. That's not to say that these programs won't run on a Windows platform—they will, with very little tweaking.

The book is divided into five parts. The first part covers what comes to mind for many people when they think of Perl and web development—namely, CGI development and database interaction. The CGI module is examined, and I present tips for programming CGIs, such as the Carp module for debugging. The second part of the book widens the focus into Internet interaction with Perl. The Net:: family of modules is covered, along with the LWP for retrieving web pages through Perl. Coverage of XML and RSS make up the third part of the book, where you'll learn about XML parsing through Perl, consumption of SOAP web services, and RSS feeds. The fourth part of the book looks at mod_perl for development. The fifth and final part of the book examines templating through the Template Toolkit and HTML::Mason.

What You Should Know

To use this book successfully, you'll need to know about Perl basics such as scalar variables, arrays, and hashes; the use of control structures such as if/else, for, and while; and other topics such as those you'd find in a book like *Beginning Perl, Second Edition* (Apress, 2004). Essentially, you should be comfortable with Perl before reading this book. You should also know how to install Perl modules, whether through your distribution's mechanism, such as apt for Debian, or through the use of CPAN. The book's appendix is an excerpt from the aforementioned *Beginning Perl* title. If you haven't used Perl in a while, the appendix can provide a good refresher into the language, but you'll find that reading the entire *Beginning Perl* book will be helpful to pick up where the appendix leaves off.

This book will use Perl on a Linux system. The exact flavor of Linux isn't important, though I likely have some references to Debian. Perl being Perl means that the programs will run successfully with little modification on any system that can run Apache, including Microsoft Windows.

Why Apache?

Simply put, Apache works. Apache is overwhelmingly the most popular web server in use on the Internet, according to the Netcraft survey (`http://news.netcraft.com/archives/web_server_survey.html`). Apache is open source and configurable for just about any need. Apache is stable and predictable, even under heavy load. Apache is robust, serving web without using too many resources, and it's able to use resources effectively to serve heavy traffic loads.

This is not to say that Microsoft's IIS hasn't made good strides toward meeting its competition in Apache. IIS has indeed improved its stability with version 6, but with the benchmark being IIS 5 and its predecessors, it didn't take much to improve on the stability. However, IIS is still not as good as Apache at serving web and has a long way to go before getting there.

PART 1

###

CGI Development with Perl

## CHAPTER 1

The CGI Module

The CGI module is central to web development with Perl. In fact, the CGI module is as far as some people go with Perl web development. However, there's more to Perl for the Web than just CGI. You have endless ways to interact with the Internet from a Perl program. This book will show you many of those methods. Even so, the CGI module is a good place to start.

In this chapter, you'll learn the basics of Perl-based CGI application development, including how to use both the function-oriented and object-oriented styles, some of the functions offered by the CGI module, how to use environment variables, tips for debugging and troubleshooting CGI applications, and the all-important security considerations. Let's begin with an introduction to CGI.

An Overview of CGI

CGI, or Common Gateway Interface, is a standard of communication between a web server and a client, such as a user with a web browser. Over time, CGI has come to refer to a class of programs that work with web servers. The programs themselves are considered to be external or separate from the web servers, but they provide a gateway between the client and server—thus the Gateway portion of the name Common Gateway Interface.

CGI is a standard unto itself. The current standard provides a common interface, which means that CGI programs can be written in a number of languages. Of the languages with which a CGI program can be written, Perl is arguably the most common.

Perl provides an easy-to-use syntax with a gently sloped learning curve. Yet Perl, along with its myriad modules, is incredibly powerful and robust. The Apache web server, which is usually run on Unix/Linux, continues to hold the dominant market share over all web servers on the Internet.[1] Perl is also very common on these same Unix/Linux systems. Being available and powerful leads to the ubiquity of Perl for CGI development.

Note If you're unfamiliar with Perl, please flip to this book's appendix for an overview of the language. In that appendix, you'll find excerpts from *Beginning Perl, Second Edition* by James Lee (Apress, 2004). I recommend picking up a copy of *Beginning Perl* for a full introduction to the language.

---

1. The surveys conducted by Netcraft (http://news.netcraft.com/archives/web_server_survey.html) confirm this fact.

For quite a long time (in Internet time), CGIs were frequently developed with help from a library called cgi-lib.pl. The CGI library, or cgi-lib, was a function-oriented way to simplify development of CGI programs in Perl. A developer could use the common functions of the library, rather than needing to rewrite those functions from scratch. The cgi-lib also enabled developers with less experience to write very powerful applications to interact with the Web.

As the Internet grew, so did the needs of Perl-based CGI developers. The CGI module, referred to as CGI.pm after the name of the module file itself, gives developers a very powerful interface to common CGI writing tasks. CGI.pm became available with Perl 5.

CGI.pm can be used both in the function-oriented approach of cgi-lib and also in an object-oriented fashion, allowing developers to use more than one CGI object within their program. The main difference between the two approaches is the way in which you call methods. With the function-oriented approach, you must call each method during the declaration of the CGI module. The object-oriented approach makes these methods available to you, regardless of whether you explicitly specify that they should be included in the program beforehand.

When using the CGI module in a function-oriented fashion, you can choose to import only the individual methods that you'll be using, or you can import just those functions within predefined logical groupings of methods. CGI.pm currently has several such groupings, as shown in Table 1-1. You'll see how to use these methods later in the chapter.

Table 1-1. *CGI.pm Method Groupings*

Group	Description
:all	Contains all of the methods available in the CGI.pm module
:cgi	Contains methods specific to the CGI protocol
:form	Contains methods used to generate forms
:html	A superset of the :html2, :html3, :html4, and :netscape groups
:html2	Contains methods that enable the developer to quickly use elements from the HTML version 2 specification
:html3	Like the :html2 group, contains methods that enable the developer to quickly use elements from the HTML version 3 specification
:html4	Contains methods that enable the developer to quickly use elements from the HTML version 4 specification
:netscape	Contains the Netscape extensions for the HTML 3 specification, including a shortcut to my favorite HTML tag <BLINK>
:multipart	Contains methods used to help work with MIME types
:standard	Probably the most frequently used group of methods, a superset of the :html2, :html3, :html4, :form, and :cgi groups

What You Need for This Chapter

The examples in this chapter use version 3.04 of CGI.pm on a Linux-based Apache (version 1.3.N) server. Even though Apache 2 has been released, the 1.3 branch is stable and quite common as of this writing. The 1.3 branch is also easier to work with for beginners, making it a good choice for this book. However, the routines in this chapter should work on many different versions of Apache or another CGI-compliant web server, and with different versions of the CGI.pm module as well. You can always obtain the latest version of CGI.pm from http://search.cpan.org/dist/CGI.pm/.

You'll also need to be able to execute CGI programs on your web server of choice. For example, on an Apache server, you would need a directive such as this:

```
Options ExecCGI
```

Any CGI testing performed must be done from a directory that has the ExecCGI option enabled in Apache.[2]

Although it's obvious (I hope), I'll point out that you'll need Perl on your system. You'll also need to know where Perl is located on the system. Perl is usually located in /usr/bin, but it's sometimes found in /usr/local/bin or elsewhere. When in doubt, use the which command to find the Perl interpreter:

```
% which perl
```

The system will respond with the first instance of Perl in its search path. In this case, my system happened to respond with this:

```
/usr/local/bin/perl
```

This was somewhat confusing to me, since I know that Perl is installed on this system in /usr/bin/perl as well. Looking at /usr/local/bin/perl revealed that it's merely a symbolic link[3] to the real Perl in /usr/bin:

```
% ls -la /usr/local/bin/perl
lrwxrwxrwx 1 root staff 13 Feb 24 2002 /usr/local/bin/perl -> /usr/bin/perl
```

Hello World, CGI Style

Before going too far, and to assist in testing your CGI environment, the requisite "Hello World" example is now provided. I'll show you how to create this example using both the function-oriented approach and the object-oriented approach, to highlight the basic differences between the two methods.

Function-Oriented Hello World

As I stated previously, the function-oriented method requires that the developer explicitly call or import the desired functions into their program. This is sometimes done by importing the method groups rather than the individual methods themselves. Recall the method groups listed in Table 1-1.

---

2. For more information about setting up Apache for CGI, see the Apache documentation at http://httpd.apache.org/docs/howto/cgi.html.
3. Now, if I could only remember why I created that symbolic link back in 2002. The joys of system administration on a long-lived system never cease to amaze.

The most common method grouping that I've seen used in practice is the `:standard` group. This method group contains the most frequently used methods, including those that make it easy to create and use of web forms, as well as the HTML that surrounds those forms. You'll use the `:standard` group in this first Hello World example.

■Caution New developers may be tempted to use the `:all` group of methods in `CGI.pm`. However, doing so can create a security risk, since unnecessary methods are imported into your namespace. It's a good idea to use only those methods that are necessary for the functionality of your program. The `:standard` group provides a good compromise in the never-ending battle between security and complexity.

Creating the Script

The function-oriented method of CGI development allows you to rapidly develop small CGI scripts. Using the function-oriented method, the individual methods within the script can be called directly, rather than creating an object through which to call the methods, which can add overhead during development. This makes creation of the first script rather trivial, but it should give you a taste for a few of the functions involved when developing a CGI. The code in Listing 1-1 shows a Hello World script written using the function-oriented approach.

Listing 1-1. *Hello World in Function-Oriented Fashion*

```
#!/usr/bin/perl -T

use strict;
use CGI ':standard';

print header;
print start_html('Hello World');
print h1('Hello World');
print end_html();

exit;
```

You can place this code in your favorite text editor and save it to a location defined to run CGI scripts within your web server. For example, I saved this script as `hello.cgi` in the directory `/usr/lib/cgi-bin` on a server running Debian 3.0.

Don't forget that the CGI will need the correct permissions in order to run. This can usually be accomplished with the `chmod 755 <scriptname.cgi>` command:

```
chmod 755 /usr/lib/cgi-bin/hello.cgi
```

To view the code in a web browser, point the browser to the URL of the CGI script. For example, my script is on a server at the IP address 192.168.1.10. Combining the server address plus the aliased script location results in the following URL:

```
http://192.168.1.10/cgi-bin/hello.cgi
```

Obviously, the URL for your server will likely vary from this example. If all goes well, you should see a page similar to that in Figure 1-1. If all doesn't go well, skip ahead to the "Debugging and Troubleshooting" section of this chapter.

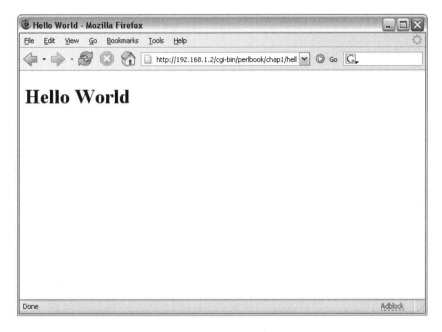

Figure 1-1. *The Hello World example viewed in a web browser*

That's all there is to programming your first CGI script. Of course, if that's all there truly were to the Perl CGI module, this book wouldn't be as thick. In the upcoming chapters, I'll expand on the CGI module to show you how to use it to interact with web forms and build applications.

Reviewing the Code

In Listing 1-1, you see the standard invocation of the perl interpreter #!/usr/bin/perl. However, there is also a -T option added to the invocation:

```
#!/usr/bin/perl -T
```

Refer to the "Security Considerations with CGI Programs" section later in this chapter for more information about the -T option. For now, just be happy that it's there.

The next line of code enables strict checking for the script:

```
use strict;
```

Like the -T option, the strict directive has to do with security, and it's explained in "Security Considerations with CGI Programs" section later in this chapter. This line will show up in every script in this chapter.

Following use strict; is the code that actually calls the CGI.pm module, and more specifically, calls the :standard method group of the CGI.pm module.

```
use CGI ':standard';
```

You may see this method group call made using the qw() operator, like this:

```
use CGI qw(:standard);
```

or

```
use CGI qw/:standard/;
```

The qw() operator is a *quote* operator that separates the given string into individual elements based on white space. All of these calls (and others using qw) are valid and essentially result in the same thing, which is the :standard method group being called. Perl has a number of quote and quote-like characters, aside from qw(). For more information about these, and all of the other Perl operators, see the perlop documentation (http://perldoc.perl.org/perlop.html).

Four functions of the CGI module are used in this script, as shown here:

```
print header;
print start_html('Hello World');
print h1('Hello World');
print end_html();
```

The first function, header(), sends the Content-Type to the browser. In this instance, the header() function is equivalent to using this bit of code in the script (see Chapter 5 for more information about the Content-Type and why the extra newline is present):

```
print "Content-Type: text/html\n\n";
```

The header() function can also be used for other HTTP headers, such as cookies.

The next CGI function used is start_html(). This function begins the HTML portion of the page with elements like <title>, <html>, <head>, and so on. In this instance, the script calls the start_html() function with a string parameter 'Hello World'. As you saw in Figure 1-1, this parameter was placed into the title bar of the web browser.

Another CGI function called in this script is h1(). This function places an <h1> element around its parameter. In this case, the parameter passed is 'Hello World', and as you saw from the results in Figure 1-1, the phrase "Hello World" was indeed given <h1> size. Finally, the end_html() function is called to provide the </body> and </html> closing tags.

The code in the example uses a semicolon (;) to end each line and then another print statement to begin the next line. This was done to make the code easier to read. However, it's quite common to use a comma in place of the semicolon when programming a CGI application, so the code would look like this:

```
#!/usr/bin/perl -T

use strict;
use CGI ':standard';

print header,
   start_html('Hello World'),
```

```
  h1('Hello World'),
  end_html();
```

```
exit;
```

This code is functionally equivalent to the form in Listing 1-1, but it does save some keystrokes.

Object-Oriented Hello World

When programming CGI applications in object-oriented fashion, you must instantiate a new CGI object. This effectively means that you can use multiple CGI objects within the program.

Creating the Script

The object-oriented Hello World script, presented in Listing 1-2, uses only one CGI object. In fact, it's not all that common to use more than one CGI object within most CGI programs.

Listing 1-2. *Hello World in Object-Oriented Fashion*

```
#!/usr/bin/perl -T

use strict;
use CGI;

my $cgi = new CGI;

print $cgi->header;
print $cgi->start_html('Hello World');
print $cgi->h1('Hello World');
print $cgi->end_html();

exit;
```

Like the code in the function-oriented example, you can place Listing 1-2 in your favorite text editor and save it to a location defined to run CGI scripts within your web server. For example, I saved this script as hello-oo.cgi (the oo stands for object-oriented—how clever) into the directory /usr/lib/cgi-bin on a server running Debian 3.0. Again, remember that the CGI will need the correct permissions in order to run, which is usually accomplished with the chmod 755 <*scriptname*.cgi> command, as in this example:

```
chmod 755 /usr/lib/cgi-bin/hello-oo.cgi
```

To view the code in a web browser, point your browser to the URL of the CGI script, as in this example, for my server with the IP address 192.168.1.10:

```
http://192.168.1.10/cgi-bin/hello-oo.cgi
```

You should see a page similar to that in Figure 1-2. Again, see the "Debugging and Troubleshooting" section later in this chapter if you have problems with the script.

Figure 1-2. *The object-oriented Hello World example viewed in a web browser*

Reviewing the Code

If you think that the code for hello-oo.cgi looks eerily similar to the hello.cgi code, you're right. The key differences are in how the functions within the CGI module are called in this version.

Recall that in the function-oriented example, the program calls a method grouping, :standard, on the use CGI line. With the object-oriented model, that call is not necessary. Thus, the line is simply written like this:

```
use CGI;
```

The next line is new to the object-oriented approach and is responsible for instantiating the CGI object so that you can call methods within it later. This line of code creates a CGI object called $cgi:

```
my $cgi = new CGI;
```

Note that the script could have used any scalar variable name instead of $cgi. Many examples use $q as a variable name for this CGI object.

The four CGI functions are called next. Notice that these calls look different from the ones in the function-oriented version.

```
print $cgi->header;
print $cgi->start_html('Hello World');
print $cgi->h1('Hello World');
print $cgi->end_html();
```

Each instance of a function call must be called through the CGI object ($cgi) created earlier. Attempting to call one of these functions without qualifying it through the $cgi object will result in an Internal Server Error message.

As with the example in Listing 1-1, the code in the example uses the semicolon format, but the comma format is acceptable and common. In that format, the code looks like this:

```perl
#!/usr/bin/perl -T

use strict;
use CGI;

my $cgi = new CGI;

print $cgi->header,
    $cgi->start_html('Hello World'),
    $cgi->h1('Hello World'),
    $cgi->end_html();

exit;
```

A Closer Look at the CGI.pm Functions

The CGI module has a large number of functions to make the life of the programmer easier. These functions range from those that create HTML tags, HTTP headers, and cookies to those for working with web forms. This section looks at some of the most commonly used functions.

HTML Shortcuts

The HTML functions within the CGI module save time and make the code look cleaner. Without the HTML functions, a CGI program would be forced to include bits of HTML interspersed with Perl, read in external files with HTML, or (more commonly) use a combination of these techniques. This makes the code much more difficult to troubleshoot and debug.

Most of the HTML version 3 and 4 tags are available through a function in the CGI module. Simply calling the HTML function with a print statement will cause it to be sent to the outputted page. Recall the Hello World examples in Listings 1-1 and 1-2. These examples use the h1() function to create an <h1></h1> HTML tag around the phrase "Hello World." Viewing the source from the resulting page shows this HTML:

```
<?xml version="1.0" encoding="utf-8"?>
<!DOCTYPE html
        PUBLIC "-//W3C//DTD XHTML Basic 1.0//EN"
        "http://www.w3.org/TR/xhtml-basic/xhtml-basic10.dtd">
<html xmlns="http://www.w3.org/1999/xhtml" lang="en-US">
<head><title>Hello World</title>
</head><body><h1>Hello World</h1></body></html>
```

The CGI module functions will usually create both the starting and ending HTML tags. However, should you wish to manually create these tags, you can do so by calling the function with start_ or end_ prepended, as in this example:

```
print start_h1;
print "This is some text";
print end_h1;
```

This code produces an opening <h1> tag followed by some text and then a closing </h1> tag. See the CGI module documentation (type perldoc CGI from a terminal window) for more information about HTML element generation.

You can also define your own functions for HTML tags. This allows you to define and call HTML tags that aren't already provided for within the CGI module. For example, suppose that a new HTML tag called <snow> is available in a certain browser, and you want to use it within your CGI program. You only need to define the function, like so:

```
use CGI qw/:standard snow/
```

Then you can call it in the same way that you would call any other HTML function:

```
print snow('Fall');
```

The resulting HTML looks like this:

```
<snow>Fall</snow>
```

Dynamic Pages and Forms

Just as standard HTML elements are available through functions in the CGI module, so are form elements. For example, tags to start and end forms, code for text fields and other input fields, and code for buttons are available as CGI module functions. The syntax for these functions is the same as the syntax for calling HTML tag functions. Consider the code shown in Listing 1-3.

Listing 1-3. *Code to Accept Input with the CGI Module*

```
#!/usr/bin/perl -T

use strict;
use CGI qw/:standard/;

print header,
start_html('Hello'),
start_form,
"Enter your name: ",textfield('name'),
submit,
end_form,
hr,
end_html;

exit;
```

When the code is saved to a web server and viewed through a browser, it should look like Figure 1-3. It looks like a regular form, but don't bother filling in the name and clicking on submit yet. There's no code to handle it!

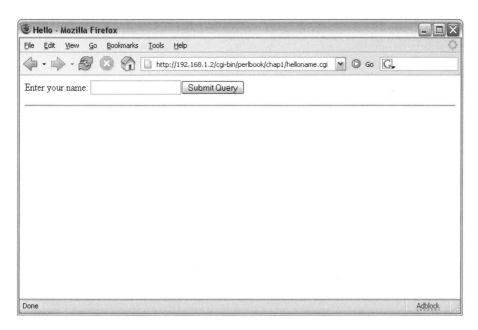

Figure 1-3. *A form created with CGI module functions*

Viewing the source code for the resulting HTML page reveals what this bit of Perl code did in the background:

```
<?xml version="1.0" encoding="utf-8"?>
<!DOCTYPE html
PUBLIC "-//W3C//DTD XHTML Basic 1.0//EN"
"http://www.w3.org/TR/xhtml-basic/xhtml-basic10.dtd">
<html xmlns="http://www.w3.org/1999/xhtml" lang="en-US"><head><title>Hello</title>
</head><body><form method="post" action="/cgi-bin/name.cgi"
enctype="application/x-www-form-urlencoded">
Enter your name: <input type="text" name="name" />
<input type="submit" name=".submit" /></form></body></html>
```

As you can see, the start_form() function inserted a <form> tag into the page. It automatically made the method a POST and set the action to itself—"/cgi-bin/name.cgi", in this case. You could change both of these parameters by providing them within the call to the start_form() function, as in this example:

```
start_form(-method=>'GET',-action=>"/cgi-bin/someothercgi.cgi")
```

The code would then produce a form tag like this:

```
<form method="get" action="/cgi-bin/someothercgi"
enctype="application/x-www-form-urlencoded">
```

However, for this example, leave the form method and action at their defaults (POST and /cgi-bin/name.cgi).

Making the form actually perform some action means that you need to handle parameters within the program. To do so, you can simply check whether the param() function returns true.

```
if (param()) {
#do something
}
```

Listing 1-4 shows a more complete function added to the code shown in Listing 1-3.

Listing 1-4. *Printing the Name Input Using the CGI Module*

```
#!/usr/bin/perl -T

use strict;
use CGI qw/:standard/;

print header,
start_html('Hello'),
start_form,
"Enter your name: ",textfield('name'),
submit,
end_form,
hr;

if (param()) {
  print "Hello ",
  param('name'),
  p;
}

print end_html;

exit;
```

■**Tip** The basic if (param()) type of check is commonly used to determine whether to serve the default page or whether to process the CGI parameters. For example, if there are parameters within param(), then the CGI will output "Hello," along with the value that was filled in for the text field that is contained in param('name').

Update your code on the web server with this new code. Don't forget to click the refresh button in your web browser to ensure that you have the new code within your version of the page. If you fail to reload the page after saving the new code, you won't get the same results as the rest of us.

Now you can fill in your name and click the Submit Query button. If your name is Steve, you'll see the output shown in Figure 1-4.

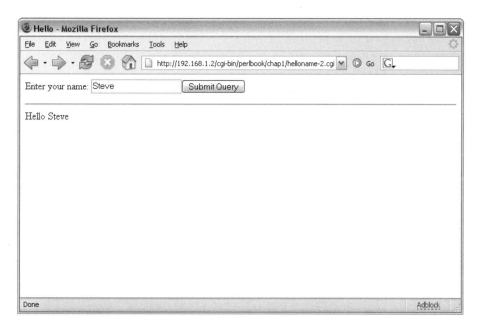

Figure 1-4. *Printing the name based on what was submitted*

Cookies

Cookies are tokens or data sent in the HTTP header. Cookies sometimes reside in volatile memory for the duration of the browser setting and can also be saved as persistent text files on the user's computer. You can use cookies for many reasons, including carrying information about users to enhance their browsing experience. Cookies offer a very useful way to maintain state between visits or during a session.

■**Caution** Cookies are often overused and relied upon unnecessarily. Additionally, some users overestimate the risks of allowing cookies and misunderstand the privacy concerns related to their use. For these reasons, some users will disable cookies in their browsers. Therefore, you shouldn't design an application that relies on cookies for session state or other client-side settings.

The CGI module includes powerful functions to assist in creating and managing browser cookies. Here, I'll show you some examples. But first, let's see what goes into a cookie. (I find it difficult to resist clever but overdone metaphors when writing about cookies; therefore, I'll apologize in advance for some of the titles of the forthcoming sections.)

Cookie Ingredients

Cookies consist of up to the following six parameters:

- *Name*: This is the name of the cookie itself and is the only required parameter for a cookie.

- *Value*: The value of a cookie is an optional item that contains the object or subject of the cookie. In other words, if you have a cookie with a name of sessionid, the value for that sessionid might be 515093028943.

- *Domain*: The domain parameter refers to the Internet domain within which the cookie is valid. Cookies are valid only within the domain in which they are set. For example, as an operator of example.com, you cannot read cookies that are tied to the domain example.net.

- *Secure*: The secure parameter refers to whether or not the cookie will be transmitted over an unsecure connection; that is, a connection that doesn't use SSL. The default for this parameter is off, meaning that cookies can be transmitted over SSL and non-SSL connections alike.

- *Path*: The path parameter further refines the area of the domain in which the cookie is valid. For example, a cookie with a path of /shoppingcart will be sent only to pages below /shoppingcart within the domain. That cookie would be sent to http://www.example.com/shoppingcart/checkout.cgi, but would not be sent to http://www.example.com/index.html, since index.html is not hierarchically below the /shoppingcart path in the URL.

- *Expiration date*: The expiration date is the time at which the cookie will no longer be valid. If no expiration date is set, or—and this is important—if the expiration date is set incorrectly, the cookie will expire at the close of the browser session. Some browsers won't accept the cookie at all if the expiration date is not set correctly. The format for the expiration date is specific and is as follows: *Weekday, DD-MM-YYYY HH:MM:SS GMT*.

■**Tip** To clear a cookie, it's usually sufficient to set the value to null, or "".

Cookie Limitations

The following are some inherent limitations set by the cookie standard itself:

- A 4KB total size for any single cookie

- A total of 300 cookies stored by a browser

- A total of 20 cookies for any given server or domain

While some of these limitations are merely recommendations, it's a good idea to keep these in mind when working with cookies. In addition, although not required, it is recommended that elements within a cookie be properly encoded. Usually, this means escaping reserved characters into their hex equivalents. For instance, a single space in the cookie would be represented as %20.

Sampling the Cookies

Setting up your computer to test cookies means configuring your web browser to prompt when a cookie is received. You set up prompting on cookie receipt through the options or preferences within your browser of choice. Doing so will cause a dialog box to be displayed when a cookie is received. This is quite an annoyance for general browsing, but it is very helpful when working with cookies to ensure that the cookies are being set with the correct parameters.

Baking Cookies by Hand

Cookies get set as part of the header. You can set cookies without the use of the CGI module, just as you can accomplish any of the tasks of writing a Perl-based CGI application without the CGI module. To send a cookie to the browser, you need to create a program to output the necessary elements. This is as simple as the code shown in Listing 1-5.

Listing 1-5. *A Simple Cookie Example*

```perl
#!/usr/bin/perl -T

use strict;

print "Content-type: text/html\n";
print "Set-Cookie: testcookie=testvalue;";
print "\n\n";
print "You've received a cookie<p>\n";

exit;
```

If you have prompting for cookies enabled in your browser (as recommended in the previous section), pointing the browser to this code on the server results in a dialog box similar to that in Figure 1-5. You can see the cookie is being set with a name of testcookie and a value of testvalue. The cookie will expire at the end of the session, since no expiration date parameter was included in the cookie.

Figure 1-5. *The cookie being set*

Baking Cookies with CGI.pm

As you've seen, setting cookies by hand isn't the most difficult thing to do, yet the CGI module makes it even easier, especially in the area of setting the expiration date. Cookie functions are included within the :standard method group of the CGI module.

Just as with the manual method for sending cookies to the browser, you need to output the necessary elements when using the CGI module. Listing 1-6 shows how to re-create the simple cookie set in Listing 1-5 using the CGI module.

Listing 1-6. *A Simple Cookie Example Using the CGI Module*

```
#!/usr/bin/perl -T

use strict;
use CGI qw/:standard/;

my $cookie = cookie(-name=>'testcookie',-value=>'testvalue');
print header (-cookie=>$cookie);
print "You've received a cookie<p>\n";

exit;
```

Notice that in Listing 1-5, the path for the cookie was set to /cgi-bin/, or the directory from which the program was run. However, in Listing 1-6, the path is set to /, or the root of the site from which the program is run. Since the path is not set explicitly, the default for the module will be used, with the result being the root directory set for the path.

As with the manual example, you can view this code from the server through a browser with cookie prompting enabled to see the cookie contents as the cookie is being set.

Consuming Cookies

You've now seen how to set simple cookies in browsers both by hand and by using the CGI module. It might be nice to find out how to actually read those cookies back into your program.

Cookies are sent as part of the request header and can be accessed as an environment variable. As you've probably come to expect, the CGI module also includes a built-in function for cookie retrieval. You just call the cookie() function with the name of the cookie as an argument. Listing 1-7 shows the code to retrieve the cookie named testcookie (created in Listing 1-6).

Listing 1-7. *Retrieving Cookies*

```
#!/usr/bin/perl -T

use strict;
use CGI qw/:standard/;

my $retrievedcookie = cookie('testcookie');
```

```
print header,
start_html,
p("You sent a cookie and its value was $retrievedcookie\n"),
end_html;

exit;
```

But note that since the cookie set in Listing 1-6 didn't have an expiration date set, if you've closed your browser, the cookie will be gone, and this example won't work!

Setting Cookie Expiration

As I just noted, because the cookie created in Listing 1-6 contained only a name and a value parameter, it expired when the browser session closed. When you set an expiration date for a cookie, the cookie will be available on the user's computer until the expiration date, which means that it will be available when she visits your application until that date, regardless of whether or not she closed the browser. However, the format for the expiration date is very specific, and if formatted incorrectly may cause the cookie to expire at the end of the session or not be set at all!

Assume that you want to set an expiration date seven days in the future. Without the help of the CGI module, you would first have to figure out the current date, then add seven days to it, and then format the string in the correct format for the cookie's expiration date parameter. The code might look something like Listing 1-8.

Listing 1-8. *Setting Cookie Expiration Without Using the CGI Module*

```perl
#!/usr/bin/perl -T

use strict;

my @monthnames = qw/Jan Feb Mar Apr May Jun Jul Aug Sep Oct Nov Dec/;
my @weekdays = qw/Sunday Monday Tuesday Wednesday Thursday Friday Saturday/;

my $nextweek = time+604800;

my ($sec,$min,$hour,$mday,$mon,$year,$dayname,$dayofyear) = gmtime($nextweek);
$year += 1900;

print "Content-type: text/html\n";
print "Set-Cookie: testcookie=testcookievalue;";
printf ("expires=%s, %02d-%s-%d %02d:%02d:%02d GMT",$weekdays[$dayname],$mday,➡
$monthnames[$mon],$year,$hour,$min,$sec);
print "\n\n";
print "You've received a cookie<p>\n";

exit;
```

■**Note** There are certainly other valid methods for performing this operation, setting the date, and setting the expiration date. However, it's not very common to set a cookie expiration manually. Instead, it's much more likely that you'll be using the CGI module for this purpose.

On the other hand, the CGI module makes setting the expiration date rather easy. Instead of having to worry about the format or calculate the date in the future, you can simply call the expires() function of the cookie method with an argument indicating when the cookie will expire. Listing 1-9 shows an example that sets the same expiration date as Listing 1-8.

Listing 1-9. *Setting Cookie Expiration Using the CGI Module*

```
#!/usr/bin/perl -T

use strict;
use CGI qw/:standard/;

my $cookie = cookie(-name=>'testcookie',value=>'testcookievalue',-expires=>'+7d');
print header (-cookie=>$cookie),
start_html('CGI Cookie Test'),
p("You've received a cookie\n"),
end_html;

exit;
```

Notice first that the code is much, much simpler. You don't need to set the month names, get the date in a week's time, or format the date correctly. Notice also that the only difference in this code from the code in Listing 1-6 is that the code for the expiration date has been added:

```
my $cookie = cookie(-name=>'testcookie',value=>'testcookievalue',-expires=>'+7d');
```

Using this syntax, you can expire a cookie with just about any given time period. The time periods for cookie expiration are shown in Table 1-2.

Table 1-2. *Time Period Abbreviations for the CGI Module's Header and Cookie Functions*

Abbreviation	Definition	Example
d	Days	+1d (expire 1 day from now)
h	Hours	+8h (expire 8 hours from now)
M	Months	+1M (expire 1 month from now)
m	Minutes	-1m (expire immediately)
now	Immediately	now (expire immediately)
s	Seconds	+30s (expire 30 seconds from now)
y	Years	+1y (expire 1 year from now)

Setting Multiple Cookies

You may find that one cookie isn't sufficient for your application. In that case, you have two primary solutions:

- You could simply set multiple cookies, each corresponding to a different setting or preference. This method works well for a few cookies, but remember that there's a limit of 20 cookies per domain.

- If the application has a large number of cookies, a better solution is to create a session ID, store that session ID in a database, and tie that database into the settings and preferences that need to be stored for the application.

Storing a session ID in a database has the advantage of giving your application virtually unlimited settings that it can store in the background, since only one cookie is sent to the browser. Also, since only one cookie is sent to the browser, you will save bandwidth, thus making the site seem quicker to the user. Granted, this is less important for LAN-based applications, but any savings of bandwidth are good savings. This section shows how to set and read multiple cookies using the CGI module.

You can send multiple cookies to the browser by first creating the cookies, as you've done, and then passing the cookies as an array reference to the cookie() function. Listing 1-10 shows an example.

Listing 1-10. *Sending Multiple Cookies Using CGI.pm*

```perl
#!/usr/bin/perl -T

use strict;
use CGI qw/:standard/;

my $cookie1 = cookie(-name=>'testcookie',value=>'testcookievalue',expires=>'+7d');
my $cookie2 = cookie(-name=>'secondcookie',value=>'secondcookievalue',➥
expires=>'+1d');
print header (-cookie=>[$cookie1,$cookie2]),
start_html('CGI Cookie Test'),
p("You've received a cookie\n"),
end_html;

exit;
```

This code has only two differences from the code in Listing 1-9:

```perl
my $cookie2 = cookie(-name=>'secondcookie',value=>'secondcookievalue',➥
expires=>'+1d');
print header (-cookie=>[$cookie1,$cookie2]),
```

The first line creates a scalar containing a cookie with a name of secondcookie, a value of secondcookievalue, and an expiration of one day into the future. Notice that the expiration of $cookie2 is different from that of the other cookie in this example.

The second line of code looks strikingly similar to the call to the header() function from previous examples. Notice that this time, the call is setting two cookies, separated by a comma, within a set of brackets, which you'll recognize as an anonymous array. As you might come to expect by now, trying to accomplish this same task without the help of the CGI module is possible but much more time-consuming.

Reading the values from multiple cookies calls for the same process as reading one cookie (shown earlier in Listing 1-7), except that you read all of them! Listing 1-11 shows the code to read both of the cookies sent by the example in Listing 1-10.

Listing 1-11. *Retrieving Multiple Cookies*

```
#!/usr/bin/perl -T

use strict;
use CGI qw/:standard/;

my $retrievedcookie1 = cookie('testcookie');
my $retrievedcookie2 = cookie('secondcookie');

print header,
start_html,
p("You sent a couple cookies and their values were $retrievedcookie1 and ➥
$retrievedcookie2\n"),
end_html;

exit;
```

This code has only two changes from the code to retrieve one cookie. One is the addition to create a scalar to retrieve the second cookie:

```
my $retrievedcookie2 = cookie('secondcookie');
```

And the other to print the results to the resulting web page:

```
p("You sent a couple cookies and their values were $retrievedcookie1 and ➥
$retrievedcookie2\n"),
```

Setting the Secure Flag

Setting the secure flag in a cookie makes that cookie readable only if done so over an SSL connection (using HTTPS). This is useful if your cookie will be used to store personal information (which I wouldn't generally recommend for anything but a few applications, and then only if the cookie is a session cookie and not a cookie to be stored on a hard drive).

You set the secure flag as another argument within the call to the cookie function, as in this example:

```
cookie(-name=>'cookiename',-value=>'cookievalue',-secure=>1);
```

Note that if you don't have an SSL-enabled web server, you won't be able to test the secure flag.

Environment Variables

Environment variables are values set by the environment where a process runs. In the case of a CGI script, the environment variables are set by the web server on which they run. These variables are automatically made available to your CGI script in the form of the %ENV hash.

Viewing Environment Variables

The script shown in Listing 1-12 makes it possible to view the environment variables available to a CGI script on your web server.

Listing 1-12. *Viewing Environment Variables in a CGI Script*

```perl
#!/usr/bin/perl -T

use strict;
use CGI qw/:standard/;

print header,
start_html('Environment Variables');
foreach my $variable (keys %ENV) {
  print p("$variable is $ENV{$variable}");
}
print end_html;

exit;
```

The only new items in this script are the three lines of the foreach loop, which is a standard Perl construct. Saving this script to your web server and accessing it through a browser will result in a page similar to that in Figure 1-6.

Some of the environment variables sent to your script by the web server are the result of settings on the server itself; others are sent from the server as read by the browser accessing the script. One environment variable is HTTP_USER_AGENT. This environment variable is sometimes used (and misused) to determine the browser software and version accessing the page. Chapter 2 examines the use of HTTP_USER_AGENT to present a page based on the value of the variable.

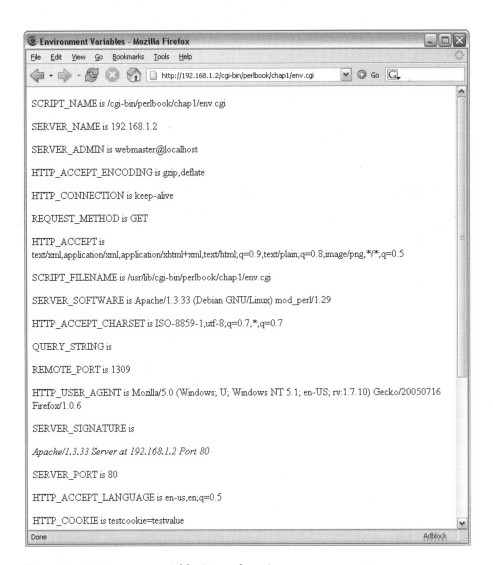

Figure 1-6. *Environment variables in a web session*

Carrying Values Between Forms

The ability to carry values between pages or forms within your application is key for all but the simplest of CGI programs. Earlier in the chapter, you saw how cookies might be used to carry values between forms. Here, I'll show you how to use the form itself to carry these values.

■**Caution** Values carried between pages through form variables—hidden or not, over SSL or not—can be faked, forged, or otherwise altered. Therefore, it is imperative that you do not rely on the data passed between forms, nor should you consider the data to be legitimate until you can check it for validity. More than one web site has been hacked this way. For example, customers have altered prices for products, and then ordered those products at that price. Always assume that data is invalid until proven otherwise.

Earlier, in Listing 1-4, you saw an example of how to accept a form value for a name and then respond with a message when the name is submitted. That code can be considered a simple two-page application. The first page presents the user with the text box, and the second page takes that result and performs an action, which is to send output to the browser. Now, assume that you want to create a third (and fourth, fifth, and so on) page, with each carrying over the values from the previous page. To do so, you need to make the second page present the user with another form for additional input. Listing 1-13 expands on the earlier example to ask the user for his favorite color and then presents the third page, based on the result.

Listing 1-13. *Values Carried Between Pages*

```perl
#!/usr/bin/perl -T

use strict;
use CGI qw/:standard/;

print header;

if (param('color')) {
   print start_html('Hello'),
   "Hello ", param('name'),p,
   "Your favorite color is: ",param('color'),p,
   hr;
}
elsif (param('name')) {
   print start_html('Hello'),
   "Hello ",
   param('name'),
   p,
   start_form,
   "Please enter your favorite color: ",textfield('color'),
   hidden(-name=>'name',-value=>param('name')),
   submit,
   end_form,
   hr;
```

```
} else {
  print start_html('Hello'),
  start_form,
  "Enter your name: ",textfield('name'),
  submit,
  end_form,
  hr;
}

print end_html;

exit;
```

This code is somewhat different from the previous example. First, notice that this script produces a new page for each step in the process, rather than simply outputting to the same page regardless of location within the script.

After the requisite interpreter opening line and the request to use the CGI module, the first thing the script does is send a header to the browser. No matter which step the user is in within the application, it will need to send a header. There's no reason to repeat the header code each time within the if-elsif-else conditionals.

The first conditional encountered within the program is one to look for the existence of the color parameter. If this parameter contains a value, then you know that the user has reached the final step within the application. If the script tested for the existence of the name parameter as before, it wouldn't be able to tell whether the user was coming from the first or second step.

The elsif conditional houses the code that you'll see on the second page of the script, after the user enters his name. This code is similar to the previous example, except that it now contains a hidden form variable that contains the name parameter from the previous step:

```
hidden(-name=>'name',-value=>param('name')),
```

Finally, the code within the else conditional is executed if neither color nor name contain a value. This means that the code is executed only when the user visits the page for the first time, prior to entering any input.

Interaction with the System

You already saw some system interaction when you looked at the %ENV environment variable hash sent by the web server to your CGI script. There's virtually no limit to the amount of interaction that's possible with both the local system and the remote system through Perl and its modules. At its most basic level, interaction with the system can simply mean reading or setting environment variables, reading from or writing to a file on the local filesystem, sending an e-mail from your script, or working with a database. You can also have more advanced system interaction, such as starting or killing processes, querying remote systems, or starting and stopping actions on the local server or remote servers.

With all of this power comes some danger as well. Any time your script interacts with the system on which it is housed, something could go seriously wrong. The problem may be the result of a bug in the code or a malicious use of the program to produce unexpected results.

No matter where the problem lies, you'll need to be mindful of the possible outcomes of working with system processes and files.

Chapter 4 looks at system interaction in detail, including some of the security risks when interacting with the system.

Debugging and Troubleshooting

An all-too frequent problem when programming CGI is the much-maligned Internal Server Error message. Figure 1-7 shows an example of such a message in a web browser.

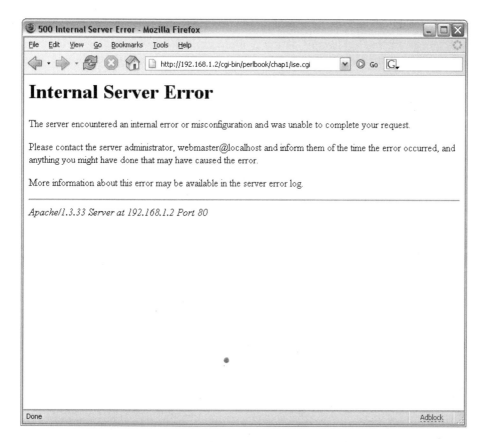

Figure 1-7. *The dreaded Internal Service Error message*

Unfortunately, it's sometimes difficult to determine the cause of the error. The task is much easier if you have access to the error log for the web server. An examination of the error log for the web server will usually get you much closer to finding the cause and then the solution to the error. Refer to your web server configuration file and/or web server administrator for the location (and for access to) the error log file for the web server.

A frequent error seen in the error logs for the web server is "Premature end of script headers." Like the Internal Server Error message, this error could be the result of any number of problems within the CGI script. Usually, the server will output additional information. For example, while writing one of the scripts for this chapter, I forgot a comma within some CGI code. The result of this oversight was an Internal Server Error message in the browser, along with a "Premature end of script headers" error in the log file. But what was more interesting was another entry in the log file:

```
Bareword found where operator expected at /home/u030701/cgi/thirdpage.cgi
    line 16, near ")
  hr"
    (Missing operator before hr?)
```

With that information, I was able to quickly find the error within the script. However, sometimes debugging isn't quite as easy as in this example. There are times when all you'll see is a "Premature end of script headers" error or another cryptic message about a problem in the script. When this happens, only your good troubleshooting skills will help. Using numerous print statements and other temporary debugging tools to try to narrow down the location of the error is very helpful. In addition, it may be possible to run the script directly from the command line in order to better determine where the error lies. This is not always possible though, especially if the error is buried deep within the code. Here, I'll suggest some other helpful troubleshooting tools.

Verbose Output

A helpful debugging tool is to use the -w option on the Perl interpreter invocation:

```
#!/usr/bin/perl -w
```

Using this option causes Perl to be verbose with undefined variables and other oddities that it notices within the program. If you're having trouble identifying the location of a problem, using -w can help.

Syntax Check

In addition, you can perform a syntax check of the program without actually executing it by using the -c command-line option. For example, you could check the syntax of a program called webform.cgi with this command, issued from the shell:

```
perl -c webform.cgi
```

You'll then receive an indication of any syntactical errors within the program. If you're lucky, you'll see something like this:

```
webform1.cgi syntax OK
```

If a syntax error is found, you'll see output indicating the error and the line where the error was found. For example, I removed a right bracket to produce an error in a script (really, I removed it to produce the error—I didn't forget it!). When I ran the program with the -c option, I received this output:

```
syntax error at webform.cgi line 25, near "else"
webform.cgi had compilation errors.
```

The Carp Module

One of the most important and helpful modules available to help debug an error is the
`CGI::Carp` module, or `Carp` for short. Using the `Carp` module, you can redirect more verbose
error messages to the web browser or to a log file. Consider the code shown in Listing 1-14.

Listing 1-14. *Using Carp for Debugging*

```
#!/usr/bin/perl

use CGI::Carp qw(fatalsToBrowser);
use CGI qw/:standard/;

print "Content-type: text/html\n\n";

die "I killed it here";
```

The result of viewing this code through a browser is shown in Figure 1-8.

Figure 1-8. *Using Carp to send errors to the browser*

The Carp module was instructed to send fatal errors to the browser using the fatalsToBrowser namespace. This is fine for initial debugging of a CGI, but I strongly recommend against using this method on a line-production system, since it could reveal many details about your configuration to a potential attacker. That said, using fatalsToBrowser can reduce your debugging and trouble-shooting time immensely when you're faced with a difficult-to-find bug in a CGI program. If you don't have access to the Apache log files, as might be the case in a shared hosting environment, fatalsToBrowser might be your only option. Just be sure to disable it prior to going live with your CGI program.

Luckily, fatalsToBrowser isn't required in order to take advantage of the Carp module. You can have error messages logged to the file of your choice by placing a BEGIN block at the top of the CGI script:

```perl
BEGIN {
        use CGI::Carp qw(carpout);
        open LOG, '>>', '/var/log/apache/carperror.log' or die
        "Cannot open file: $!\n";
        carpout(LOG);
}
```

In this example, a log file is opened for appending and the carpout() method is used to send messages to the specified file.

■Note You will likely have to manually create the log file, as well as make sure that it is owned by the user running the Apache server. For example, I created the carperror.log file with the command touch /var/log/apache/carperror.log and then chown'ed the file to the www-data user and group using the command chown www-data.www-data /var/log/apache/carperror.log. The user www-data is the user that Apache runs as on a Debian system. On other systems, such as Red Hat and Fedora, this may be the httpd user.

Joining the BEGIN block with a slightly modified version of the code from Listing 1-14 produces the code shown in Listing 1-15.

Listing 1-15. *Logging Carp Messages to a File*

```perl
#!/usr/bin/perl

BEGIN {
        use CGI::Carp qw(carpout);
        open LOG, '>>', '/var/log/apache/carperror.log' or die
        "Cannot open file: $!\n";
        carpout(LOG);
}

use CGI qw/:standard/;
```

```
print "Content-type: text/html\n\n";

$dbi->connect();

print "hi";
```

In the example shown in Listing 1-15, Carp logging is set up. Then the rest of the CGI continues. I purposely call an undefined $dbi->connect() method to produce an error. When viewed through a browser, this causes a fatal error, and the "hi" never gets printed to the client's browser. However, the following line is now inside the carperror.log file:

```
Can't call method "connect" on an undefined value
    at /usr/lib/cgi-bin/perlbook/chap1/isecarp.cgi line 14.
```

The Carp module enables other debugging options as well. Use perldoc, the Perl documentation program, to look up further information on CGI::Carp, by typing the following:

```
perldoc CGI::Carp
```

Other Troubleshooting Tips

The following are some other tips for debugging and troubleshooting:

- Check the permissions on the program. Many times, the permissions are set incorrectly. The correct permissions are usually set as rwxr-xr-x, which corresponds to octal 755. You should never set the permissions to rwxrwxrwx, or octal 777. See the next section on security for more information.

- Check the ownership of the program. On systems that use the suEXEC feature, the ownership must exactly correspond to the ownership set up in the Apache configuration file. If it doesn't, the program won't run and errors will be sent to the log file.

- Check log files! One of the strongest points of open-source software is logging. Examining the Apache error log is almost always helpful.

Security Considerations with CGI Programs

CGI programs and their security have been much maligned over the years. However, by themselves, CGI programs usually present no more of a security risk than any other application that can be run by anyone in the world, all things being equal. Of course, the fact that the CGI script can be run by anyone visiting the web site makes the security of the program and the server particularly important.

A competent system administrator can secure a CGI environment in such a way as to make up for many kinds of programmer mistakes. That said, CGI programmers are not relieved of the duty to make their programs safe. This section examines some of the security considerations when creating a CGI application.[4]

---

4. This section does not examine security of the server itself. Such things are best left to other titles such as *Hardening Apache* by Tony Mobily (Apress, 2004).

File Permissions

Too often, I've seen CGI programs that have improper permissions on the web server. When something goes wrong in the CGI application, some programmers immediately blame server settings and go overboard by changing the permissions on the application to the widest, most open, and insecure setting of all: chmod 777. This permission enables any local user to over-write and, yes, delete the application. While you may not think that anyone would do this, it takes only one inadvertent command by one lowly newbie to wipe out the application.

CGI permissions should be 755 (rwxr-xr-x), 775 (rwxrwxr-x), or even more restrictive in certain circumstances. By no means should "other" or "world" be given write permission on a CGI script.

Taint Mode

Although very simple, the examples in this chapter have all included two things that you as a CGI programmer can do to help make your program more secure. The first is using the -T option when invoking the Perl interpreter. The other is using the strict pragma, as described in the next section.

The -T option enables Perl's taint mode, whereby untrusted input into your program will not be allowed to perform certain operations, such as interaction with the system, writing to files, and so on. In a way, this option saves you from yourself. A simple mistake using tainted data can result in a malicious user being able to execute a system process or gain access to areas they are not authorized to enter.

Data is untainted by running it through a regular expression, and the -T option prevents the use of untrusted input. This means that only acceptable data will be allowed within the script once it passes through the regular expression. For example, the script in Listing 1-4 looks for input from the user through a form variable. This input consists of a person's name. Therefore, it would be a fair assumption that the only acceptable input consists of letters, maybe alphanumeric values, and possibly an apostrophe (though you would be surprised at how many applications break if an apostrophe is included as input). If you wanted to untaint the name parameter as it came into the script, you might do something like this:

```
my $name = param('name');
if ($name =~ /^\w+('\w+)?$/) {
  $name = $1;
} else {
  warn "Bad data found in $name";
  $name = "";
}
```

The code essentially looks for any number of word characters, followed by an optional apostrophe, followed by any number of alphanumeric values. If this matches, the resulting $1 variable is assigned to $name. If this doesn't match, a warning is sent to the log file, and $name is set to nothing.

Using taint mode will likely seem like a hassle, but it will certainly make your application safer. I recommend making a function to untaint regularly used inputs. For example, it's quite common to untaint the same types of data repeatedly, such as names, telephone numbers, domain names, e-mail addresses, and so on. Creating a function and then calling that function to untaint the data is usually simplest.

Also, a number of existing Perl modules are available on CPAN (http://www.cpan.org/) to assist in the process of untainting data. Helpful routines include ones to untaint and check the validity of e-mail addresses, IP addresses, and credit cards. If you're writing a CGI application that requires untainting, don't reinvent the wheel. Instead, leverage these modules in your application.

Taint mode is a runtime option. This effectively means that you might not find out about the tainted use of a variable until that variable is used within the program for an unsafe operation. The only way to find these types of issues if they are hidden is to test the program before release.

Strictness

The use strict; statement, included in the scripts in this chapter, is something that, as a Perl developer, you should be using in all of your scripts, not just CGI programs. When you include this line in your code, the Perl interpreter will look for variables and functions that have not been predeclared or variables that are out of scope.

The use strict; directive is a compile-time option. This means that any such errors will be caught immediately when the program runs. This is in contrast to a runtime option such as taint checking, which will cause an error only when a tainted variable is encountered.

Untrusted Data from Forms

One of the most common mistakes historically with CGI programs is the use of untrusted data in an application. The problem usually begins by passing hidden form variables between forms in the application, and then taking some action based on this data without doing some sanity checking on the data itself. Shopping cart programs have been broken in this way, as have other applications. The problem isn't limited to Perl-based CGI applications; any application that relies on user input could fall victim to this type of vulnerability.

The options for strictness and taint mode will help to only a certain extent against this type of attack. The best way to guard against untrusted data is to not use hidden form fields at all. This isn't always possible or, more appropriately, it isn't always practical to create an entire application without hidden form variables. The important thing to remember is that when you have any form variable, hidden or otherwise, you must perform a sanity check on the data received from the user. This frequently includes going through a number of conditionals to ensure that the data is not only in an acceptable format (think: taint checking), but also is within a valid range.

Take a shopping cart application as an example. With taint checking enabled, you could only verify that the form parameter was a series of numbers, usually in the form of N numbers followed by a period (or a comma in some locales) and then two numbers, like 5.15. However, all taint mode checking has done is to ensure that you have a series of numbers with a period or comma; it has done nothing to actually check the amount of the number. This means that there's nothing to prevent a user from changing that form field to 0.01. Since 0.01 is an acceptable number according to the taint checking, it would pass through without a problem, except now instead of purchasing the item at $5.15, the attacker is purchasing it for $0.01!

Does the example seem far-fetched? It shouldn't. Similar things have happened repeatedly to web sites with poorly designed applications that don't do proper checking of data being passed into the application.

Rather than fix the underlying problem, some developers use tricks to ensure that the data is correct. One of the most popular among these tricks is to use JavaScript to check that data is valid on the client side, to prevent a round-trip to the server before finding out there is a problem with the data. Unfortunately, it's trivial to get around a JavaScript check. Again, the only place that you can check data is within your program after it can no longer be accessed by the user.

Reliance on any JavaScript tricks to try to block access to the source code or try to prevent the user from doing something is a sign of a fragile, poorly designed application in the same way that reliance on a certain browser is a sign of poor coding. Fragile Internet applications rely on client-side settings; good applications work using widely recognized standards and handle errors and unexpected conditions gracefully.

Another flawed trick is to use the HTTP_REFERER (yes, that's the correct spelling in this case) variable to ensure that the only place from which a user might visit is a valid page. In other words, the developer is trying to make sure that someone isn't trying to come into the middle of a shopping cart with her own prices and quantities. As you might expect, HTTP_REFERER can be forged without much difficulty. Therefore, you shouldn't rely on this value to be sure that the data you're receiving is valid; rather, you should check the data against a known set of good values.

Untrusted Data from Cookies

Just as form data should always be untrusted, cookies are client-side objects sent to your application and should be treated appropriately. Cookies can be altered, just as form values can be modified. Any data received from cookies must be taint-checked and value-checked to ensure that it is the same as when it was sent to the user. The examples from the previous section apply equally to cookies. Always check data coming from the user, and always design the application to fail gracefully when the user does something unexpected.

Summary

Building an entire Perl-based CGI application such as a shopping cart is a matter of handling form values across multiple pages, sometimes using cookies, sometimes passing the values across the pages themselves, interacting with a database, possibly managing sessions, and using environment variables. I've found that knowledge and talent at designing web pages is more of a challenge than getting the background CGI programs working.

In this chapter, you learned about the CGI module including some of its functions. You also learned how to work with cookies through the CGI module, as well as debugging a CGI with the help of the Carp module. In the next chapter, you'll take a closer look at the Carp module, as well as some other modules that are commonly used when building web applications.

CHAPTER 2

■■■

Popular CGI Modules

Along with the CGI module, introduced in Chapter 1, a number of other modules and helper applications can make your Perl application quite powerful. This chapter examines some of those modules and helper applications. It also provides an example of coding program behavior based on environment variables, another concept introduced in Chapter 1. Finally, you'll look at the security considerations related to using the modules discussed in this chapter.

Integration with Other Modules

The CGI module is central to development of CGI applications in Perl. However, the CGI module is not the only module useful to the Perl CGI programmer. This section examines a couple of the popular modules used with CGI programs developed in Perl, including CGI::Carp, URI::Escape, Net::SMTP, mod_perl, and HTML::Mason.

■**Note** Like the previous chapter (and subsequent chapters) of the book, this chapter assumes that you are familiar with Perl programming basics. If you're unfamiliar with Perl, refer to this book's appendix.

CGI::Carp

The Carp module, introduced in Chapter 1, assists in the handling of error messages by providing more useful information. The CGI::Carp module is the CGI version of that module.

Using CGI::Carp, you can send errors to a custom log file rather than to the default web server log. You can also send errors directly to the browser in place of the dreaded Internal Server Error message.

You call the CGI::Carp module with a use statement, just as you invoke as any other module:

```
use CGI::Carp;
```

By default, many useful methods are exported by this simple invocation. However, some methods are not exported by default. Some of these will be highlighted in upcoming sections.

Table 2-1 shows the Carp functions for outputting warnings and errors. By default, these are sent to STDERR, which is usually written to the web server error log. As you'll see next, you can change the destination for Carp-generated errors.

Table 2-1. *Carp Functions for Outputting Warnings and Errors*

Function	Description
carp()	Sends a warning of errors. It is not fatal.
cluck()	Sends a warning of errors, including a stack backtrace. It is not fatal.
confess()	Sends a fatal error, including a stack backtrace.
croak()	Sends a fatal error.

Sending Fatal Errors to the Browser

With CGI::Carp, you can configure errors to be sent to the browser window rather than to the log file. This might be useful for debugging and other purposes. However, you should be aware of the potential for this method to divulge too much information to the end user. In other words, using this method makes debugging and testing easier, but it also may give out too much information about the script, including its location and other items that you might not wish disclosed. Therefore, if you're going to use this method, it's a good idea to disable it before going live with the application.

To send errors to the browser, you need to use one of the methods that is not exported by default; therefore, you must call it explicitly. Listing 2-1 provides an example of using CGI:Carp to send fatal error messages to the browser.

Listing 2-1. *Sending an Error to the Browser with CGI::Carp*

```
#!/usr/bin/perl -T

use strict;
use CGI qw/:standard/;
use CGI::Carp qw/fatalsToBrowser/;

print header,
  start_html("Testing CGI Carp");
  die ("This is a test die");
print end_html;

exit;
```

Viewing the code in a browser reveals a page like the one in Figure 2-1.

CGI::Carp takes care of most of the background work for you once you call the correct method, with this line of code:

```
use CGI::Carp qw(fatalsToBrowser);
```

From there, if the script dies, the error will be sent to the browser.

As you can see in Figure 2-1, the error message also shows contact information. You can configure this message by calling the set_message() function. Like the fatalsToBrowser() function, set_message() needs to be explicitly imported into your namespace:

```
use CGI::Carp qw(fatalsToBrowser set_message);
```

Figure 2-1. *A fatal error sent to the browser*

Then call the set_message() function, supplying an argument of the message you want to appear:

```
set_message("This is a better message for the end.");
```

Incorporating the set_message() function into the example in Listing 2-1 yields the code shown in Listing 2-2.

Listing 2-2. *Using set_message with CGI::Carp*

```
#!/usr/bin/perl -T

use strict;
use CGI qw/:standard/;
use CGI::Carp qw(fatalsToBrowser set_message);
set_message("This is a better message for the end.");
```

```
print header,
start_html("Testing CGI Carp");
die ("This is a test die");
print end_html;

exit;
```

The results are displayed in Figure 2-2.

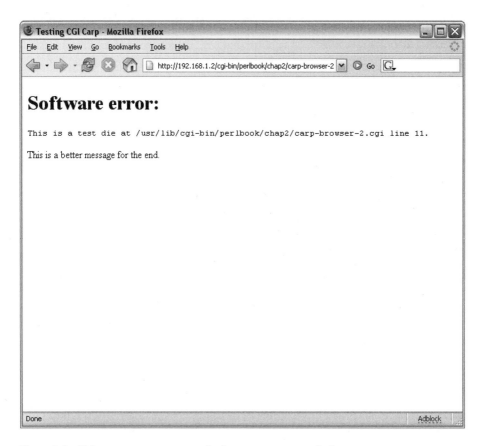

Figure 2-2. *Using set_message to send a better message to the browser*

Writing to an Alternate Log File

Normally, errors that occur in CGI programs are sent to the Apache error log. Actually, errors are sent to STDERR, which is normally picked up by Apache and written to the error log. It can be helpful to have this information written to a different error log. Doing so is possible with the help of CGI::Carp, which outputs to a log file located in /home/u030701/logs/.

However, before you attempt to write to an alternate log file, you need to ensure that the web server has permissions to write to the log file. In the case of Apache, the server usually runs as a nonprivileged user such as www-data, apache, httpd, or the like. Therefore, to enable

Apache to write to this log file, you need to explicitly grant the permission. Here is an example of the commands for granting permission on Debian Sarge server, which means that the server runs as the user www-data (you don't need to restart the server):

```
touch /home/u0307/1/logs/cgierrors.log
chown www-data.nogroup /home/u030701/logs/cgierror.log
```

Failure to grant the server permission to write to the log file will result in a Permission Denied error in the normal error log.

Listing 2-3 shows an example of writing to an alternate log file.

Listing 2-3. *Writing to an Alternate Log File*

```perl
#!/usr/bin/perl -T

use strict;
use CGI qw/:standard/;

BEGIN {
    use CGI::Carp qw(carpout);
    open (ERRORLOG, '>>', '/home/u030701/logs/cgierrors.log') or
        die("Unable to open log file: $!\n");
    carpout('ERRORLOG');
}

print header,
start_html("Testing CGI Carp");
warn ("This is a test warning");
print p("Hello, this is a test, check the logfile"),
end_html;

exit;
```

The script in Listing 2-3 is driven by the code contained within the BEGIN{} block:

```perl
BEGIN {
    use CGI::Carp qw(carpout);
    open (ERRORLOG, '>>', '/home/u030701/logs/cgierrors.log') or
        die("Unable to open log file: $!\n");
    carpout('ERRORLOG');
}
```

The BEGIN{} block is evaluated and executed immediately, thus making the code within that block effective immediately. That code effectively traps any error conditions and writes (appends) them to the specified log file.

URI::Escape

Working with CGI scripts sometimes means working closely with Universal Resource Identifiers (URIs) and Universal Resource Locators (URLs). It also means playing by a certain set of rules or standards for characters that are acceptable in a URI or URL.[1] RFCs 2396 and 2732 define the characters that are restricted when they appear in a URL.

In essence, you must escape reserved and unsafe characters if they appear in the query string of the URI. Usually, you escape characters by changing the value for the reserved character to its hexadecimal (hex) equivalent preceded by a % instead of 0x. For example, the hex equivalent for a dollar sign ($) in a URL is %24; the URI hex for a space character is %20. Programmers familiar with Microsoft Windows web design might recognize the %20 as a space, since it's more common to see spaces in filenames on Windows systems than on Unix and Unix-like systems.

In Perl, there's more than one way to accomplish a given task, and escaping characters is no exception. There's nothing preventing you from manually escaping each invalid character within a URI, and, in fact, a regular expression wizard could account for all instances of reserved and unsafe characters, and substitute them with their hex equivalents in one line of code. That's an enjoyable exercise for learning regular expressions, but I've found that the URI::Escape module saves a lot of time in this area.

You can download the URI::Escape module from your favorite CPAN mirror (find mirrors at http://www.cpan.org/). This is probably one of the easiest Perl modules to use.

The URI::Escape module includes two primary functions: uri_escape($string) and uri_unescape($string). The uri_escape() function accepts an optional second argument containing a set of characters to be escaped, as opposed to the default set of restricted characters from RFC 2396. These characters include the following: ;, /, ?, :, @, &, =, +, $, ,, [,], -, _, ., !, ", *, ', (, and).

When a string containing one of these characters is passed to the uri_escape() function, it will return a string with the restricted characters replaced with their safe counterparts. Conversely, when the uri_unescape() function receives a string with escaped characters, it will replace those escaped characters with their restricted, unsafe counterparts. Sometimes, the best way to explain things is with an example. Consider the code in Listing 2-4.

Listing 2-4. *A Safe String Example with uri_escape*

```perl
#!/usr/bin/perl -T

use strict;
use URI::Escape;
use CGI qw/:standard/;

my $unsafestring = "\$5/[3454]/this is a windows filename.asp";
my $safestring = uri_escape($unsafestring);
```

---

1. The difference between a URL and URI is subtle. A URL is a type of URI meant to show the location of the resource. The Internet Engineering Task Force (IETF) has published a number of Request For Comments (RFC) documents that define these and many other Internet standards. For more information, see the IETF's web site (http://www.ietf.org/) or the RFC Editor's web site (http://www.rfc-editor.org/).

```
print header,
start_html("Making URLs Safe Is Our Business"),
p("The string that is unsafe for a URL is: $unsafestring\n"),
p("When fed through the url_escape() function it becomes:
$safestring\n"),
end_html;

exit;
```

The code is pretty simple but illustrates the uri_escape() function very well. As usual, the URI::Escape functions are imported into the namespace with this code:

```
use URI::Escape;
```

From there, a string is created with all sorts of unsafe characters, including a $, brackets, and spaces. Notice the \ included in the string. The backslash doesn't actually appear in the output, since it's used to escape the $5, so that Perl doesn't interpret the $5 as a variable!

```
my $unsafestring = "\$5/[3454]/this is a windows filename.asp";
```

The string is then run through the uri_escape() function, with the results placed into a variable called $safestring:

```
my $safestring = uri_escape($unsafestring);
```

The next lines of code in the example are ones that you've seen in earlier examples, beginning the web page output and so on. Two lines of output to the resulting web page are based on the output from the uri_escape() function:

```
p("The string that is unsafe for a URL is: $unsafestring\n"),
p("When fed through the url_escape() function it becomes: $safestring\n"),
```

First, you're shown the string as it would appear before any escaping of unsafe characters (the variable $unsafestring). Next, the result of the uri_escape function is shown as the contents of the $safestring variable. Viewing the page through a browser, as shown in Figure 2-3, illustrates the results of the program.

Parsing an escaped URI string is a useful task, not only when programming for the Web, but also when performing forensics or monitoring security logs. Attackers and malicious code will frequently disguise their code by escaping it using the hex equivalent. Feeding that encoded string into the uri_unescape() function can help reveal the intent of such an attack. Listing 2-5 shows an example of using uri_escape().

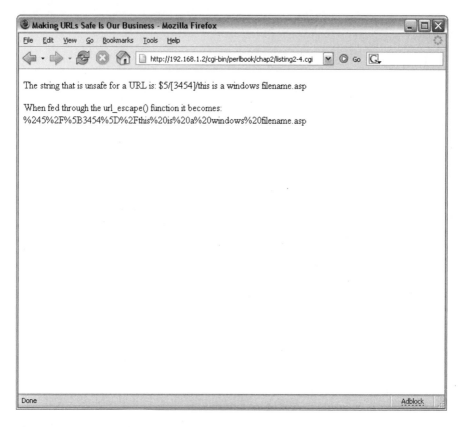

Figure 2-3. *An escaped string viewed through a web browser*

Listing 2-5. *Using uri_unescape to Make a String Without Escape Characters*

```perl
#!/usr/bin/perl -T

use strict;
use URI::Escape;
use CGI qw/:standard/;

my $unsafestring = "\$5/[3454]/this is a windows filename.asp";
my $safestring = uri_escape($unsafestring);
my $unescstring = uri_unescape($safestring);

print header,
start_html("Making URLs Safe Is Our Business"),
p("The string that is unsafe for a URL is: $unsafestring\n"),
p("When fed through the url_escape() function it becomes: $safestring\n"),
p("When the escaped string is unescaped, it becomes: $unescstring\n"),
end_html;

exit;
```

This code is similar to that shown in Listing 2-4. The additions to this code show the uri_unescape() function being run, as well as the results of that function call. As you can see in Figure 2-4, the string is indeed unescaped correctly.

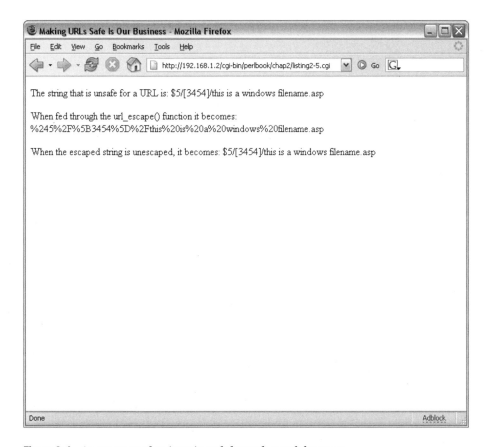

Figure 2-4. *An unescaped string viewed through a web browser*

Two other functions within URI::Escape enable the developer to escape characters with a code above 255: uri_escape_utf8($string) and uri_unescape_utf8($string). These functions encode the characters as UTF-8 prior to escaping them. As with the normal uri_escape() function, the uri_escape_utf8() function also accepts an optional second argument containing a string of unsafe characters.

Net::SMTP

A somewhat common element in a web site is a contact form. These forms usually consist of a few form fields that enable the visitor to send a message to the business or web site operator. In the background, the contact form sends an e-mail message to the site operator or the intended recipient.

Like so many other things in Perl, there are multiple way to accomplish the task of sending e-mail. One method is to use a `mailto` script such as `FormMail.pl` or another prebuilt mailer script. These scripts solve the problem, but many of them have historically had security holes or other issues that have allowed them to be abused. With that in mind, another solution is to use the `Net::SMTP` module to send the e-mail. Chapter 6 examines the use of `Net::SMTP` to send e-mail from a Perl script.

Mod_perl and HTML::Mason

Two essential characteristics of popular, high-traffic web sites are speed and frequent updates. Speed can be accomplished through many means, including the all-too-frequently used method of adding more and more servers to meet demand. While this is certainly necessary for the most popular sites and helps with redundancy, a better solution is to first look at ways to improve the performance of the server itself and the pages being served.

Updating a site frequently means that visitors will always have something new to view when they visit the site. Too often, companies put up a web presence and leave it as is, in a static and unchanging mode forever. These same companies then wonder why no one visits their site. Updating a site is not a difficult task, but maintaining it over a long period of time can be a headache. Therefore, it's important to make site maintenance as easy as possible.

To meet both the goals of adding speed through server optimization and making updates easy, many sites turn to an Apache module known as `mod_perl` for speed and the Perl module called `HTML::Mason` for easing the burden of frequent updates.

`Mod_perl` is an Apache module that greatly enhances the speed of CGI applications. `Mod_perl` embeds the Perl interpreter into the web server, thus making any CGI or Perl-based responses much faster.[2] By preloading the CGI code, `mod_perl` maintains the application in a ready-to-run state, as opposed to needing to compile the CGI each time it's run.

The drawback to `mod_perl` is that it is not recommended for use in a shared-hosting environment. In other words, if you use a web hosting provider and share the server with other users, the use of `mod_perl` makes it easier for malicious users to gain access to your application as it is running. `Mod_perl` will be discussed further in Chapters 10 and 11.

`HTML::Mason` (or just `Mason`) is a Perl module that enables execution of Perl code from within "Masonized" HTML files, and thus enables advanced templating. Such templating allows you to define a basic look and feel of a web site and plug text into the look and feel, thus easing ongoing maintenance of the site.

Designing an entire site from within a CGI application is cumbersome at best. Having to write each bit of HTML code as a line of Perl code is tedious and drives web developers positively mad. By using `Mason`, the HTML can be designed and then interspersed with Perl bits as appropriate. This frees the web developer to concentrate on the design of the web site. `Mason` requires `mod_perl` and is very powerful in its own right. `Mason` will be discussed in detail in Chapter 13.

---

2. `Mod_perl` does much more than merely enabling CGIs to be served faster. It also enables advanced usage of the Apache web server at a lower level than is possible through a normal CGI.

Interaction Based on Environment Variables

As noted in Chapter 1, environment variables, which are available to your programs from the server itself, can be useful for CGI programming. Using variables like the system time or the browser used by the client, you can change the behavior of your program. As an example of using environment variables, let's look at displaying a page to the browser based on that browser and browser version.

Some sites misuse the HTTP_USER_AGENT and attempt to block visitors based on the value of this variable. Such sites frequently claim to work only in certain browsers. These sites are the result of poor design by someone who doesn't understand the Internet. Since HTTP_USER_AGENT is based on a client-side setting, it can be forged or made to look like an acceptable browser. The user agent is covered in Chapter 5, where you'll see how to change this value. You should *not* rely on any values coming from the client side when designing a web application, and you certainly don't want to design a site that works with only certain browsers.

With that in mind, since different browsers and different versions of a browser render web pages differently, in some cases, it's helpful to customize the page to suit the browser. But be aware that the customization may not work in all cases. In the end, it's much better to design a site that adheres to well-defined and widely adopted standards, or at least default to these settings when the user agent cannot be determined.

Performing an action based on the HTTP_USER_AGENT variable is more of an exercise in Perl programming than an exercise in anything specific to CGI programming. Programming a set of conditional statements on the value of the variable is all that's necessary, as shown in the example in Listing 2-6.

Listing 2-6. *Determining the User Agent and Printing the Appropriate Result*

```perl
#!/usr/bin/perl -T

use strict;
use CGI qw/:standard/;

my $useragent = $ENV{'HTTP_USER_AGENT'};

print header,
start_html('User Agent Example');
if ($useragent =~ /Firefox/) {
    print p("You are visiting with a Firefox browser");
} elsif ($useragent =~ /MSIE/) {
    print p("You are visiting with an Internet Explorer browser");
} else {
    print p("Could not determine browser: $useragent");
}
print end_html;

exit;
```

The relevant bits of code within this program include the line to set the user agent into a local variable:

```
my $useragent = $ENV{'HTTP_USER_AGENT'};
```

Next is the Perl conditional `if-elsif-else` to take an action based on a word found within the $useragent variable that is unique to the browser:

```
if ($useragent =~ /Firefox/) {
    print p("You are visiting with a Firefox browser");
} elsif ($useragent =~ /MSIE/) {
    print p("You are visiting with an Internet Explorer browser");
} else {
    print p("Could not determine browser: $useragent");
}
```

Notice that if the browser cannot determine the browser, the default action is to do something sane to handle the problem—as opposed to producing an error or, worse yet, crashing, when this variable isn't present or is something unexpected.

The result when viewing this program through a web browser is shown in Figure 2-5.

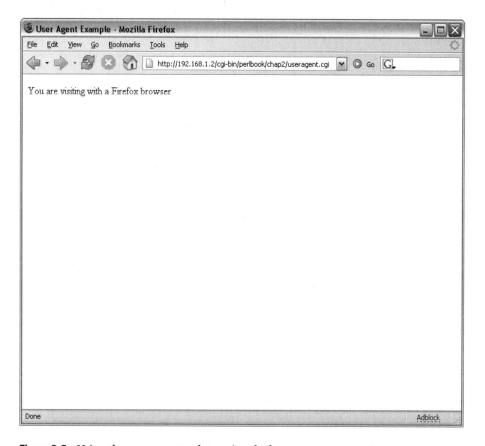

Figure 2-5. *Using the user agent to determine the browser*

Security Considerations with CGI Modules

Each module presents its own set of security issues. The `CGI::Carp` module, for example, can return too much information to the web browser with the `fatalsToBrowser()` method, which can result in information disclosure to potential attackers.

You should never trust input from any source, regardless of whether you're using Perl or any other language. Any and all input should be sanitized and cleaned using things like `uri_escape()`, taint mode (discussed in Chapter 1), and other such modules and helpers. Disallow all input by default, and then allow only the very smallest subset of valid input possible.

When you begin interacting with other systems and external clients such as web browsers, the potential for attack increases. I've seen countless web applications try to hide things from the client by disabling things like the View Source option in the web browser or by using other cute tricks that just don't work. Some of the worst applications place database information directly within the code of the page and assume (or hope) that no one will bother to look at the source. Or the designers believe they can effectively hide those details from the client when they output them to the page.

In addition, these same designers employ only client-side validation using JavaScript and never bother to check the data on the backend. This leads directly to exploits against their database, such as SQL injection attacks and their related vulnerabilities. *Always* validate input from within your server-side program, regardless of what you do to validate that input from the client side. Never rely on anything that you get from the web browser, including things like the user agent.

Summary

This chapter examined some additional Perl modules used in web development. You saw the use of the `CGI::Carp` module to help debug programs. Then you looked at how to use the `URI::Escape` module to work with URLs and URIs in order to make them safe for use within your programs and for display. You were also introduced to some other modules that will be covered in greater detail later in the book, including `Net::SMTP` and `HTML::Mason`.

One item that was not covered in this chapter was interaction with databases, which is an important part of many CGI applications. The next chapter covers working with databases in your CGI applications.

CHAPTER 3

■■■

Databases and Perl

Databases are vital to countless applications and play an important part in bringing applications to the Web. This chapter examines the elements involved in connecting to relational databases using Perl.

This chapter assumes that you are familiar with SQL. If SQL is just another acronym to you (it stands for Structured Query Language), I recommend that you refer to any number of excellent books on SQL or web sites that concentrate on SQL and the specific database server that you'll be using for development.

LAMP is another acronym that you may have heard in the world of web development. LAMP is an abbreviation for Linux-Apache-MySQL-Perl/PHP/Python. The MySQL database portion of that acronym is of interest in this chapter. However, there's nothing preventing you from using any other relational database with Perl, including Microsoft SQL Server. This chapter will look almost exclusively at MySQL, simply because it is so popular and well suited for web applications.

Interacting with a Database

Interacting with a database in Perl involves two pieces: the DBI and the database driver, or DBD. Each of these pieces is a Perl module. The DBI provides the software interface that is independent of the database, and the DBD provides the software that is database-dependent. This section discusses the DBI and the DBD for MySQL, and the role they play in connecting to a database through Perl.

The DBI

The DBI, an abbreviation for database independent or database interface (more commonly database independent), contains data-access libraries that are independent of the type of database. In other words, the DBI provides a generic interface on which you call a driver to access a database. This general interface allows you to use some common methods, regardless of the backend database.

The DBI is a module in itself, and thus is called into your program's namespace with a use pragma:

```
use DBI;
```

The DBI loads one or more database drivers (generally referred to as DBD, for database dependent). The DBD, which will be discussed shortly, has the specific software and code required to access a given type of database. It provides the interface between the DBI and the type of database for the connection.

Without a DBD, the DBI in and of itself isn't terribly useful. However, the DBI provides the methods that you use to work with the database itself. When coupled with the appropriate DBD, the DBI is the key to making database connections work.

The DBI gives you three objects, called *handles*, that enable you to work with the database. These are the driver, database, and statement handles. Driver handles are not commonly used within a CGI program, and will not be discussed here. Database handles are used within a program in order to make a connection to the database. Statement handles are children of database handles that are used to send SQL statements to the database. These two types of handles are discussed in detail later in this chapter, in the "Database Handles" and "Statement Handles" sections.

Database Drivers

A database driver provides the database-interaction methods that are specific to the individual database implementation. It is commonly referred to as the DBD, for database dependent, since its code depends on which database is being used. For example, a MySQL database has different syntax than an Oracle database. The DBI operates independently of the database, leaving the implementation-specific bits to the DBD.

You might be curious as to which drivers are installed on your server. The DBI module provides a function for listing all of the currently installed drivers. Listing 3-1 uses the available_drivers() function of the DBI module to retrieve the drivers available on the server.

Listing 3-1. *Listing Currently Installed Drivers*

```
#!/usr/bin/perl

use strict;
use DBI;

my @drivers;
@drivers = DBI->available_drivers();

foreach my $dbd (@drivers) {
  print "$dbd driver is available\n";
}

exit;
```

You run this program from the command line. The output will look something like this:

```
ExampleP driver is available
Proxy driver is available
mysql driver is available
```

The program incorporates the DBI into the namespace with this line:

```
use DBI;
```

The available drivers are placed into an array called @drivers with this line:

```
@drivers = DBI->available_drivers;
```

Finally, the array is expanded within the foreach loop and printed to STDOUT, producing the output.

As you saw from the output, the MySQL DBD is installed on this server. If you wanted to connect to a different type of database, you would need to obtain the DBD module from your favorite CPAN mirror or install it from your distribution's repository. For example, Debian 3.0 includes a number of DBDs, a listing of which is available by searching the repository with the command apt-cache search dbd.

Some of the more popular DBDs include the following:

- *MySQL*: As previously stated, MySQL is one quarter of the prized LAMP (Linux-Apache-MySQL-Perl) development platform that's so popular around the world.

- *PostgreSQL*: Another popular open-source database is PostgreSQL. The DBD for PostgreSQL is similar to that of MySQL.

- *ODBC*: The ODBC DBD is commonly used to connect to databases that run on Windows systems, such as Microsoft SQL Server and Microsoft Access, but the ODBC driver could be used to connect to virtually any database that offers ODBC connectivity.

- *Sybase*: Another popular DBD is used with the Sybase database server. This server and the DBD for it won't be covered in this book. For more information about running Sybase on Linux and the DBD for Sybase, see http://www.peppler.org/.

Data Source Names, Credentials, and Attributes

A data source name, or DSN for short, is the information needed by the DBI in order to connect to the database. This information includes the DSN itself, as well as other information such as the hostname of the server hosting the database, the name of the database, a port number, and so on. The exact information that you must supply depends on the DBD that you're using to connect. For example, an Oracle DBD might require or accept different parameters than the MySQL DBD uses.

The DSN is a simple string, frequently stored in a variable called $dsn. DSNs begin with the characters dbi:, followed by the name of the driver. For example, the DSN for a MySQL database is dbi:mysql. You can expand the code in Listing 3-1 to show the valid DSNs for the given database drivers on your system by using the data_sources() DBI method, as shown in Listing 3-2.

Listing 3-2. *Listing Valid DSNs*

```
#!/usr/bin/perl

use strict;
use DBI;
```

```perl
my @drivers;
@drivers = DBI->available_drivers;

foreach my $driver (@drivers) {
  print "$driver driver is available\n";
  my @dsns = DBI->data_sources($driver);
  foreach my $dsn (@dsns) {
    print "\tDSN: $dsn\n";
  }
}
```

When executed, the output contains valid DSNs corresponding to the drivers that are on the system. For example, here is output for the MySQL driver on my system:

```
mysql driver is available
        DSN: DBI:mysql:books
        DSN: DBI:mysql:maildb
        DSN: DBI:mysql:music
        DSN: DBI:mysql:mysql
```

Here's a sample DSN for connecting to a MySQL database called books located on a server at the IP address 192.168.1.10.

```perl
my $dsn = "dbi:mysql:books:192.168.1.10";
```

An alternate syntax is more explicit:

```perl
my $dsn = "dbi:mysql:database=books;hostname=192.168.1.10"
```

Following the DSN are optional (but usually required) credentials, including a username and password, for the database connection. When calling the connect() method, the username and password are passed as additional arguments to the method, separated by commas:

```perl
$dbh = DBI->connect($dsn,"username","password");
```

The $dbh refers to the database handle, as discussed in the next section.

Like the DSN, the username and password are frequently placed into variables and passed as such to the DBI's connect() method:

```perl
$dbh = DBI->connect($dsn,$username,$password);
```

You can send additional attributes along to the connect() method. These are attributes that apply to the handle and can be represented individually or as a hash. Two attributes that are often applied are RaiseError and PrintError. Both of these attributes are discussed in the "Error Handling" section later in this chapter.

Database Handles

As stated previously, the process of connecting to a database is mostly generalized among databases, although there are some considerations for specific types of databases. Connecting to a database creates a database handle object, which is used as a marshalling point to create statement handles and interact with the database server.

Database handles represent a connection to the database, and you could have multiple connections to multiple (or the same) database by defining multiple database handles. Database handles are usually referred to in code as $dbh.

Creation of a database handle through the DBI requires a DSN. Most databases today are multiuser, which means that credentials such as a username and password are also required in order to connect to the database and create the database handle. It is good practice to connect to the database as few times as possible (usually once) within a program, rather than connecting and disconnecting for each statement or query.

The DBI connect() method connects to the database and returns the database handle:

```
$dbh = DBI->connect($dsn, ...);
```

■**Note** Though you'll frequently see the database handle object referred to as $dbh, there is no reason why it couldn't be called any other valid variable name. The $dbh is a long-standing convention, and I will use it in this book to refer to a database handle.

Statement Handles

Just as database handles are created from the DBI, statement handles are children of a database handle. As the name implies, statement handles are used for individual statements, such as SELECT, INSERT, UPDATE, DELETE, and so on, to be executed on the database server. Multiple statement handles can (and usually are) defined based on one database handle within a given program.

Statement handles are created on a per-statement basis. This means that if you have multiple statements to execute against a given database handle, you will need multiple statement handles. However, you can reuse a statement handle if the statement needs to be rerun against a database. In fact, you can use parameters to execute the same statement but with different values, as explained in the "Binding Parameters" section later in this chapter.

Statement handles are not always necessary in order to issue statements to the database. Statement handles are necessary when you need to retrieve, or fetch, information from the database. However, statements also can be executed directly against the database through the database handle's do() method, as explained in the "Executing Other SQL Statements" section later in this chapter.

As previously stated, a statement handle is created from the database handle. In practical terms, this means that you create a variable, commonly called $sth, to hold the statement handle object. The statement handle variable's prepare() method is called on the database handle. Here's an example:

```
my $sth = $dbh->prepare("SELECT user,host FROM mysql.user");
```

By itself, the statement handle created in the code example may not actually do anything! For some database types, including MySQL, interaction with the database has not yet taken place. Rather, the DBI has simply *prepared* the statement for later execution. This prepare() method call is used to enable parameterizing of the statement before executing the statement later. The statement won't actually be executed against the database until the execute() method is called on the statement handle, $sth:

```
$sth->execute();
```

At this point, the statement—in this case, a SELECT statement—has been run against the database, although no results have been retrieved.

■**Note** Some databases will parse the statement when prepare() is called and thus can return errors if the server encountered problems while trying to parse the SQL statement given in the prepare() method. Refer to the documentation for the given database driver to determine if statements are parsed at the time of the prepare() call.

Error Handling

It's important to check and handle error conditions when working with databases. The DBI itself automatically handles errors when it detects that one has occurred. The DBI uses two attributes— PrintError and RaiseError—to automatically report errors. The PrintError attribute uses the warn() function to report errors, and the RaiseError attribute uses the die() function. Automatic error checking is useful for many situations, but as a developer, you may find it desirable to manually check for and handle errors for better programmatic control in case an error pops up.

You can disable both the PrintError and RaiseError attributes by setting the value of each to 0. This can be done at any time, on the fly if you will, or more commonly, at the time of database handle creation and connection to the database. As you might expect, you can also reenable a previously disabled attribute, setting the value to 1. For example, recall the database connection method called earlier. It looks like this:

```
my $dbh = DBI->connect($dsn,$username,$password);
```

You can disable the PrintError and RaiseError attributes like so:

```
my $dbh = DBI->connect($dsn,$username,$password, PrintError => 0, RaiseError => 0);
```

As previously stated, these values can be set in a hash as well. (If you're unfamiliar with hash references, refer to *Beginning Perl, Second Edition* by James Lee.) To set them this way, the hash—let's call it %attr—first needs to be created and then added to the connect() method call as a hash reference:

```
my %attr = (
  PrintError => 0,
  RaiseError => 0
);
my $dbh = DBI->connect($dsn,$username,$password, \%attr);
```

By default, the DBI enables warnings only through the PrintError attribute, whereas RaiseError is not enabled when using the connect() method.

Knowing that PrintError and RaiseError are available is helpful. Both PrintError and RaiseError can be enabled on any handle, although they are most often used with database handles. As previously stated, the attributes can be enabled and disabled on the fly, as needed. Assume that you have a database handle called $dbh. You can set the attributes on this handle at any time in this way:

```
$dbh->{PrintError} = 1;
$dbh->{RaiseError} = 1;
```

To turn the attributes off, change the value from 1 to 0.

Even with PrintError and RaiseError, it may be easier to manually call the die() function. This is especially important when initially connecting to the database. The DBI connect() method returns an undef when the connection fails, which makes it easy to check to ensure that the connection was successful. A common method for doing so is to use die() with the DBI connect() method call:

```
my $dbh = DBI->connect($dsn,$username,$password)
  or die "Cannot connect to database: $DBI::errstr";
```

This example also uses the $DBI::errstr method, which returns a description of the actual error.

■**Caution** It's a best practice to not fail quite so loudly when programming a web application. In other words, you wouldn't want to give too verbose of an error message and possibly divulge information to a web site visitor when a connection fails. For that reason, if you will be outputting errors to the browser, don't include the $DBI::errstr variable in that output.

There's nothing preventing you from using a combination of automatic and manual error checking within your code. In addition, you can use three other methods to help when debugging:

- The err() method returns the error number.

- As just noted, the errstr() method returns a string containing a description of the actual error.

- The state() method returns the SQLSTATE error string.[1]

You'll likely find that the errstr() method is the most useful of the three debugging methods.

Using SQL Databases with the DBI

Now that you have a grasp of the objects involved in database connectivity through Perl, including the DBI, various DBDs, database handles, and statement handles, it's finally time to

---

1. This method is not supported by all drivers.

connect to the database and do something. This section examines the steps necessary to connect to a database, retrieve some results, and perform other actions necessary for successful database interaction.

Connecting to the Database

The first step is to load the DBI into your namespace and then create a database handle by connecting to the database. For example, putting everything together to form a connection string and create a database handle for connecting to a MySQL database called `mysql` on the host 192.168.1.10 looks like this:

```perl
#!/usr/bin/perl

use DBI;
use strict;

my $dbh = DBI->connect("dbi:mysql:mysql:192.168.1.10","dbuser","dbpassword");
```

Alternatively, if you've stored the DSN information in its own variable and stored the username and password in variables, you can create the database handle as follows:

```perl
#!/usr/bin/perl

use DBI;
use strict;

my $username = "dbuser";
my $password = "dbpassword";
my $dsn = "dbi:mysql:mysql:192.168.1.10";
my $dbh = DBI->connect($dsn,$username,$password);
```

This database connection does not perform any fatal error checking, relying instead on the DBI's internal error checking, which in this case, will be the `PrintError` attribute. The result will be that any connection errors are only warnings, rather than fatal errors. To cause a fatal error on connection failure, you can call the `die()` function explicitly:

```perl
my $dbh = DBI->connect($dsn,$username,$password)
  or die "Cannot connect to database: $DBI::errstr";
```

From this database handle, `$dbh`, you create statement handles that all tie back to this database handle. This means that any queries or other SQL statements run will do so with the permissions and privileges of the database user for that database handle. If the user that you used to connect to the database has only `SELECT` privileges, you will not be able to perform another operation, such as `INSERT`, through that database handle.

In addition, it's important to note that database handles connect to an individual database. While you can use as many tables within that database as your privileges permit, you cannot (usually) work with tables in other databases. If you need to work with multiple users to gain additional privileges or work with more than one database, you'll need to create additional database handles and subsequent statement handles from there.

Disconnecting from the Database

When you're finished executing queries and working with the database handle, it's good practice to explicitly disconnect from the database. Database servers such as MySQL may automatically end the session after N seconds of idle time and N seconds of session life-time, where N is dependent on the server configuration. However, most servers will also have a connection limit as well, which could easily be reached under heavy load or when something goes wrong and a program continues to execute. For these reasons, explicitly disconnecting makes life easier in the long run.

The disconnect() method is a database handle method and thus, when you're finished executing queries, retrieving results, and flushing statement handles (as explained in the following sections), you can disconnect from the database by calling disconnect():

```
$dbh->disconnect();
```

Executing a Query

Executing a query against a relational database using the DBI is a multistep process:

1. You create a statement handle by calling the prepare() method of the database handle.

2. For databases such as MySQL, you call the execute() method on the statement handle in order to actually execute the SQL statement on the server.

3. To retrieve the results of the query, you use one or more methods of the statement handle. Retrieving the results is explained in the next section.

Let's build on the statement handle you saw earlier:

```
my $sth = $dbh->prepare("SELECT user,host FROM mysql.user");
```

Executing the query against the database requires calling the execute() method against the statement handle:

```
$sth->execute();
```

It's a great idea to check for fatal errors when executing a SQL statement due to a plethora of issues that can avail themselves at this late hour. Therefore, if you haven't enabled RaiseError on the database handle (remember, PrintError is enabled by default, but is only a warn() level), you should check for success by using or with the statement handle's execute() method:

```
$sth->execute() or die "Cannot execute sth: $DBI::errstr";
```

■**Note** Even though you've executed the statement on the database, it may still be running on the server. Queries that return a large number of rows, or otherwise overtax servers, might not be able to complete immediately, but will continue executing as you fetch the results.

Retrieving the Results

What fun would executing queries against a database be without actually being able to process the results of the query? Results from a query are returned to the statement handle. It's your job to programmatically iterate through the results. This is usually accomplished by looping through the result set and performing some action on each row as it is retrieved. The method usually used for this purpose is the `fetchrow_array()` method[2] of the statement handle.

Let's continue with the sample statement handle prepared and then executed:

```
my $sth = $dbh->prepare("SELECT user,host FROM mysql.user");
$sth->execute or die "Cannot execute sth: $DBI::errstr";
```

This query will retrieve the username and the host from the MySQL user table, which holds the usernames and passwords for the MySQL server. To iterate through this result set, construct a while loop to call the `fetchrow_array()` method on each loop:

```
while (my($username,$hostname) = $sth->fetchrow_array()) {
  print "Username is $username. Host is $hostname\n";
}
```

The entire program is shown in Listing 3-3.

Listing 3-3. *Retrieving Query Results Listing MySQL Users and Hosts*

```
#!/usr/bin/perl

use DBI;
use strict;

my $username = "dbuser";
my $password = "dbpassword";
my $dsn = "dbi:mysql:mysql:192.168.1.10";
my $dbh = DBI->connect($dsn,$username,$password)
  or die "Cannot connect to database: $DBI::errstr";

my $sth = $dbh->prepare("SELECT user,host FROM mysql.user");

$sth->execute() or die "Cannot execute sth: $DBI::errstr";

while (my($username,$hostname) = $sth->fetchrow_array()) {
  print "Username is $username. Host is $hostname\n";
}

$dbh->disconnect();
```

---

2. There also are variations of the `fetchrow_array()` method, including `fetchrow_arrayref()` to retrieve an array reference, `fetchrow_hashref()` to retrieve a reference to a hash, and others. For more information about these other methods, refer to the documentation on the DBI (`perldoc DBI`).

When run, the program will retrieve each username and hostname defined in the MySQL user table. Here's some sample output from one of my servers:

```
Username is postfix Host is localhost
Username is root Host is localhost
Username is  Host is localhost
Username is testuser Host is localhost
Username is user Host is localhost
```

■**Note** Some fields may be blank, depending on what's defined in the MySQL user table.

Within the while loop to retrieve results, you can perform any action necessary on the data retrieved. The example in Listing 3-3 prints the results. A common task is to push the results into an array for later use, as shown in the example in Listing 3-4, which looks for hosts with the MySQL wildcard character, %.

■**Note** A percent sign within the MySQL user table indicates a wildcard. In other words, it stands for any host. For example, a wildcard host entry of simply % means essentially any host, anywhere, with that user. A wildcard host entry of 192.% would require only the first octet of the IP address to match in order for the connection to be allowed from that host. Of course, a valid username (and hopefully a password) would also be required.

Listing 3-4. *Pushing Query Results to an Array to Find Wildcard Hosts*

```perl
#!/usr/bin/perl

use DBI;
use strict;

my $username = "dbuser";
my $password = "dbpassword";
my $dsn = "dbi:mysql:mysql:192.168.1.10";
my $dbh = DBI->connect($dsn,$username,$password)
  or die "Cannot connect to database: $DBI::errstr";

my $sth = $dbh->prepare("SELECT host FROM mysql.user");

$sth->execute() or die "Cannot execute sth: $DBI::errstr";
```

```
my @mysqlhosts;
while (my $hostname = $sth->fetchrow_array()) {
    push (@mysqlhosts,$hostname);
}

while (<@mysqlhosts>) {
    if ($_ =~ /%/) {
        print "Wildcard host found: $_\n";
    }
}
$dbh->disconnect();
```

Most of the early portion of this example is the same as Listing 3-3, but notice that the query itself is different, this time retrieving only the host from the MySQL user table. Instead of printing the output directly while fetching, it is pushed into an array, @mysqlhosts, for later use. The later use comes next, when that array is expanded and each entry is examined for the offending percent sign.[3]

My output looks like this:

```
Wildcard host found: %
Wildcard host found: 192.168.1.%
```

Your output may vary if you don't have any wildcard hosts on your server.

Another use might be to take the results and build another query based on the data retrieved. The possibilities are without limit and entirely dependent on the needs of your program.

Dumping the Results

In some cases, you may not want to build the loop for fetching the results from a query. In such instances, you can use the DBI's dump_results() method on the statement handle. Using dump_results() enables you to quickly see if a query was successful. It returns the rows themselves, followed by the number of rows returned. Listing 3-5 shows the program in Listing 3-4 altered to use dump_results() instead of the fetchrow_array() method.

Listing 3-5. *Dumping a Query's Results*

```
#!/usr/bin/perl

use DBI;
use strict;

my $username = "dbuser";
my $password = "dbpassword";
my $dsn = "dbi:mysql:mysql:192.168.1.10";
```

---

3. It would be better practice to place the if{} test within the database fetch itself, in order to save memory. I guess you'll have to wait for version 2 of the software!

```
my $dbh = DBI->connect($dsn,$username,$password)
  or die "Cannot connect to database: $DBI::errstr";

my $sth = $dbh->prepare("SELECT user,host FROM mysql.user");

$sth->execute() or die "Cannot execute sth: $DBI::errstr";

print $sth->dump_results();

$dbh->disconnect();
```

The output is as follows:

```
'postfix', 'localhost'
'root', 'localhost'
'', 'netserver'
'testuser', 'localhost'
'user', 'localhost'
3 rows
```

Finish()-ing the Statement

It is a good idea to be aware of the result set that you're working with from a given statement handle. If you don't retrieve all of the rows from a query, the result set will still hold data. This can mean extra memory usage for the database server and can also result in warnings when you attempt to execute the disconnect() method. Therefore, if you won't be retrieving all of your results, be sure to use the finish() method on the statement handle to flush the results.

In the examples shown, all of the results were retrieved by iterating through them using fetchrow_array() or dump_results(). However, if this hadn't been the case, I would have used the finish() method, like this:

```
$sth->finish();
```

Using the Quote Method for Dynamic Statements

In the examples shown so far, there's no reason why you couldn't substitute a valid variable within the SQL statement. In other words, instead of merely using this:

```
SELECT host FROM mysql.user;
```

you could, assuming a variable of $username, use this:

```
SELECT host FROM mysql.user WHERE user = '$username';
```

In this example, the variable $username is interpolated, and whatever is in $username will be sent with the query. This interpolation of $username is as opposed to parameterizing or binding for dynamic statements, as you'll see in the "Binding Parameters" section, coming up soon.

A popular vector for attackers exploiting database connectivity (particularly in web applications) is to include characters or other anomalies in an attempt to get the program, and therefore the database server, to execute additional commands. These types of attacks are made possible when input is allowed unchecked or the program executes a SQL statement without first properly sanitizing it for the database's consumption. The DBI contains an aptly titled quote() method to properly escape or sanitize SQL statements for you.

You should use the quote() method for any statement that will use parameters or other variables or input that could possibly be dirty. The quote() method belongs to a database handle, since nearly every database server has its own set of rules for quoting. Consider this code, assuming a database handle of $dbh has already been created:

```
my $dirtystring = "This is some %really% \"weird\" \\* input";

my $cleanstring = $dbh->quote( $dirtystring);

my $sth = $dbh->prepare("SELECT * from tablename where something = $cleanstring");
```

So, the example shown earlier in this section might look like this:

```
my $usernamein = "suehring";

my $sth = $dbh->prepare("SELECT host FROM mysql.user WHERE user = " .
    $dbh->quote($usernamein . "        ");
```

While it may seem like a hassle to need to clean up input and other parameters before using them in a statement, the trade-off is well worth the extra typing. I could go into a story akin to the age-old "I used to have to walk 18 miles a day to school" of how life was prior to the quote() method, but rest assured that using quote() is much easier and simpler than needing to do the same function manually against all input.

Executing Other SQL Statements

Not all statements must go through the prepare() and execute() methods, or even create a statement handle prior to being run against the database server. The database handle's do() method executes a statement immediately against the database. This is useful for performing actions like DELETE, INSERT, and UPDATE, which don't actually retrieve any results from the database, but merely perform an action against the database.

The do() method is used in the context of a database handle. Assuming a database handle of $dbh with a table called table, you might use do() like this:

```
my $rows = $dbh->do("DELETE from table where id = '4'");
```

The $rows variable would contain the number of rows affected by this statement. If the statement executes successfully, regardless of the number of rows deleted, the do() method will return true. In other words, the rows affected could still be zero, even though the statement executed successfully.

Binding Parameters

As you saw earlier, you can use the quote() method to create dynamic SQL statements. However, another method exists for creating such statements, namely *parameters*. Parameters are also known by a few other names or concepts, such as *binding* or *placeholders*. When you hear one of these terms, it's referring to the concepts described in this section.

You may be asking why you would use binding instead or interpolated value queries. Binding speeds up the execution of the same SQL statement. Therefore, if you're going to be executing the same statement but with different values, you can gain speed by using parameters. Whether or not you should use parameters also depends on the database that you're using; not all databases implement binding.

Recall a previous example that used variable interpolation to build the statement handle for a dynamic query:

```
my $sth = $dbh->prepare("SELECT host FROM mysql.user WHERE user = " .
    $dbh->quote($usernamein . "        ");
```

Using parameters, that statement handle would look like this:

```
my $sth = $dbh->prepare("SELECT host FROM mysql.user WHERE user = ?");
$sth->bind_param(1, $username);
```

The bind_param() method on the statement handle accepts an index value, beginning with 1, to specify the order in which the parameters should be bound, and it then accepts the value itself, this time in the variable $username.

Notice that the quote() method is not used here. Since bind_param() hands off the parameters to the database separate from the SQL statement, the quote() method isn't necessary.

You can (and many times will) bind multiple values. Consider this example:

```
my $sth = $dbh->prepare("SELECT host FROM mysql.user WHERE user = ? AND host = ?");
$sth->bind_param(1, $username);
$sth->bind_param(2, $hostname);
```

It's important to understand that not all portions of a statement can be parameterized. For example, most databases won't allow you to parameterize the entire WHERE clause of a SQL statement. However, binding the values used within that WHERE clause is valid on many databases.

Rather than using bind_param() to bind parameters to their values, you can also send the values when you call execute(). You must specify the values in the same order in which they appear in the SQL statement. So, based on the SQL statement in this example:

```
my $sth = $dbh->prepare("SELECT host FROM mysql.user WHERE user = ? AND host = ?");
```

username should be specified first and host second. Therefore, this would be correct:

```
$sth->execute($username,$hostname);
```

and this would be incorrect:

```
$sth->execute($hostname,$username);
```

Inserting Data into a Database

Inserting rows into a database is largely the same syntactically as retrieving rows from it, with the obvious changes to the SQL syntax itself. For example, you could use the do() method or the prepare() method for inserting into a database. You create the database handle as you would for any other database operation, create the statement handle the same way, and call execute() if you've used prepare().

Assume that this INSERT statement would execute against a database table:

```
INSERT INTO urls VALUES
    ('','http://www.braingia.org/','suehring',unix_timestamp(),'query words');
```

The equivalent DBI code is shown in Listing 3-6.

Listing 3-6. *Inserting into a Database*

```perl
#!/usr/bin/perl

use DBI;
use strict;

my $username = "dbuser";
my $password = "dbpassword";
my $dsn = "dbi:mysql:goo:192.168.1.10";
my $dbh = DBI->connect($dsn,$username,$password)
  or die "Cannot connect to database: $DBI::errstr";

my $sth = $dbh->prepare("INSERT INTO urls VALUES
('','http://www.braingia.org/','suehring',unix_timestamp(),'query words')");

$sth->execute() or die "Cannot execute sth: $DBI::errstr";

$dbh->disconnect();
```

As you can see, much of this code is the same as previous examples, with the exception being the INSERT syntax for the actual statement. You can also bind parameters with INSERT statements and use the do() method.

One common task when inserting data into a table is to retrieve the value for an auto-incremented index ID for the newly inserted row. The MySQL DBD includes a function for retrieving this value. Note that this is dependent on the database itself and also on the data layout. If there is no auto-incremented field in the database table, this value might be meaningless. Additionally, some databases don't implement this. Check the Perl documentation for your DBD.

In the case of the example in Listing 3-6, the first field was an auto-incremented field. Therefore, it's possible to add some code to the example to retrieve the value for that ID field. The new code is shown in Listing 3-7.

Listing 3-7. *Retrieving an Index ID*

```perl
#!/usr/bin/perl

use DBI;
use strict;

my $username = "dbuser";
my $password = "dbpassword";
my $dsn = "dbi:mysql:goo:192.168.1.10";
```

```perl
my $dbh = DBI->connect($dsn,$username,$password)
  or die "Cannot connect to database: $DBI::errstr";

my $sth = $dbh->prepare("INSERT INTO urls VALUES
('','http://www.braingia.org/','suehring',unix_timestamp(),'query words')");

$sth->execute() or die "Cannot execute sth: $DBI::errstr";

my $insertid = $dbh->{'mysql_insertid'};
print "$insertid\n";

$dbh->disconnect();
```

Notice the two new lines in Listing 3-7:

```perl
my $insertid = $dbh->{'mysql_insertid'};
print "$insertid\n";
```

In this case, the output from each run should increment, assuming that no one else is inserting data into the table at the same time! For example, I called this program insert2.pl. Running the program from the command line outputs the $insertid variable:

```
netserver% ./insert2.pl
41
```

Running the program again reveals that the value is indeed incrementing:

```
netserver% ./insert2.pl
42
```

Interacting with the Web

Thus far, this chapter has looked at only the basics of the DBI, and with good reason. Understanding how the DBI works enables you to write powerful web applications. What you do with the data contained in the database is entirely up to you.

Outputting to HTML

You could simply output the statements to plain HTML by combining the DBI functions with what you've learned about CGI programming.

Reworking the example from Listing 3-4 into a plain web page yields the result shown in Listing 3-8.

Listing 3-8. *Creating a Web Page Integrated with SQL Data*

```perl
#!/usr/bin/perl

use DBI;
use strict;
use CGI qw/:standard/;
```

```perl
my $username = "dbuser";
my $password = "dbpassword";
my $dsn = "dbi:mysql:mysql:192.168.1.10";
my $dbh = DBI->connect($dsn,$username,$password)
  or die "Cannot connect to database: $DBI::errstr";

my $hosttolookup = "%";

my $sth = $dbh->prepare("SELECT host FROM mysql.user WHERE
    host LIKE ?");

$sth->execute($hosttolookup)
    or die "Cannot execute sth: $DBI::errstr";

my @mysqlhosts;
while (my $hostname = $sth->fetchrow_array()) {
    if ($hostname =~ /%/) {
        push (@mysqlhosts,$hostname);
    }
}

print header,
    start_html('MySQL Hosts Using Wildcards');

my $count = @mysqlhosts;
if ($count == 0) {
    print p("No Hosts Using Wildcards");
}
else {
    while (<@mysqlhosts>) {
        print p("Host Wildcard: $_");
    }
}

print end_html;

$dbh->disconnect();
```

Essentially, the program is largely the same as those previously shown. The main difference is that, instead of printing to STDOUT, this program outputs HTML. The core of the "HTMLized" portion of the program is here:

```perl
print header,
    start_html('MySQL Hosts Using Wildcards');

my $count = @mysqlhosts;
if ($count == 0) {
    print p("No Hosts Using Wildcards");
}
```

```
else {
    while (<@mysqlhosts>) {
        print p("Host Wildcard: $_");
    }
}

print end_html;
```

None of this code should be new to you after going through the previous chapters on CGI programming. If there are no hosts using wildcards, the program will output a message indicating that. If there are hosts using wildcards, that list is sent to the HTML instead, as shown in Figure 3-1.

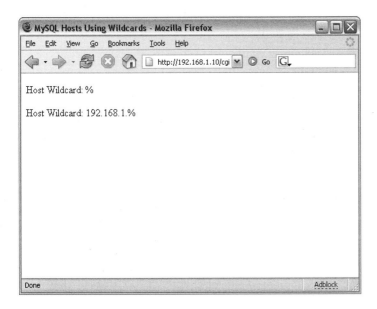

Figure 3-1. *The output from the script indicating that hosts were found with wildcards*

Building HTML Tables

The output from Listing 3-8 is nice for a simple program, but when you're building a more complex CGI program, you'll likely find that you want to use HTML tables for the output. You can build a table manually or by using the CGI's table() method. The example in Listing 3-9 uses the table() method to print each user and host on a MySQL server in tabular format.

Listing 3-9. *Creating an HTML Table*

```
#!/usr/bin/perl

use DBI;
use strict;
use CGI qw/:standard/;
```

```perl
my $username = "dbuser";
my $password = "dbpassword";
my $dsn = "dbi:mysql:mysql:192.168.1.10";
my $dbh = DBI->connect($dsn,$username,$password)
  or die "Cannot connect to database: $DBI::errstr";

my $sth = $dbh->prepare("SELECT host,user FROM mysql.user");

$sth->execute()
    or die "Cannot execute sth: $DBI::errstr";

print header,
        start_html('MySQL Hosts and Users'),
        table({-border=>1}),
                Tr({-align=>'CENTER',-valign=>'TOP'},
                [
                        th(['User','Host'])
                ]);

while (my ($hostname,$username) = $sth->fetchrow_array()) {
        if ($hostname eq "") {
                $hostname = "<b>undef</b>";
        }
        print Tr({-align=>'CENTER',-valign=>'TOP'},
                [td(["$username","$hostname"])
                ]);

}

print end_html;

$dbh->disconnect();
```

Running this program shows that the data has been placed into an HTML table, as shown in Figure 3-2.

In Listing 3-9, first the table is created using CGI.pm's table() method:

```perl
print header,
    start_html('MySQL Hosts and Users'),
    table({-border=>1}),
        Tr({-align=>'CENTER',-valign=>'TOP'},
        [
            th(['User','Host'])
        ]);
```

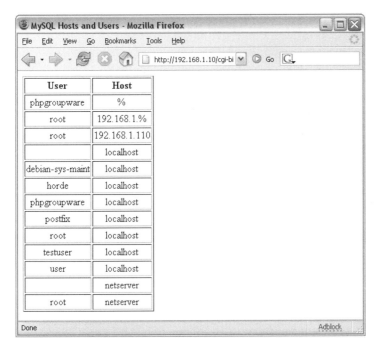

Figure 3-2. *Data from a SQL query has been placed into an HTML table.*

Next, the results are iterated through and the table dynamically created on the fly:

```
while (my ($hostname,$username) = $sth->fetchrow_array()) {
        if ($hostname eq "") {
                $hostname = "<b>undef</b>";
        }
        print Tr({-align=>'CENTER',-valign=>'TOP'},
                [td(["$username","$hostname"])
                ]);

}
```

Each row of the table must be created within the while() loop in order for it to make sense in an HTML table format.

You could also place values retrieved into a hash within the while() loop, or you could use other methods, including fetchrow_hashref() and others. See the DBI documentation (type perldoc DBI from a terminal window) for more information about other methods.

Troubleshooting Database Interaction

Many a Perl DBI developer has been perplexed by database connectivity. Troubleshooting a database connection is no different from troubleshooting another bit of code. Well, it may be a little different, because troubleshooting a database connection is easier! Most servers will have a command-line interface (CLI) into the database or another means for you to test your connection apart from the program itself.

Here are some troubleshooting tips for working with database connectivity issues in a Perl program:

- If a connection to a database isn't working, the first thing you should do is examine the amount of error reporting that you have coming from the database. Be sure that `PrintError` and `RaiseError` are enabled, and use the `or die()` construct as much as possible.

- One of the most helpful debugging and troubleshooting techniques is the frequent use of simple `print` statements to help determine where the problem might lie. In the context of a SQL statement, it's very helpful to print out the statement exactly as it's about to be run on the database. Doing so can help you to see that a parameter isn't being filled in correctly or might help you spot another error.

- On some systems, you can enable logging of all queries for certain database servers such as MySQL. Be careful in doing so, however, as this can lead to a massive amount of logging and can also log potentially sensitive information, depending on what's stored in your database.

- Databases that have a CLI are especially helpful. Connect to the CLI as the same user that you're using for the program, and attempt to execute the same SQL statement to see if it works. You would be surprised how many issues can be solved by connecting to the CLI to imitate the program's behavior in an interactive way. Refer to the documentation for your database server to determine the syntax for connecting to the CLI.

Security Considerations with Data Access

Accessing a database from a Perl program, especially one that's on the Web, presents its own set of security risks and challenges. You most definitely don't want to allow unauthorized access to the database and the data it contains. This section looks at some of the risks involved and gives suggestions for mitigating those risks.

Stored Credentials

One of the most obvious risks in connecting to a database from a program is that the credentials (username and password) are stored in the program itself or within a file that the program can read for those values. Unfortunately, there's no truly effective method for mitigating this risk. If you're running the program on a shared server, such as some web hosting provider's server, you need to ensure that other users cannot read the program's code to see the password. This is usually easier said than done. However, many web hosting providers now have users running in their own chroot'ed shell, which means that the risk of another user reading your files is greatly reduced. (For more information about chroot, see http://www.braingia.org/projects/.)

Unnecessary Privileges

There's always a chance that someone might get access to the credentials stored in your program. For this reason, it's important that the user credentials stored in that file allow only the minimum amount of privileges necessary to perform the task for that program. For example, if you have one program that performs SELECT statements for a catalog and another that updates a shopping cart database, it's much better to use two separate users for these programs, each with separate privileges, than to have one "super-user" with all privileges.

■Tip Grant only the exact privileges necessary to perform the task at hand on only the databases (and even tables) necessary to perform that task from only the necessary host.

Having performed a number of security audits, I can't count the number of times that I've seen developers grant their users full privileges (with grant option in MySQL, for example). By doing so, they've effectively made a super-user who even has the power to add other users! I can't think of a worse scenario than having attackers get that username and password and be able to not only control the database, but also to add hidden users for themselves to get back in later! Again, it's important to keep privileges at a minimum and separate privileges whenever possible.

Unsanitized Statements and Input

Another common mistake is to execute statements on a database that haven't been properly sanitized. The DBI includes the quote() method to make sanitization easy. Employ the quote() method whenever you'll be using a variable within a SQL statement.

Putting data on the Web through a database magnifies the problem of unsanitized input. Improperly checking (or not checking at all) the input that arrives from a web form or elsewhere is only asking for trouble when the input can lead to database interaction. Be sure to untaint the data, as discussed Chapter 1, and be sure to use the quote() method to clean the input and prevent users from executing more than they should on a database.

Summary

This chapter looked at database access through Perl. Much of the chapter was devoted to the DBI, which provides the interface into databases in Perl. The DBI uses database-dependent code, or DBDs, to connect to various database server implementations. Much of the chapter's material was not specific to web programming per se, but rather covered how to work with databases.

The chapter included examples of connecting to databases, running queries, and retrieving query results. You also saw some examples of how to create HTML pages using data retrieved from SQL with the DBI.

The final section discussed security considerations with data access. It's very important to ensure that any data you use—whether in a SELECT statement or any other SQL statement—is sanitized.

In the next chapter, you'll learn about system interaction through Perl programs, with specific focus on the interaction from web programs. This will include a discussion of working with files through a CGI program.

CHAPTER 4

■■■

System Interaction

Interacting with the system means many things to a Perl script. Naturally, by the simple act of executing, a Perl script is interacting with the system on many levels. Exactly how the interaction at that low level occurs isn't of much concern to most Perl programmers. The system interactions of interest to Perl programmers are those that involve files and system processes. These types of interactions with the system are the focus of this chapter.

Perl Scripts and the Operating System

When a Perl script interacts with the system, it normally does so with the rights and privileges of the user executing the script. If the user is root, then the script usually executes with the rights of root. If the script runs as a normal user, then it has the rights of that user. However, Perl scripts can change their userid (uid), real or effective, within the program by using mechanisms such as suidperl and Apache's suEXEC feature.

When a CGI program interacts with the system, it usually does so with the permissions of the web server. On modern Linux systems, Apache runs as a nonprivileged user such as httpd, www-data, or the like, rather than the root user. This means that any CGI script executed as part of a web application will be run as this nonprivileged user, so it likely won't be able to write to files on the system, to kill processes, and so on.

The Apache suEXEC feature is an option to enable CGI scripts to be run as a user other than the httpd web server user. Using suEXEC, the CGI scripts might be owned and therefore run as a normal user account, and thus be able to read and write to that user's directories and files. The Apache suEXEC mechanism makes administrators and most web developers happy, if that's possible. Administrators are happy because CGI scripts aren't run as a system account (such as httpd). Web developers are happy because they can read from and write to their own set of files without worrying about another developer on the computer overwriting their files.

Working with Filehandles

File input and output (I/O) is accomplished in Perl through the use of filehandles. Three filehandles are provided by default: STDIN, STDOUT, and STDERR (standard input, standard output, and standard error, respectively).

■**Note** Having these three default filehandles available means that you can use shell redirect characters such as greater-than and less-than (> and <) to receive output from and send input to a Perl program. For the most part, with CGI scripts, these redirection features aren't used.

When working with a CGI program written in Perl (or any Perl program, for that matter), you can also open, or create, additional filehandles other than STDIN, STDOUT, STDERR. These filehandles are logical connections between the filesystem and the Perl program. You can open filehandles for reading, writing (create and write), or appending. This section examines the basics of using filehandles to work with files from within your Perl program.

Opening Filehandles

The call to open a filehandle consists of three main elements: the name of the filehandle, the mode for opening, and the name of the file to open. This is most easily shown with a timely example:

```
open MYFILE, '<', 'thefilename';
```

This example makes the call to open a filehandle named MYFILE. This name, MYFILE, will be used internally by your program when referencing the filehandle. The name MYFILE resides in its own namespace. The file as it exists on the filesystem is called thefilename, and the mode in which this file will be opened is for reading.

You can also open a file for writing by using a single greater-than sign (>), using a slightly different syntax:

```
open (MYFILE, ">thefilename");
```

Most Perl programs written over the past several years will use this format for the open() statement. The previous example uses a newer syntax for opening a filehandle. If thefilename file already exists on the system, it will be overwritten because of the single greater-than sign.

■**Caution** It's important to use extra care when writing to files. It's quite possible to overwrite important system files (such as /etc/passwd) by including only one greater-than sign (overwriting) instead of two (appending).

Using a double greater-than sign (>>) indicates that the file will be opened for appending. Building on the previous example, opening a file called thefilename for appending using a filehandle named MYFILE looks like this:

```
open (MYFILE, ">>myfilename");
```

All of the examples assume that the file myfilename is located in the same directory as the Perl script. As often as not, the file is located in a different directory. In that case, you need to tell the Perl program where to find the file, whether using a location relative to the current directory or an absolute path. I've found that it's best to fully qualify the location with an absolute path. Doing so ensures that the program will always be able to find the file (assuming that it actually exists).

Opening a file for reading located in the /tmp directory looks like this:

```
open (FILE, "/tmp/thefile");
```

File-open operations return true if they are successful and false if they are not, but Perl programs will silently continue and even let you use filehandles that haven't been created successfully. This can wreak havoc on Perl programs, unless the status of the file-open operation is checked for errors. As the programmer, it's your job to check the result, which is where the die() function comes in.

Using die() to Trap Errors

File-open operations can fail for any number of reasons, including because the file or a component of its path does not exist or because the user does not have sufficient privileges. What happens if the file that you're opening within a Perl program doesn't exist? For create and append file operations, the file will automatically be created if it doesn't exist. Remember that for create operations (the single greater-than sign), the file will be created or re-created, even if it already exists. If the path to a file being opened doesn't exist, Perl will silently continue as if the file had been created successfully. The same applies for files that are opened for reading: Perl will continue executing, regardless of whether the file or path actually exists. Therefore, it's important that you trap errors when working with files and directories.

Using the die() function, you can effectively stop the program from executing if an error is encountered while opening a file. The die() function prints to STDERR when called. Since the open() function returns true on success and false on failure, you can use the die() function when the open() function returns false, as would be the case when a file-open operation fails.

The easiest way to use the die() function is with a logical OR when opening a file, as in this example:

```
open (MYFILE, ">thefilename") or die "Cannot open file 'thefilename': $!";
```

The logical OR can also be written as ||.

Reading from Filehandles

To read from a filehandle, you essentially read each line individually, in much the same way you read from STDIN. Consider this example:

```
open (FILE, "/tmp/file") or die("Cannot open file: $!");
while (<FILE>) {
    chomp;
    print "The line just read was: $_\n";
}
```

This example uses the chomp() function, which takes a scalar argument and removes the newline character from the end, assuming that there is indeed a newline character present. In the context of this example, chomp() acts on the $_ built-in variable, which holds the contents of the line just read in from the filehandle.

The chomp() function is used frequently when reading from a file to remove the newline character from the end of the line. The chop() function is also available, but it isn't as useful in this context, because it removes the last character from the line, regardless of whether that character is a newline or another character.

Writing to Filehandles

To write to a filehandle, place the filehandle after the print function call, like so:

```
open (NEWFILE, ">/tmp/thenewfile");
print NEWFILE "Printing to the new file like this.\n";
```

Closing Filehandles

None of the examples so far have shown how to close a filehandle. That is because Perl automatically closes the filehandle when the program exits or if the file is opened again. However, I almost always explicitly close any open filehandles. I do so simply to be thorough in coding. I recommend that you do the same. It's a simple method:

```
close (FILEHANDLE);
```

Here's a better example:

```
open (NEWFILE, ">/tmp/thenewfile") or die (Cannot open file: $!");
print NEWFILE "Printing to the new file like this.\n";
close (NEWFILE);
```

Using File Tests

One final area of basic file usage that I'll touch on are the file tests, known within the perlfunc documentation (where you can find more information about them) as the "-X" tests. These functions test the given argument, a filename or filehandle, for something. That doesn't sound like much fun, but it is really. Using a -X file test, you can quickly determine whether a file exists, if it's a directory or a symbolic link, whether it's a text file or a binary file, it's age, and other such useful bits of information that you might find necessary in a given Perl program. Table 4-1 is a partial list of the -X file tests.

Table 4-1. *Some -X File Tests*

-e	File or directory exists.
-z	File is empty (zero size).
-s	File is not empty; function returns size in bytes.
-f	Argument is a plain file.
-d	Argument is a directory.
-l	Argument is a symbolic link.
-p	Argument is a named pipe.
-S	Argument is a socket.
-b	File is a block special file.
-c	File is a character special file.
-t	Filehandle is an open tty (isatty()).
-f	Argument is readable by effective uid/gid.

Some -X File Tests

-w	Argument is writable by effective uid/gid.
-x	Argument is executable by effective uid/gid.
-o	Argument is owned by effective uid.
-R	Argument is readable by real uid/gid.
-W	File is writable by real uid/gid.
-X	File is executable by real uid/gid.
-O	File is owned by real uid.
-T	File is an ASCII text file.
-B	File is a binary file.
-u	Argument has setuid bit set.
-g	Argument has setgid bit set.
-k	Argument has sticky bit set.
-M	Time in days from argument modification time to Perl program start time.
-A	Time in days from argument access time to Perl program start time.
-C	Time in days from argument change time to Perl program start time.

A Slight Aside: Directory Listings

I know that I said I was done with basic filesystem usage in Perl, but before I conclude the section, I want to address a common task that you might encounter in your Perl program: obtaining a directory listing or a listing of files in a directory.

Using readdir, you can obtain a listing of files in a given directory by using its directory handle. Directory handles are much like filehandles, insofar as how you create them within your Perl program. You create a directory handle with the opendir() function:

```
opendir (TMP, "/tmp") or die "Cannot open /tmp";
```

Then you can read from the directory handle in a manner similar to reading from a file:

```
while ($file = readdir(TMP)) {
    print "The file $file is in /tmp\n";
}
closedir(TMP);
```

You can also close the directory handle by using the closedir() function, as shown in this example.

Uploading Files with CGI.pm

So far, this chapter has laid some groundwork for dealing with files from within Perl programs, both CGI and non-CGI. Now, it's time to look at filesystem interaction specifically from a CGI program.

Uploading files through a web browser is a multifaceted task that confronts many web developers. Not only must developers code the basic framework for the upload, but they must also consider the security aspects of allowing users to put files on the web server. If those files contain malicious code that a user can then execute, the user might very well be able to compromise the entire web server. If a size limitation isn't put on the file, a user might upload a file big enough to fill the disk of the web server.

As with seemingly everything in Perl, there are multiple ways to upload files through a CGI program. It's quite possible to build your own handlers for file uploads. However, the CGI module includes functions to assist with file uploads. Here, I'll describe using the CGI module functions.

Note The Apache::Request module, which works with mod_perl, offers another method for working with uploaded files. It provides greater control over the file-upload process than the CGI module functions. For example, the Apache::Request module can help limit the maximum size for the file, thus making the entire process of allowing uploads just that much safer. Chapter 11 provides more information about the Apache:Request module.

Creating a File-Upload Field

CGI.pm includes a function to create a file-upload field within a web form, much like the one shown in Figure 4-1. The upload field created must then be processed within your program.

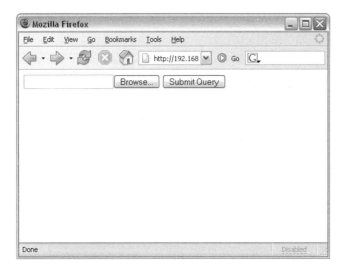

Figure 4-1. *A form with a file-upload field*

In order to use the file-upload field function, called upload(), you must use the special multipart encoding scheme, which is accessed by calling start_multipart_form(), rather than the normal `start_form()` function that you're accustomed to using. Timely code snippets always seem to help. Here's an example of the `upload()` function in action:

```
start_multipart_form();

$handle = $q->upload(-name=>'filename',
    -default=>'the_initial_text',
    -size=>75,
    -maxlength=>150);
```

The `upload()` function accepts four parameters:

- `-name`: This is the name for the field itself. It will be the name that you use to access the field within your code. It has no significance outside the web page and your program. In other words, users never see this name unless they view the HTML source of the web page. The `-name` parameter creates a filehandle within your Perl program, which means that you can work with the file just as you would work with any other filehandle in Perl. Now you know why all that material about filehandles in the previous section was so important.

- `-default`: This parameter specifies the default text to appear in the field. This text isn't necessarily honored by all browsers, so you should be wary of its use or test extensively using different versions of different browsers (which you should do anyway).

- `-size`: This parameter indicates the physical size of the field as it will appear on the web page. Note that this size doesn't have any correlation to the size of the file to be uploaded; rather, it's akin to the size parameter for an everyday, run-of-the-mill form field. Like the `-default` parameter, the `-size` parameter is optional.

- `-maxlength`: This parameter specifies the maximum length in characters that the field will accept on the web page. Like `-size`, `-maxlength` has nothing to do with the actual size of the file to be uploaded. And like the `-size` parameter, the `-maxlength` parameter is optional within the call to `upload()`.

So, of the four parameters, only the first, `-name`, is required. The remaining three parameters are not required. In fact, many browsers ignore the `-default` option. Since three of the four parameters are optional, the code example shown previously can be written more tersely, as follows:

```
$handle = $q->upload('filename');
```

As mentioned, the `upload()` function creates a filehandle that you then need to deal with in your code. Since it's a filehandle, you can do a few things with the uploaded file. Most commonly, the filehandle will be used to simply print (or output) to a file on the filesystem. Expanding on the code example just given and what you've learned about writing to files already, here's an example that takes the filehandle and writes to standard output:

```
$handle = $q->upload('filename');
while (<$handle>) {
    print;
}
```

Accessing Uploading File Header Information

The CGI module also includes a function called uploadInfo(), which gives you access to header information which may (or may not) be sent from the web browser along with the uploaded file. The headers sent by the browser are actually sent as a reference to a hash or associative array. Using the uploadInfo() function along with a header like Content-Type, it's possible to determine the type of document being uploaded in order to allow only certain types to be uploaded. Be forewarned though, browsers can lie. Don't ever rely on user input or on any data coming from a user's browser. As I've emphasized in previous chapters, no input should be used within your program until it has been validated.

For example, it's possible to incorporate a CGI program into the form shown in Figure 4-1 in order to print the Content-Type of the file being uploaded. Listing 4-1 contains a basic CGI script for accomplishing this task.

Listing 4-1. *Printing the Content-Type of an Uploaded File*

```perl
#!/usr/bin/perl

use strict;
use CGI qw/:standard/;

my $q = new CGI;

my $filename = $q->param('uploaded_file');
my $contenttype = $q->uploadInfo($filename)->{'Content-Type'};

print header;
print start_html;
print "Type is $contenttype<P>";
print end_html;
```

The Content-Type is placed into the variable $contenttype, and then printed to the output stream of an HTML page as an example. Figure 4-2 shows an example of choosing to upload an HTML file, and Figure 4-3 shows the output produced from Listing 4-1.

In practice, you would likely check the content type in order to make sure that it's one of the acceptable types of files that your program expects as input. Consider the example in Listing 4-2.

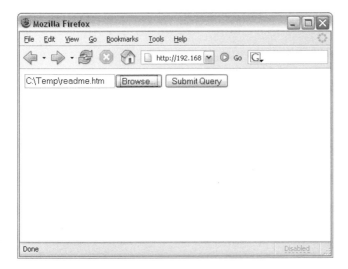

Figure 4-2. *Uploading an HTML file*

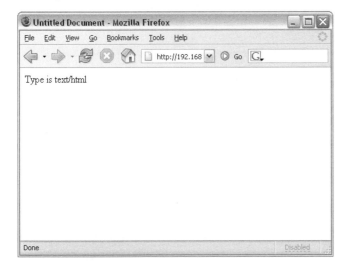

Figure 4-3. *Output showing the Content-Type*

Listing 4-2. *Checking for Acceptable File Types*

```
#!/usr/bin/perl

use strict;
use CGI qw/:standard/;
```

```
my $q = new CGI;

my $filename = $q->param('uploaded_file');
my $contenttype = $q->uploadInfo($filename)->{'Content-Type'};

print header;
print start_html;
if ($contenttype !~ /^text\/html$/) {
    print "Only HTML is allowed<P>";
    print end_html;
    exit;
} else {
    print "Type is $contenttype<P>";
}

print end_html;
```

When a file with a Content-Type that isn't text/html is uploaded to this CGI script, its output indicates that only HTML types are allowed, as shown in Figures 4-4 and 4-5, where an executable file is uploaded. Figure 4-4 shows an example of choosing to upload an executable file, and Figure 4-5 shows the output produced from Listing 4-2.

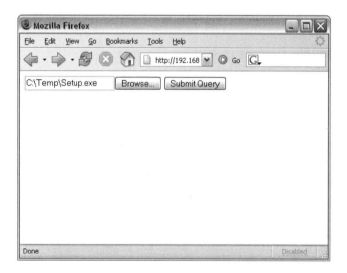

Figure 4-4. *Uploading an executable file*

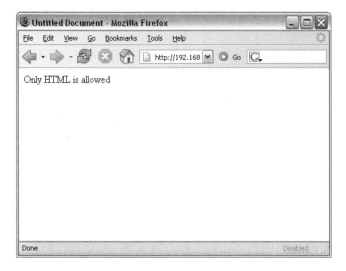

Figure 4-5. *Output produced when a file with a Content-Type other than text/html is uploaded*

Protecting Temporary Files

Whenever a file is being uploaded from the web client to the server, the content of that file is being stored in a temporary location on the server. This creates a number of problems, not the least of which is that the file, while being stored in that temporary location, might be exposed to other users local to the server itself. To lessen (but not completely remove) this risk, you can use the -private_tempfiles pragma when you invoke the CGI namespace—in other words, with the use CGI lines that usually appear at the beginning of the program. Where before you might have something like this:

```
use CGI qw/:standard/;
```

you now have this:

```
use CGI qw/:standard -private_tempfiles/;
```

Working with System Processes

By the phrase "working with system processes," I'm specifically referring to spawning programs external to your Perl program—such as cat, ls, and others—in order to obtain information and interact with the operating system itself.

When working with processes, or really anything outside your Perl program, there is an inherent danger of introducing unknown and possibly unsafe elements into the program. Refer to the "Security Considerations with System Interaction" section later in this chapter for more information about this aspect of programming with Perl.

Since this book does assume at least some familiarity with Perl, it's logical to assume that you have some experience with spawning external processes from a Perl program. This section won't be a rehash of every bit of information about such an undertaking. Rather, this section will provide some refresher material to ensure we're all talking the same language.

Executing System Processes from a Perl Program

When Perl runs a system process, it inherits the traits of its parent. Recall from the earlier section on filehandles that a Perl program inherits the three standard filehandles: STDIN, STDOUT, and STDERR. The Perl program also inherits other things, like the uid of the parent, the umask, the current directory, and other such environmental variables. Perl provides the %ENV hash as means to access and change the environment variables that are inherited by your Perl program. You can iterate through this hash in the same way that you would any other hash to see the environment variables.

```
foreach $key (keys %ENV) {
    print "Environment key $key is $ENV{$key}\n";
}
```

The fork() and exec() methods of firing a system command are the most flexible method of working with system commands available in Perl. Unfortunately, they're also the most complex and arguably the least used, especially when it comes to CGI programming. I'm not going to clutter these pages with a discussion of fork() and exec(), but rather refer you to the perlfunc document pages for more information about fork(), exec(), kill(), wait(), and waitpid().

Here, we'll look at using the system() function, run quotes, and system processes as filehandles.

The system Function

The system() function is a common way to fire off a new process from a Perl program. When you use the system() function, a new process is created or handed off to /bin/sh, and the Perl program waits until the process is finished running.

The exit status from the system() function is passed back to the Perl program. It's important to note that this exit status is not the exit status of the command that the system() function actually runs, but the exit status of the shell in which the command is run. This is an important distinction because it means that you can't rely on the exit status of the system() function as an indication of whether or not the actual command run by the function completed successfully.

Here's an example of the system() function in action:

```
system("uptime");
```

Run Quotes

The next method to execute a system process from within a Perl program goes by a few names—*backquotes*, *backticks*, or *run quotes*. I'll be using the name run quotes for no reason other than that's the name that I've heard used the most often.

Run quotes are different from the system() function in that they return the output of the command. If you want to capture the output of the command, using run quotes provides an easy way to accomplish the task, as this example shows:

```
$uptime = `uptime`;
```

When executed, the variable $uptime would contain the output from the uptime command:

```
21:20:07 up 202 days,  5:52,  3 users,  load average: 0.01, 0.02, 0.00
```

Obviously, the output from your uptime command probably will be different.

System Processes As Filehandles

You learned about filehandles earlier in this chapter. You can also use system processes as file-handles by using the same open() function as you use to create a filehandle. Like file-flavored filehandles, you can open process filehandles for reading and writing.

The syntax of the open() function is largely the same for processes as it is for files, except that the pipe character (|) is used instead of the greater-than/less-than characters. The location of the pipe character determines whether the process handle is opened for reading or writing.

Creating a process handle for reading looks like this:

```
open(UPTIME, "uptime|");
```

Creating a handle for writing looks like this:

```
open(PRINTER, "|lpr ");
```

Then you could print to that handle, similar to how you print to a filehandle:

```
print PRINTER "Printing something from this handle\n";
```

Using System Processes Within a CGI Program

Using a system call from within a Perl-based CGI script is no different from using the same system call from within another Perl program. The one exception is that you must pay particular attention to the environment within which the script will be run.

Many times, the environment will be that of the web server user. This means that the Perl program might not have access to the same commands, files, and other environmental bits as your user on the same system. A common symptom is that the script will appear to run fine when you execute it from your shell, but when you attempt to access the script through the web browser, it won't work, possibly giving the infamous Internal Server Error message that Perl programmers everywhere have come to love.

Some web servers use Apache's suEXEC feature for the execution of CGI scripts. With suEXEC, CGI scripts are executed as the user who owns the program, which is frequently the same as your userid for many installations.

Security Considerations with System Interaction

When working with the system—files or processes—from within a Perl program, you must pay additional attention to your surroundings. It's quite possible and unfortunately easy to over-write existing and essential files by opening a file for writing instead of appending.

Whenever you work with anything outside your Perl program, there is always a risk of introducing unknown data into your Perl program or doing something unintentional to the system itself. The former is an important concern for developers; the latter is primarily a concern for the system administrator. For those of us who frequently wear both hats, it's important to perform rigorous sanity checks against data and against all external system interactions. This means, among other things, liberal use of the print() function to ensure that the script is doing what you think it should be doing, and use of the die() function or, at least, the warn() function to report on unexpected conditions. Otherwise, the program may continue as normal, even though the file-open operation failed. The die() function is helpful to prevent the script from getting itself into an unknown state. Also, you'll want to enable taint mode and strict checking, as explained in Chapter 1.

Summary

This chapter covered system interactions that involve files and system processes. You work with files from a Perl script through filehandles. You can open files for reading, writing, or appending. When creating a filehandle, the file is opened in read mode by default, except when using the three-argument version of the open() function, and unless you use a single or double greater-than sign, to indicate either writing or appending, respectively. Whenever you're working with filehandles, it's always a good idea to use the die() function to ensure that the filehandle was created successfully.

System processes can also be created or spawned from within a Perl program. There are four methods for working with external system processes from within a Perl program: the system() function, run quotes (or backquotes), the fork() and exec() functions, and the open() function. With the system() function or the run quotes method, the Perl program waits until the process is finished running. The system() function returns the status from the shell to the Perl program. Run quotes return the resulting value from any command(s) run outside the Perl program. You can use the open() function to spawn external processes in much the same way as you create a filehandle, except that you use the pipe character (|) to denote that you want to run a process, rather than a filehandle. Putting the pipe character after the command indicates the process handle is for reading; putting the pipe character before the command indicates that the process handle is for writing.

When working with system processes, you must pay attention to the environment variables that the program will inherit when it runs. Since many CGI scripts are executed as the web server user, the script might not run the same when it is executed by the web server.

When your CGI program is interacting with the system, you need to take great care to ensure that the program is written with security in mind. This is especially the case for programs that will be accessed through the Web. The use of taint and strict modes is essential, along with use of the die() function.

This chapter marks the end of the first part of the book. The next part of the book will look at some additional interaction that Perl programs can take with the Internet. So far, you've seen how to create web pages with Perl. The next chapter describes how to consume and work with web pages from within Perl.

PART 2

■■■

Internet Interaction with LWP and Net:: Tools

CHAPTER 5

■■■

LWP Modules

LWP is an abbreviation for library of WWW modules in Perl. LWP modules enable you to incorporate common web tasks into your Perl program through a set of functions that can be imported into your namespace.

Using the LWP modules (the LWP, for short), you can perform tasks such as retrieving web pages, submitting web forms, and mirroring a web site. As with other tasks in Perl, you could accomplish these same things without the help of the LWP. However, this chapter will concentrate on using the LWP modules (thus the title). The LWP contains a number of protocol methods, including ones to work with HTTP, HTTPS, FTP, NNTP, and others. This chapter looks at how to use the LWP with HTTP and HTTPS.

Getting Started with the LWP

To use the LWP modules, you need to first obtain and install them. Distributions such as Debian have the LWP prepackaged, which makes installation rather trivial (`apt-get install libwww-perl`). If your distribution doesn't contain a prepackaged version of the LWP, you can download and install the software manually. The LWP modules are available from your favorite CPAN mirror.

It's always a good idea to check whether the modules are already installed prior to going through the job of installing them. An easy method for testing this is with the following command, executed from the shell:

```
perl -MLWP -e 'print "$LWP::VERSION\n"'
```

You have the LWP installed if you see a version number such as this output:

```
5.803
```

If you don't have the LWP installed, you'll need to perform the installation in order to accomplish most of the tasks in this chapter.

The LWP primarily works with the HTTP request and response model. This means that the module is an excellent choice for retrieving and parsing web pages on the Internet. Here's a quick example to get your feet wet. The code (`Getua.pl`) retrieves a web page and prints it all to STDOUT.

SOLVING A REAL-WORLD PROBLEM WITH THE LWP

The LWP even helped me to get a console gaming system. In 2004, a popular beverage company had a contest that involved collecting a number of points to earn prizes. These prizes were made available online, but limited quantities of specific prizes were available. For the more popular items, these quantities were quickly depleted. In order to ensure that I was one of the lucky people to get the item I wanted—a gaming console—I needed a method to monitor the web page to see when the item became available. Perl to the rescue!

Using the LWP I was able to quickly create a script to look for certain text ("Now Available," for example) to appear on the page, and then send an e-mail alert when the text was found. With this script set to check every five minutes, I got the gaming console.

Of course, this is just one example of how the LWP can be used to solve a real-world problem, albeit a simple one.

```perl
#!/usr/bin/perl -w

use LWP;
use strict;

my $browser = LWP::UserAgent->new(agent => 'Perly v1');
my $result = $browser->get("http://www.braingia.org/ewfojwefoj");
die "An error occurred: ", $result->status_line( ) unless \
$result->is_success;

#Do something more meaningful with the content than this!
print $result->content;
```

When you run this code, it will output the raw web page. It will probably fly past on the screen, likely ending with something like this:

```
    </script>
</body>
</html>
```

You'll take a closer look at this code later in the chapter, in the "Retrieving a Web Page" section.

HTTP from 29,999 Feet

While not quite a high-altitude flyover of HTTP—thus 29,999 feet instead of 30,000 feet—this section gives you a primer on HTTP's inner workings. RFC 2616 (which can be found at http://www.rfc-editor.org/) defines the Hypertext Transfer Protocol (HTTP) and provides the model under which web traffic operates. HTTP is based on requests and responses. In HTTP communications, the requester of a document is the client, and the responder is the server. When you visit a web page in a browser such as Mozilla Firefox, the browser sends the request to the server, which then responds accordingly.

HTTP Requests

An HTTP request contains the method for the request, information about the resource being requested, and the protocol version. These three pieces of information are contained on the first line, known as the *request line*. Next follow one or more optional header lines, which normally consist of *key:value* pairs. Finally, an optional body is included in the HTTP request. The body of the HTTP request frequently contains form values being passed as part of the request, but it can include any number of other objects.

Consider this example, which is created with the following command:

```
telnet www.braingia.org 80
```

The HTTP request looks like this:

```
GET / HTTP/1.1
Host: www.braingia.org
```

The first line is the request line, which contains three pieces of information: the method (GET), the resource (/, to indicate the root directory or that the default file be served from this directory), and the protocol version (HTTP/1.1). Following the request line is a header. In this case, this is the Host header, and it specifies the host (www.braingia.org) should receive the request. The Host header enables multiple web sites to share the same physical IP. It's up to the web server itself, such as Apache, to handle the request correctly, based on the value of the Host header.[1] Notice the extra empty line after the header. This carriage return/line feed (CRLF) is key for an HTTP request.

HTTP Responses

The web server will receive the HTTP request and respond to it. The first line of the response, known as the *status line*, contains the protocol version, followed by a numeric status code and the text response corresponding to that code.

Following the status line are optional response headers and entity headers. Finally, the optional body is included after an additional blank line (CRLF), as is the case in the request.

Here's an example of a response, based on the request shown in the previous section:

```
HTTP/1.1 200 OK
Date: Wed, 06 Apr 2005 15:47:45 GMT
Server: Apache/1.3.26 (Unix) Debian GNU/Linux mod_mono/0.11
mod_perl/1.26
Transfer-Encoding: chunked
Content-Type: text/html; charset=iso-8859-1

<body follows here. . .>
```

---

1. The Host header is quite common in HTTP requests, but that was not always the case. Prior to the existence of the Host header, every web site with its own host and domain name was required to have its own IP address. This contributed to IP address space depletion as the Internet grew. By using the Host header, a single IP address can house thousands of web sites, all using different domain names and all serving different content.

As you can see from this example, the first line (the status line) contains the protocol version (HTTP/1.1), the status (200), and the text associated with that numeric response (OK). The numeric status codes are divided into classes based on the first digit in the code, as listed in Table 5-1.

Table 5-1. *HTTP Status Codes*

Code Class	Type
1*nn*	Informational
2*nn*	Success
3*nn*	Redirection
4*nn*	Client error
5*nn*	Server error

Following the status line are a number of optional header lines, including the date and the server version, Transfer-Encoding, and Content-Type. A blank line (CRLF) is included, followed by the body. In this case, I've snipped the body of the response, which was the HTML and other bits from the actual web page.

■**Note** Some of the headers that I referred to as optional may be required, depending on the type of request and response. However, most requests and responses won't require additional headers. Additionally, for most HTTP transactions, the body is almost always included, since the body is the content of the web page itself, but realize that the body is indeed optional according to the RFC 2616, notably for HEAD requests. For more information about HTTP requirements, see RFC 2616 (http://www.rfc-editor.org/).

Without the LWP, the Perl programmer would need to manually code each portion of the HTTP request, in much the same way that the CGI programmer would need to code each portion of the HTTP response if it weren't for the CGI module. The LWP modules provide functions and object-oriented classes for working with HTTP.

Keeping It Simple with LWP::Simple

The LWP::Simple module gives the programmer a simple interface into common uses of the LWP for working with web resources. It provides five functions that enable you to use the GET HTTP method very easily: get(), getprint(), getstore(), head(), and mirror(). These functions give the programmer just enough control to be dangerous, but they don't offer full power provided with the LWP through the LWP::UserAgent module, which I'll cover after describing the LWP::Simple functions.

Get Functions

Most requests for web pages on the Internet use the GET method. LWP::Simple includes functions to perform GET requests on Internet resources. including the aptly titled get() function:

```
$page = get("http://www.braingia.org/");
```

Using this function, the body of the resulting resource will be saved to the variable $page. If the GET request fails, the value of $page will be undefined.

Related to the get() function are two other functions: getprint() and getstore(). The getprint() function usually returns output directly to STDOUT, but it can return output to whatever the currently selected filehandle happens to be. Since STDOUT is usually that filehandle, getprint() will normally just output to the screen. This function is useful for simple Perl commands executed from the shell, as opposed to commands from within full-blown Perl programs. For example, a cron job could be created to automatically check the contents of a web page using a command line such as this:

```
> perl -MLWP::Simple -e "getprint('http://www.braingia.org/') or die"
```

The getstore() function takes the output of a web page and automatically stores it in an external file. Obviously, if you actually want to work with that resulting output from within your Perl program, you will need to then open the file and read in its contents.

The getstore() function also returns the status of the GET method and sets is_success() if the status is in the 200 range. It sets is_error() if the status is in the 400 or 500 range. This effectively means that you can test to ensure that the GET request was successful by looking to see if is_success() is true. Consider the example shown in Listing 5-1 (Example1.pl).

Listing 5-1. *Using is_success() with getstore()*

```perl
#!/usr/bin/perl -w

use LWP::Simple;
use strict;

my $status = getstore("http://www.braingia.org/","/tmp/braingia");
unless (is_success($status)) {
    die "Couldn't retrieve page: $status";
}
open (PAGE, "/tmp/braingia") or die "$!";
while (<PAGE>) {
    print();
}
close(PAGE);
```

If the getstore() function is successful, the raw HTML and other page items will be printed to STDOUT, similar to the output shown for the first example in this chapter (Getua.pl).

If you would like to see what happens when an error is returned, simply point the URL for the getstore() function to a file that doesn't exist, as shown in Listing 5-2 (Example2.pl).

Listing 5-2. *Using getstore() to Print an Invalid Page*

```perl
#!/usr/bin/perl -w

use LWP::Simple;
use strict;

my $status = \
    getstore("http://www.braingia.org/nofile.aspx","/tmp/braingia");

unless (is_success($status)) {
        die "Couldn't retrieve page: ${$status}";
}
open (PAGE, "/tmp/braingia") or die "$!";
while (<PAGE>) {
        print();
}
close(PAGE);
```

There won't be a file named nofile.aspx on my web site (I'd be surprised if I ever have anything named *.aspx on my site), so the getstore() function will return a 404, for a Page Not Found error, which will, in turn, cause is_success to be false. The script will die and output the status message:

```
Couldn't retrieve page: 404 at ./example2.pl line 10.
```

The Head Function

The HEAD method is normally used to test hypertext links for validity and, when implemented by the server, returns the header information in the same way that a GET request would. The HEAD method never returns the body of the resource.

■**Caution** Unfortunately, the HEAD method is not supported by all web servers and is turned off by others. This means that the use of the HEAD method is unreliable.

LWP::Simple implements the HEAD method with the head() function. You can use this function in either a scalar or list context.

In a scalar context, head() returns true or false based on the status of the return code. You can use this form in an if/then or unless control structure to test for success:

```perl
die "Wasn't able to run the HEAD method on the URL" unless \
head('http://www.braingia.org');
```

When called in a list context, the head() function returns five items from the response header:

- Content type

- Document length

- Modified time

- Expires

- Server

For example, the head() function might be called in this manner in order to capture the five values:

```
($content_type,$doclen,$modified,$expires,$server) = \
head('http://www.braingia.org');
```

The Mirror Function

The mirror() function works in much the same was as the getstore() function, but also includes a check to compare the modification time of the local file and the modification time of the remote resource, based on the If-Modified-Since response header. Listing 5-3 shows an example of the mirror() function in action (Example3.pl):

Listing 5-3. *Using the mirror() Function*

```
#!/usr/bin/perl -w

use LWP::Simple;
use strict;

my $url = "http://www.braingia.org/";
my $file = "/tmp/braingiamirrorweb";

my $status = mirror($url,$file);

die "Cannot retrieve $url" unless is_success($status);
```

This program won't produce any output to the terminal unless there is an error. If it's successful, there will be a file in /tmp called braingiamirrorweb. Inside that file will be raw output such as HTML and other bits as found on the web page. The contents will be similar to the following:

```
<!DOCTYPE html PUBLIC "-//W3C//DTD XHTML 1.1//EN"
"http://www.w3.org/TR/xhtml11/
DTD/xhtml11.dtd">
<html>
```

```
<head>
<meta http-equiv="Content-Type" content="text/html; charset=iso-8859-1"/>
<script type="text/javascript">
<!--
```

The user agent object also has a `mirror()` method, and the `lwp-mirror` program implements the `mirror()` function. Both of these are discussed in the "Using Mirroring a Web Site" section later in this chapter.

Getting More Functionality with LWP::UserAgent

The user agent plays a central role in web transactions. The user agent is roughly synonymous with the browser or client side of an HTTP request and response transaction. The LWP includes a `UserAgent` namespace, `LWP::UserAgent`, which implements many functions and has numerous attributes that you would find in a web browser.

The user agent is frequently used to create a new browser object. This object can have a number of attributes set to define the behavior and operation of the resulting browser object. Table 5-2 summarizes the `LWP::UserAgent` attributes and their corresponding default values for the browser object.

Table 5-2. *LWP::UserAgent Attributes*

Attribute	Default Value
agent	libwww-perl/*NNNN* (where *NNNN* is the version)
conn_cache	No default
cookie_jar	No default
from	No default
keep_alive	No default
max_redirect	7
max_size	No default
parse_head	1
protocols_allowed	No default
protocols_forbidden	No default
requests_redirectable	GET HEAD
timeout	180

To set one or more of the attributes, pass them as a key pair to the `new()` call when invoking `UserAgent`. Here's an example:

```
use LWP;

my $browser = LWP::UserAgent->new(agent=>'Mozilla');
print "the browser agent is ", $browser->agent(), "\n";
```

These attributes can also be changed after the browser object has been created, as shown here:

```
use LWP;

my $browser = LWP::UserAgent->new();
$browser->agent("Mozilla");
print "the browser agent is ", $browser->agent(), "\n";
```

■**Caution** Some (poorly designed) web sites use the user agent value to prevent users of certain browsers from accessing the site. As you just saw, the user agent can be trivially changed by the user. Stick to the web standards set by organizations such as the W3C, and you won't have to use stupid tricks such as these on sites that you design.

In the upcoming examples of using the LWP, you'll see how many of the attributes for the user agent object are put into action.

Using the LWP

Now that you've seen some of the LWP components, this section looks at some common uses of the LWP. These include retrieving a web page, submitting a web form, handling cookies, handling password-protected sites, mirroring a web site, and handling proxies.

Retrieving a Web Page

The LWP makes the process of screen scraping rather trivial. *Screen scraping* refers to programmatically capturing the document being served in an HTTP request, through a means other than a standard web browser. A common goal of screen scraping is to look for certain text on the document and do something if that text is found. Listing 5-4 shows an example of how to do this (Get.pl).

Listing 5-4. *Retrieving a Web Page with get()*

```
#!/usr/bin/perl -w

use LWP::Simple;
use strict;

my $webpage = get("http://www.braingia.org/");

if (($webpage) && (grep {/Steve/} $webpage)) {
    print "I found the text\n";
}
```

This example uses the get() function from LWP::Simple, which enables you to quickly and easily retrieve a web page using the GET method, as explained earlier in the chapter. The program will perform a GET against the web page at http://www.braingia.org/, and then search for some text within the page, including any HTML, scripts, or other material returned. If that text is found, the program will print a simple message to STDOUT indicating that it found the text, something like this:

```
I found the text
```

The choices for working with the resulting text from the get() function are limited only by what you would like to do with the results.

Setting Additional Parameters

The get() function works well for simple GET method requests. However, some sites require you to set additional parameters, such as authentication, user agent, and other values. When you need to set these additional parameters, use the LWP::UserAgent class.

Consider the example in Listing 5-5 (Getua.pl), which performs a GET on a URL and also sets the agent parameter.

Listing 5-5. *Setting a User Agent and Retrieving a Web Page*

```perl
#!/usr/bin/perl -w

use LWP;
use strict;

my $browser = LWP::UserAgent->new(agent => 'Perly v1');
my $result = $browser->get("http://www.braingia.org/ewfojwefoj");
die "An error occurred: ", $result->status_line( ) unless
$result->is_success;

#Do something more meaningful with the content than this!
print $result->content;
```

You may recognize this as the example I showed you at the beginning of this chapter. The program will report itself as "Perly v1" to the web server. You can use this to mimic any web browser or make up your own, as shown in the example. The output from this program is raw HTML and JavaScript, as shown previously.

■**Note** For more information about user agent strings, see the appropriately titled "User-Agent Strings" document at http://www.mozilla.org/build/revised-user-agent-strings.html.

Setting Timeouts

Sometimes, the web server is slow to respond, or other network-type issues cause the browser to time out. You can set the timeout of the browser to a value appropriate for your application.

Recall that the default is 180 seconds. You can set the timeout either when you create the browser object or at any time during its life. Assume you have a browser object called $browser. In this example, you set the timeout to 30 seconds, instead of the default 180:

```
$browser->timeout(30);
```

Controlling Browser Redirects

Browser objects created through the LWP::UserAgent class accept HTTP redirects for the GET and HEAD methods. You can change this behavior to accept redirects for other combinations of HTTP methods or disallow redirects entirely. The requests_redirectable attribute accepts a list of HTTP methods that can be redirected:

```
$browser->requests_redirectable([\@methods]);
```

This list is inclusive, so if you merely call the function with one method as an argument, you overwrite what's already there. To accept redirects for the POST method (discussed in the "Submitting a Web Form" section a little later in this chapter), you add it to the list by calling requests_redirectable:

```
push @{$browser->requests_redirectable}, 'POST';
```

Realize that the requests_redirectable attribute already contains two values: GET and HEAD. Therefore, if you want to add a method to that list, you must use a method such as push (as in this example). If you don't push a new value onto the stack, you'll be replacing what's already there. This can cause no end to confusion.

Based on that note of caution, it's sometimes helpful to see if a particular method will indeed accept a redirect for a given browser object. A call to the redirect_ok() method will return true if a redirect would be permitted for the given method. Consider this example:

```
if ($browser->redirect_ok(GET)) {
    print "The browser object would accept a redirect for GET\n";
}
```

Sending Additional Headers

In some cases, you may need to specify additional header lines as part of the request for a URL. In these instances, you can send them along with the request as key/value pairs. For example, a GET method using the get() function would normally look like this:

```
$browser->get($url);
```

To include additional headers, place them after the URL, as in this example:

```
$browser->get($url, Header => Value, Header => Value . . .)
```

A use for this might be to send the acceptable character set to the server:

```
$browser->get($url, 'Accept-Charset' => 'iso-9859-1');
```

Cloning the Browser

If you already have a browser object set up in your program and configured as you like it, you can use the clone() method to quickly create a duplicate of the browser object. Assume that you have a browser object, $browser, already created. The following code would create a duplicate of that browser object:

```
$browser2 = $browser->clone();
```

Submitting a Web Form

Two HTTP methods are used to pass form variables into a script on the web: GET and POST. Using GET, the parameters are passed as part of the URL itself in *name=value* pairs. This type of submission using the LWP is rather trivial and can be accomplished in a number of ways through various GET methods, as you've already seen in this chapter.

However, even though GET is the most commonly used method, the POST method is also frequently used, especially when working with web forms or web services.

Using GET, any parameters passed into a CGI application are passed via the URL. This can be problematic for three main reasons:

- Some browsers and servers limit the length of the URL, thus making complicated parameter passing more difficult.

- All characters in the URL must be encoded in order to be safe for URLs.

- Parameters passed on the URL are visible to anyone listening, regardless of whether or not SSL (HTTPS) is used.

In contrast, using POST, all of the parameters are passed as part of the message body. This alone effectively removes all three problems with GET. Parameters passed via POST aren't limited by length, nor do they need to be encoded. And since the parameters are passed within the body, they are indeed encrypted when passed over SSL.

Using the LWP post() method, the *name=value* pairs are passed as an array—well, actually as a reference to an array, as you'll see shortly.

When working with forms, there are a number of form elements that appear inside the <form></form> tags on the page. For example, assume a web form located at http://www.example.com/form.cgi contains text boxes to fill in with information such as the user's name, e-mail address, and zip code. The *name=value* parameters might look like this for a filled-in form:

```
name=Steve Suehring
email=suehring@braingia.com
zip=54481
```

You can send these in a POST request through the LWP by placing them as arguments within the call to the post() method of the browser object, as shown here:

```
$result = $browser->post('http://www.example.com/form.cgi',
    [
        'name' => 'Steve',
        'email' => 'suehring@braingia.com',
        'zip' => '54481'
    ]);
```

To analyze a web form, the first task is to determine the URL of the target. This is defined in the opening <form> tag as the "action" for the form. From there, it's a matter of determining which parameters, if any, are required, and the corresponding values for them. Of course, since this is Perl, it's common to substitute variables for the parameter values themselves. So instead of hard-coding the zip code, you might want to set $zip as a scalar variable that changes for the web form. Naturally, what you do with the POSTed data is up to you and the form itself.

Handling Cookies

As explained in Chapter 1, cookies are used by web sites to track state and other information about the visiting browser or user agent. It's up to you to work with the cookies that are set and expected by the web site.

The LWP's cookie_jar attribute is used with sites that set and read browser cookies. Using the cookie_jar attribute, you can store cookies both in memory or out to a file. When I monitored a site to win a gaming console (as I described earlier in the chapter), I used an existing cookie store. Since that site required authentication using a cookie, I was able to use the cookies file from Firefox to successfully authenticate to the site from within the script.

The cookie_jar attribute can read cookies based solely in memory, or it can use cookies in a file. If the cookies are based in memory, they exist only as long as the life of the user agent object created within the program itself. If the cookies are based in a file, they become persistent and can be saved and read between multiple user agents and multiple executions of the program itself.

You can create a temporary cookie store in memory by invoking the HTTP::Cookies object. For example, assume a browser object named $browser. Creating a memory-based cookie store would look like this:

```
$browser->cookie_jar(HTTP::Cookies->new);
```

On the other hand, using a file would look like this:

```
use LWP;

my $browser = LWP::UserAgent->new( );
my $cookie_jar = HTTP::Cookies->new(
        'file' => '/home/suehring/cookies.txt'
);
$browser->cookie_jar($cookie_jar);
```

Handling Password-Protected Sites

Some sites require authentication through a username and password in order to sign in and use the resources found there. This authentication is provided or indicated by a 401 Authorization Required HTTP response. Normally, a dialog box prompting for authentication pops up, as opposed to a username and password web page. The LWP includes attributes to work with sites that use basic authentication. Using the credentials() method, you add these attributes to a given browser object programmatically. The credentials() method looks like this:

```
$browser->credentials('server:port','realm','username'=>'password');
```

For example, the site www.example.com has a subscribers area for which you must supply credentials. This site uses a realm of Subscribers.

```
$browser->credentials('www.example.com:80',
    'Subscribers',
    'suehring' => 'badpassword');
```

Now when the $browser object is used to access a URL within the www.example.com domain that prompts for credentials, the credentials specified in the example will be sent.

The credentials themselves die at the end of the browser object's life. You can store as many credentials inside a browser object as you need, based on the server name and realm name for the protected resource.

Mirroring a Web Site

Earlier in this chapter, I mentioned LWP::Simple's mirror() function, as well as the lwp-mirror program. Both of these work well for mirroring an entire web site. The browser object also has a mirror() method that enables a site to be mirrored, while taking advantage of the extra power of the object's interface.

The lwp-mirror program does an excellent job of mirroring a site in a sane, easy-to-understand manner. I recommend the lwp-mirror program for nearly all mirroring operations. lwp-mirror is called from your shell and accepts a URL and an output file as arguments:

```
lwp-mirror <url> <output_file>
```

Here is an example:

```
lwp-mirror http://www.braingia.org/ local_braingia_index.html
```

The mirror() method on the browser object has two requirements as well: the URL and the output file. Here is an example of using this method:

```
$browser->mirror('http://www.braingia.org','local_braingia_index.html');
```

Handling Proxies

Proxies are sometimes required to access Internet services. The LWP includes a set of methods for working with proxies that enable you to set a proxy for a given protocol or set of protocols. When a proxy is required on a given system, it's not uncommon for it to be set among the different environment variables in the shell. The LWP can use the shell environment variable for proxy. A call to the env_proxy() method will look for environment variables that indicate the proxy server to use, such as http_proxy, as in the following example:

```
$browser->env_proxy();
```

It doesn't hurt to call this method if nothing is set for the proxy environment variable—the proxy value for the browser object will still be empty.

The proxy() method accepts two arguments: the protocol and the actual proxy to use. Here is its format:

```
$browser->proxy(protocol, proxy_server);
```

For this example, assume that you have a browser object called $browser and proxy server called proxy.example.com. If you want to set the HTTP proxy server for use within the program, the invocation of the proxy() method looks like this:

```
$browser->proxy("http","http://proxy.example.com");
```

It's quite common for a proxy server to be used for URLs that are outside the local network. Inside the network, a proxy server should not be used. For these cases, the LWP includes a no_proxy() method that accepts a comma-separated list of domains for which no proxy server should be used. Assume that you have a server located at local.example.com for which you want direct access, as opposed to access through the proxy. The no_proxy() method call looks like this:

```
$browser->no_proxy("local.example.com");
```

Calling no_proxy() with an empty list clears out the list of hosts:

```
$browser->no_proxy();
```

Removing HTML Tags from a Page

As you've undoubtedly seen if you've followed the examples in this chapter, the content that comes back from a GET request is the raw, uncensored HTML (and other language) content from the web server. To say that this is difficult for a human to read and interpret is an understatement. Unfortunately, there is no surefire method for extracting the useful text from a web page. However, you have some options for retrieving the text from a page.

For example, Listing 5-6 shows the Get.pl example shown earlier in the chapter, but modified to use HTML::FormatText to produce output that is more human-friendly.

Listing 5-6. *Using HTML::FormatText to Retrieve the Text from a Page*

```perl
!/usr/bin/perl -w

use strict;
use HTML::TreeBuilder;
use HTML::FormatText;
use LWP::Simple;

my $webpage = get("http://www.braingia.org/");

my $htmltree = HTML::TreeBuilder->new->parse($webpage);

my $output = HTML::FormatText->new();
print $output->format($htmltree);
```

Recall that when run before, the output from web page retrieval looked like this:

```
<!DOCTYPE html PUBLIC "-//W3C//DTD XHTML 1.1//EN"
 "http://www.w3.org/TR/xhtml11/
DTD/xhtml11.dtd">
<html>
<head>
<meta http-equiv="Content-Type" content="text/html; charset=iso-8859-1"/>
```

Now, rather than outputting the raw HTML and other bits, with the help of `HTML::FormatText`, the output is the actual text on the web page, which currently looks like this:

```
Braingia.org - Web Site for Steve Suehring
============================================


Home | LinuxWorld Magazine | Google Current Work Software My Bookshelf
Older Projects Webnotes Contact


Intarweb
```

As you can see, the output is much easier to read and parse by a human.

■**Tip** Using the Lynx web browser with the `-dump` option also gets the text on the web page.

The easiest (or so it may seem) method for working with the text from a web page is by using regular expressions. Since HTML and other languages are known entities, it's almost always possible to work up a regular expression to extract the text that you need.

There are also Perl modules to assist with the extraction of text from web pages. The aptly titled `HTML::Parser` module along with `HTML::Tokenizer` serve this purpose. These modules can be quite cumbersome to use though, and are highly specialized at that. The `WWW::Mechanize` Perl module provides a good interface to enable browsing through a Perl program as well.

Both regular expressions and the parsing modules have their limitations. Regardless of which method you choose, each page that you need to parse will be unique and offer its own set of challenges.

Security Considerations with the LWP

When working with the LWP, you must take extra caution to not cause unnecessary traffic. It's quite easy to begin a mirror process and consume a lot of disk space or network bandwidth. In addition, the administrators of the site being mirrored might think the site is under attack and take action accordingly.

Obviously, the same rules that apply to other Perl programming apply when you're using the LWP. Don't run as root unless absolutely necessary, be mindful of what you're doing so you don't overwrite files, and so on.

If you're allowing uploads through web forms, pay special attention to where those files are uploaded to and what the user can do with those files once uploaded. Numerous attacks have begun through a file-upload interface.

Summary

This chapter looked at some forms of interaction between a Perl program and the Internet using the LWP modules. You saw how to set up a Perl-based browser, along with attributes such as the user agent. You retrieved web pages and also learned about the GET and POST methods.

More Internet interaction through Perl is on the way in the next chapter. Where this chapter focused primarily on the LWP and web interaction, the next chapter will expand into other protocols, such as POP3, SMTP, and others.

CHAPTER 6

■ ■ ■

Net:: Tools

The things that a programmer can do with Perl never cease to amaze me. The area of network programming is no exception. Of course, it's quite possible to get down and dirty with Perl and write your own network servers and clients. I find this to be rather enjoyable, which should tell you something about me. However, sometimes I value simply getting the work done, rather than the process of writing low-level client/server code. Truthfully, that's most of the time. There's no need to reinvent the wheel when it comes to working with Simple Mail Transfer Protocol (SMTP), Domain Name System (DNS), Post Office Protocol version 3 (POP3), Internet Control Message Protocol (ICMP), Lightweight Directory Access Protocol (LDAP), and other networking protocols.

This chapter takes a look at some of the tools available to the Perl programmer for working with various Internet protocols (aside from HTTP): POP3 and SMTP for working with e-mail, DNS, and ICMP for ping. These are just a few of the numerous Net:: modules available. For example, other Net:: modules allow you to query an LDAP directory (and interoperate with Microsoft's Active Directory), query the whois database of domain names, work with FTP, and more. The libnet tools on CPAN (http://search.cpan.org/~/libnet-1.19/) provide a listing of some of these tools.

Checking E-Mail with Net::POP3

POP3 (defined by RFC 1939) is a popular protocol used to check e-mail. It's used to retrieve e-mail from a server, typically at an Internet provider, where the e-mail is stored or spooled. When you check your e-mail, a username and password are sent to the server, and the server sends back a list of messages and, optionally, the e-mail content itself. POP3 is not a protocol to send e-mail; that's SMTP. POP3 is used only to retrieve e-mail that's being stored on a POP3 server.

The Net::POP3 module is the primary module used to check e-mail with the POP3 protocol. However, in the tradition of Perl, there are several packages available that can work with e-mail. One such package is Mail::Box, which I'll cover after the discussion of Net::POP3.

The Net::POP3 module is available with many Linux distributions and also from your favorite CPAN mirror. As with other modules, a use statement is the best way to import the Net::POP3 namespace into your Perl program:

```
use Net::POP3;
```

Creating a POP3 Object

Like the browser object you encounter when working with the LWP modules (as described in the previous chapter), the Net::POP3 module works by creating a POP3 object. You create this object with a call to the new() method. The new() method returns a reference to the newly created object, which you're likely to store inside a scalar variable. Here's an example:

```
use Net::POP3;
$pop3conn = Net::POP3->new('mail.example.com');
```

The host, as provided in the example as mail.example.com, isn't required when you call the new() method. If the host is not set when you call the new() method, it must be configured in Net::Config within the POP3_Hosts parameter. However, you'll almost always define it in the program, as shown in the example.

Naturally, you can store the host inside its own variable. It's common to do so by storing the host variable in the beginning of the program or getting it from an external source. For example, you might store the host in a scalar variable called $pophost. You then invoke the call to new() like this:

```
$pop3conn = Net::POP3->new($pophost);
```

Sometimes, the mail server is stored in an environment variable.[1] It might be called MAIL_SERVER or POP3_SERVER. The name of the environment variable depends on your system; there is no set standard. Use the shell command printenv or export to see your environment variables. Alternatively, you can iterate through the environment variables from within your Perl program with the following code (introduced in Chapter 4):

```
foreach $key (keys %ENV) {
    print "Environment key $key is $ENV{$key}\n";
}
```

Here's an example that sets the POP3 host for the call to the new() method based on the environment variable, assuming an environment variable of POP3_SERVER:

```
$pop3conn = Net::POP3->new($ENV{POP3_SERVER});
```

The host can also be an array of POP3 hosts. If an array or list of hosts is given, the program will try each in turn. This is not a common scenario. Usually, the mail spool is stored on one server, and if there are multiple servers, the correct one is chosen automatically.

For the rest of this discussion, I'll use the variable $pop3conn to refer to the Net::POP3 connection object created here.

Setting and Getting Other POP3 Connection Parameters

Four other parameters are available when you're setting up a connection with Net::POP3. You can set any of the parameters when you create the connection object or later.

---

1. If an environment variable isn't set, you could set one. However, I don't see a particular advantage to doing so as opposed to just defining it within your program.

When you set options at the time of connection object creation, they are set as *name* => *value* pairs. For example, to set the `timeout` parameter to 30 seconds on creation of the connection object, do this:

```
$pop3conn = Net::POP3->new("mail.example.com", timeout => 30);
```

To set more than one parameter, separate them with a comma:

```
$pop3conn = Net::POP3->new("mail.example.com", timeout => 30, debug => 1);
```

Let's look at the Net::POP3 connection parameters `host`, `timeout`, `ResvPort`, and `debug`. The following examples shows setting options after the connection object has been created.

Host

The host must be set at creation of the POP3 object. You can find out the name of the current host for a given POP3 connection object by calling the `host()` method with no arguments:

```
$pop3conn->host();
```

Recall the example earlier in this section that created a POP3 connection to mail.example.com. Now consider this example that prints the name of the current host:

```
use Net::POP3;
$pop3conn = Net::POP3->new('mail.example.com');
print "The POP3 Server is" . $pop3conn->host() . "\n";
```

Timeout

The `timeout` value is the amount of time to wait for a response from the POP3 server. The default is 120 seconds. Like other parameters, it can be set at creation or set later by calling the option directly. This example sets the value to 30 seconds:

```
$pop3conn->timeout(30);
```

ResvPort

Don't be confused by the `ResvPort` option. This option is used to set the local port from which connections will originate. It is not used to set the port of the server. `ResvPort` can be useful if you have a firewall that allows only certain ports as source ports, for example (though that would be quite an uncommon configuration).

Debug

The `debug` option can be a lifesaver when you're having trouble getting the POP3 connection to work. When you set `debug` to 1, additional output is printed to STDOUT, including the actual POP3 conversation between the program and the server. Like other options, `debug` can be set at the time of object creation or later, within the program. The option is either disabled (default or 0) or enabled by setting the value to 1:

```
$pop3conn->debug(1);
```

The output from debug looks something like the following (yours will vary). In this example, you can see the calls to various other Perl modules, including Net::Cmd and IO::Socket. The actual POP3 conversation follows, and it shows that I don't have any mail waiting.

```
Net::POP3>>> Net::POP3(2.28)
Net::POP3>>>   Net::Cmd(2.26)
Net::POP3>>>     Exporter(5.58)
Net::POP3>>>   IO::Socket::INET(1.27)
Net::POP3>>>     IO::Socket(1.28)
Net::POP3>>>       IO::Handle(1.24)
Net::POP3=GLOB(0x81659cc)>>> USER suehring@braingia.net
Net::POP3=GLOB(0x81659cc)<<< +OK
Net::POP3=GLOB(0x81659cc)>>> PASS ....
Net::POP3=GLOB(0x81659cc)<<< +OK
Net::POP3=GLOB(0x81659cc)>>> STAT
Net::POP3=GLOB(0x81659cc)<<< +OK 0 0
```

Banner

The banner() method returns the server's connection banner. Calling banner() looks like this:

```
$pop3conn->banner();
```

Note that not all POP3 servers will return a value here. So while the call will not fail, you won't see any output either!

Checking E-Mail

Up until this point, you've seen only the methods and options related to the connection object itself. This means that the e-mail is still sitting on the server waiting to be picked up.

You check for e-mail receipt with the login() method. When you receive mail (the login() method returns more than 0), you have a choice of what to do with the mail. You can obtain a list of messages and their sizes with the list() method, you can retrieve the messages with get(), or you can do both. I'll show you how to do both. Just be aware that you aren't required to obtain a list of messages before retrieving them.

Login

Once you've created the connection object, you log in to the server by using the login() method. The login() method sends the USER and the PASS commands to the POP3 server, according to the protocol specification. Neither the username nor the password is required. If you don't provide the password, it will be read using Net::Netrc. If you don't give the username, the currently logged-in user will be sent as the username. In practice, it's just as easy and usually cleaner to specify both within the program. Doing so avoids confusion later when you need to migrate the code to a different machine or user, or just have to look at it three years later to debug it.

The basic syntax for the login() method is as follows:

```
$pop3conn->login(username,password);
```

When login() is called in a numeric context, the result is the number of messages waiting on the server for the user. If there is an error with authentication, the login() method will return undef. Therefore, you can determine if you have messages waiting by using an if/then control statement:

```perl
if ($pop3conn->login($username,$password) > 0) {
    print "You've Got Mail!\n";
}
```

Note Other methods for authentication include apop() and auth(), which provide additional security but also have additional requirements. For more information about these methods, see the Net::POP3 documentation at http://search.cpan.org/~gbarr/libnet-1.19/Net/POP3.pm.

The user() and pass() methods send the username and password for the connection by sending the POP3 USER and PASS commands. Their arguments are, not surprisingly, the username and the password, respectively. These two methods perform essentially the same functions as the login() method, which also sends the USER and PASS commands to the POP3 server. The login() method returns the number of messages, whereas these two methods do not.

List

The aptly titled list() method returns a list of the messages and their corresponding sizes. Actually, list() can also return the size of an individual message if it's called with an argument. For the first case, list() returns a reference to a hash. The hash contains the message numbers as keys and their sizes as values. Building on the example shown in the previous section, this code obtains a list of messages and prints their message numbers and sizes:

```perl
$msgs = $pop3conn->list();
foreach $msg (keys %$msgs) {
    print "Message $msg is $$msgs{$msg} bytes\n";
}
```

Listing 6-1 (Pop3complete.pl) shows a more complete example.

Listing 6-1. *Listing POP3 Messages*

```perl
#!/usr/bin/perl -w

use strict;
use Net::POP3;
my $username = "user\@example.com";
my $password = "password";
```

```perl
my $pop3conn = Net::POP3->new("mail.example.com", timeout => 30);
if ($pop3conn->login($username,$password) > 0) {
    print "You've Got Mail!\n";
    my $messages = $pop3conn->list();
    foreach my $msg (keys %{$messages}) {
        print "Message $msg is $messages->{$msg} bytes\n";
    }
}
$pop3conn->quit
```

The quit() method closes the connection. I'll explain it further in the "Deleting E-Mail and Quitting" section.

The output from the program will be similar to the following, which shows that I happen to have 12 messages in this mailbox:

```
You've Got Mail!
Message 6 is 3353 bytes
Message 11 is 4234 bytes
Message 3 is 7721 bytes
Message 7 is 2385 bytes
Message 9 is 1578 bytes
Message 12 is 257788 bytes
Message 2 is 4700 bytes
Message 8 is 1659 bytes
Message 1 is 3723 bytes
Message 4 is 1312 bytes
Message 10 is 1832 bytes
Message 5 is 2145 bytes
```

Get

You actually retrieve the message with the get() method, called with the message number as an argument. The get() method returns a reference to an array of the message itself. You can do as you please with this array reference, including simply printing the messages. Listing 6-2 (Pop3example2.pl) shows an example that retrieves a message and prints it to STDOUT.

Listing 6-2. *Getting and Printing POP3 Messages*

```perl
#!/usr/bin/perl -w

use strict;
use Net::POP3;
my $username = "user\@example.com";
my $password = "password";

my $pop3conn = Net::POP3->new("mail.example.com", timeout => 30);
my $nummsgs = $pop3conn->login($username,$password);
```

```
if ($nummsgs > 0) {
    print "There are $nummsgs messages waiting\n";
    my $message = $pop3conn->get(12);
    print "@{$message}";
}
$pop3conn->quit;
```

In this example, the number of messages available is stored in a variable called $nummsgs. Then the $nummsgs variable is checked to see if it's greater than zero. If it is, the number of messages waiting is printed, followed by message number 12. Note that I already knew how many messages were waiting and merely hard-coded message number 12 into this example. It's more likely that you'll want to iterate through each of the messages with a for loop, as shown in Listing 6-3 (Pop3example3.pl).

Listing 6-3. *Retrieving Messages with Net::POP3*

```
#!/usr/bin/perl -w

use Net::POP3;
use strict;
my $username = "user\@example.com";
my $password = "password";

my $pop3conn = Net::POP3->new("mail.example.com", timeout => 30);
my $nummsgs = $pop3conn->login($username,$password);
for (my $i=1;$i<=$nummsgs;$i++) {
    my $message = $pop3conn->get($i);
    print "@{$message}";
    print "retrieved message $i\n\n\n";
}
$pop3conn->quit;
```

In this example, each message is retrieved in turn and printed to STDOUT.

▪Note The getfh() method performs the same function as get(), but gives a filehandle, which can then be read to retrieve the given message.

Along with the get() and list(), a couple other methods stand out as being useful for working with POP3 e-mail: uidl() and top(), which get message IDs and headers, respectively. You might also find popstat() useful if you want to know the size of the mailbox.

Uidl

Many POP3 mail clients use the uidl() method to obtain a unique identifier for a given message. In this way, the program can keep track of which messages have been downloaded, so that they aren't downloaded multiple times by the same program. This would apply only when the POP3 client program doesn't delete the messages after downloading them, since the values obtained from uidl() are message-dependent. Therefore, you wouldn't use uidl() values if your program deletes the e-mail from the server after downloading it.

In order to take advantage of the values returned from uidl(), the program must keep track of which IDs have been seen, usually across multiple executions of the program. For a Perl program, this would likely mean storing the IDs in an external file, but the IDs could be stored in any valid location that can be accessed from a Perl program, such as a relational database or a DBM hash file.

Like the list() method, uidl() returns the ID for a given message when called with an argument of the message number, and it returns a reference to a hash with the message number as the key and the ID as the value when called with no argument.

Consider the example in Listing 6-4 (Pop3example4.pl), which looks nearly the same as the example for the list() method. This example uses uidl(), and then prints each ID.

Listing 6-4. *Printing Message IDs*

```perl
#!/usr/bin/perl -w

use Net::POP3;
use strict;
my $username = "user\@example.com";
my $password = "password";

my $pop3conn = Net::POP3->new("mail.example.com", timeout => 30);
if ($pop3conn->login($username,$password) > 0) {
    my $messages = $pop3conn->uidl();
    foreach my $msg (keys %{$messages}) {
        print "Message $msg is ID: $messages->{$msg}\n";
    }
}
$pop3conn->quit;
```

From here, you could store these IDs for later use or use them within the program, if the program were a long-running process. Here's typical output from this program:

```
Message 6 is ID: 5cb794e9ba2c45b2
Message 11 is ID: ac9375c45b8aca77
Message 3 is ID: 822ac7377f459093
Message 7 is ID: 3dadb5032fca6952
Message 9 is ID: e10e0bfe628f74ff
Message 12 is ID: 1420b979566679a6
Message 2 is ID: 770a0ebe8ae76b68
Message 8 is ID: b77fbf3630ea720e
Message 1 is ID: d0065fbe85999bc3
Message 4 is ID: 2e3331c08c34e0a0
Message 10 is ID: 8d63341d100e1007
Message 5 is ID: b5fc539c28da4afb
```

Top

The top() method retrieves the header of the message along with, optionally, a number of lines from the body of the message as well. This method is useful to look at the Subject line or From line of an e-mail message for something like spam filtering or just general filtering. Recall the code example given to print each message to STDOUT. Using that code as a base, the example in Listing 6-5 (Pop3example5.pl) uses top() to retrieve the header of the message, and then performs a simple grep to look for the Subject line of each message, outputting that to STDOUT.

Listing 6-5. *Printing Subject Lines*

```perl
#!/usr/bin/perl -w

use Net::POP3;
use strict;
my $username = "user\@example.com";
my $password = "password";

my $pop3conn = Net::POP3->new("mail.example.com", timeout => 30);
my $nummsgs = $pop3conn->login($username,$password);
for (my $i=1;$i<=$nummsgs;$i++) {
    my $message = $pop3conn->top($i);
    print "Message $i: ";
    print grep (/^Subject:/, @{$message});
}
$pop3conn->quit;
```

The output looks something like this:

```
Message 1: Subject: RE: Security consulting
Message 2: Subject: Re: Security consulting
Message 3: Subject: RE: Security consulting
Message 4: Subject: Meeting
Message 5: Subject: RE: Account costs
Message 6: Subject: Re: Introduction
Message 7: Subject: Re: Web design work
Message 8: Subject: Hello
Message 9: Subject: Partners Pub Website Update
Message 10: Subject: Perl help!
Message 11: Subject: Re: Perl consulting
Message 12: Subject: Files for site
```

Popstat

The popstat() method gives the number of messages along with the size of the mailbox. These are returned in list context so could be stored in an array or into individual scalars, as in this example:

```
($messages,$size) = $pop3conn->popstat();
print "There are $messages messages totaling $size bytes\n";
```

Deleting E-Mail and Quitting

At this point, you've seen how to set up a connection object, as well as how to log in to the server and view messages. The normal POP3 conversation involves two additional tasks: deleting the messages and quitting or closing the connection. These are accomplished through the delete() and quit() methods, respectively.

Delete

It's important to note that the message isn't actually deleted when you call delete(), but only marked to be deleted when the connection is closed. You could then, in theory, use the reset() method to unmark the messages to be deleted, thus preventing them from being deleted. In practice, the reset() method is not always helpful, since the connection to the server is often closed immediately after you issue delete().

To mark a message for deletion, simply call the delete() method with the number of the message as the argument. For example, to mark message number 1 for deletion, the call would look like this:

```
$pop3conn->delete(1);
```

Now when you close the connection using the quit() method, the messages that have been marked as deleted will be purged from the remote mail spool.

Quit

You've seen the quit() method used throughout the examples in the chapter. Here it is again:

```
$pop3conn->quit();
```

But wait! What if you wanted to prevent that message from being deleted? As I noted in the previous section, a call to the reset() method prior to closing the connection will prevent the message from being purged:

```
$pop3conn->reset();
```

Note that if you don't use the quit() method to actually close the connection, the messages will never be purged, even after the TCP session times out for the connection. This behavior might vary depending on the implementation of the POP3 server, so I recommend explicitly closing the connection.

■**Note** Other methods are available with Net::POP3. For more information about those methods, see the documentation for Net::POP3 at http://search.cpan.org/~gbarr/libnet-1.19/Net/POP3.pm or perldoc Net::POP3.

Checking E-Mail with Mail::Box

Mail::Box is another package, available from CPAN, for working with e-mail in Perl. In many ways, Mail::Box provides a more elegant solution to working with e-mail in Perl than the Net::POP3 package. Mail::Box is likely more appropriate for heavy lifting of POP3 and other e-mail accounts, insofar as it has multiple classes for working with messages, message bodies, headers, and so on. Mail::Box can also work with multiple formats for mailboxes, such as Maildir format, mbox format, and POP3.

■**Note** I cover Mail::Box only briefly here, but Mail::Box is a large and powerful package. See the Mail::Box web site at http://perl.overmeer.net/mailbox/ for more information about the package. Another package you might find useful is Mail::Internet, which, like Mail::Box, can be found on CPAN.

Recall the earlier example in Listing 6-2, which showed the use of Net::POP3 to check e-mail and print the number of messages. Listing 6-6 (Mailbox.pl) shows that same functionality using Mail::Box.

Listing 6-6. *Using Mail::Box to Print the Number of Messages*

```perl
#!/usr/bin/perl -w

use strict;
use Mail::Box::POP3;

my $folder = Mail::Box::POP3->new(server_name => 'mail.example.com',
    password => 'password', username => 'user@example.com') or die "$!";

my $nummsgs = $folder->messages;
print "There are $nummsgs messages waiting\n";
```

Mail::Box works with the concepts of folders. To Mail::Box, e-mail is essentially one or more folders containing zero or more messages. In the example, a virtual folder object is created, and the number of messages are determined by calling the messages() method in scalar context:

```perl
my $nummsgs = $folder->messages;
```

You can retrieve individual messages by calling the message by its index, as shown in Listing 6-7 (Mailbox2.pl).

Listing 6-7. *Printing an Individual Message*

```
#!/usr/bin/perl -w

use strict;
use Mail::Box::POP3;

my $folder = Mail::Box::POP3->new(server_name => 'mail.example.com',
    password => 'password', username => 'user@example.com') or die "$!";

$folder->message(2)->print;
```

The example prints message number 2 to STDOUT.

To print subject lines, use the get() method, as shown in Listing 6-8 (Mailbox3.pl).

Listing 6-8. *Printing Subject Lines*

```
#!/usr/bin/perl -w

use strict;
use Mail::Box::POP3;

my $folder = Mail::Box::POP3->new(server_name => 'mail.example.com',
     password => 'password', username => 'user@example.com') or die "$!";

my @messages = $folder->messages;
foreach my $message (@messages) {
    print "Subject: ", $message->get('Subject') or "<no subject>";
    print "\n";
}
```

The output from Listing 6-8 is similar to the output when using Net::POP3 to retrieve the subject lines (Listing 6-5), as shown earlier in the chapter.

Sending E-Mail with SMTP

Up until this point, you've seen examples of only how to check e-mail. Obviously, that's only half of the equation. Sending e-mail is accomplished using SMTP (defined in RFC 2821). There are multiple ways for sending e-mail from a Perl script, including opening a process handle to the local mailer (such as Sendmail or Postfix) and sending the mail to the handle, calling a system process to a local mailer, or using one or more Perl modules for the task. This section shows how to send e-mail by using one of the modules: Net::SMTP.

The Net::SMTP module was written by the same author as the Net::POP3 module. The Net::SMTP module has essentially the same types of operations as the Net::POP3 module, except, obviously, this module talks the SMTP protocol.

Creating an SMTP Object

Like Net::POP3, Net::SMTP has the new() constructor, which you use to create a Net::SMTP object. The new() constructor requires the hostname of the mail server, as shown in this example:

```
use Net::SMTP;
$smtpconn = Net::SMTP->new('mail.example.com', hello => 'mycomputer.example.com');
```

Also, as with the new() constructor in Net::POP3, you can set options when calling the new() constructor, or you can set options later. The host, as provided in the example as mail.example.com, isn't required when you call the new() method. If you don't set the host when you call the new() method, then you must configure it in Net::Config within the SMTP_Hosts parameter. However, as with the POP3 server host, you'll almost always define it in the program, as shown in the example.

You'll notice that an option, hello, is set at the time of creation. This option is important for the connection, because the default, localhost.localdomain, may cause the e-mail to be blocked by the SMTP server. I usually set the hello option explicitly on the creation of the SMTP connection object.

You can also store the server inside its own variable. It's common to do so by storing the server variable in the beginning of the program or by getting it from an external source. For example, you might store the host in a scalar called $smtpserver, and then invoke the call to new() like this:

```
$smtpconn = Net::SMTP->new($smtpserver);
```

Sometimes, the mail server is stored in an environment variable. This is much more common than storing the POP3 server as an environment variable. The name of the environment variable depends on your system; as with a POP3 server environment variable, there is no set standard. It might be called MAIL_SERVER or SMTP_SERVER. Use the shell command printenv or export to see your environment variables. Alternatively, you can iterate through the environment variables from within your Perl program with this code (as discussed in Chapter 4):

```
foreach $key (keys %ENV) {
    print "Environment key $key is $ENV{$key}\n";
}
```

■Tip You could also sort the hash: foreach $key (sort keys %ENV).

Here's an example that sets the SMTP server for the call to the new() method based on the environment variable, assuming an environment variable of SMTP_SERVER:

```
$smtpconn = Net::SMTP->new($ENV{SMTP_SERVER});
```

The host can also be a reference to an array of SMTP servers. If a reference to an array or list of servers is given, the program will try each in turn.

For the rest of this section, I'll use the variable $smtpconn to refer to the Net::SMTP connection object created here. You're welcome to use any name for this object.

Setting Other SMTP Connection Parameters

Numerous other parameters are available when you're setting up a connection with Net::SMTP. All of the parameters can be set at the time you're creating the connection object or later. When you set these options at creation time, you use *name* => *value* pairs. For example, to set the hello option to myserver.example.com upon creation of the connection object, call it like so:

```
$smtpconn = Net::SMTP->new("mail.example.com", hello => 'myserver.example.com');
```

To set more than one parameter, separate them with a comma:

```
$smtpconn = Net::SMTP->new("mail.example.com", port => 2525, debug => 1);
```

The following examples show setting options after the connection object has been created.

Hello

Part of the protocol that is SMTP requires that you, the client, identify yourself to the server on connection. This is accomplished with the HELO or EHLO command upon connection (see RFC 2821 for more details). Setting the hello option defines the host that will be sent on the connection. If you do not set this option, localhost.localdomain will be sent. Sending localhost.localdomain to a remote SMTP server is usually not a good idea, since it can get the e-mail rejected by that server. Therefore, I recommend setting this option:

```
$smtpconn->hello('mycomputer.example.com');
```

Host

The host is usually set at the creation of the SMTP connection object. You can find out the name of the current host for a given SMTP connection object by calling the host() method with no arguments:

```
$smtpconn->host();
```

Recall the example earlier in this section that created a SMTP connection to mail.example.com. Now consider this example, which prints the current host:

```
use Net::SMTP;
$smtpconn = Net::SMTP->new('mail.example.com');
print "The SMTP Server is" . $smtpconn->host() . "\n";
```

Note The domain() method returns the hostname that the server returned on connection.

LocalAddr, LocalPort, and Port

The localaddr() option is used to initiate the connection from the local computer to the server on a particular IP address; in other words, to bind the local connection to a specific local IP address. This option specifies the local IP address from which the connection will be initiated.

Like the localaddr() option, the localport() option specifies the local port from which the connection will be initiated.

The port option is used to set the remote port for the SMTP server. By default, this port is 25 and doesn't need to be specified. However, some servers listen on other ports for various reasons. In such cases, you would use the port option.[2]

Timeout

The timeout value is the amount of time to wait for a response from the SMTP server. The default is 120 seconds. Like other parameters, timeout can be set at the time you create the connection object or set later by calling directly to the attribute. This example sets the value to 30 seconds:

```
$smtpconn->timeout(30);
```

Debug

Like the debug option with Net::POP3, the debug option for Net::SMTP is very helpful. When you set debug to 1, additional output is printed to STDOUT, including the actual SMTP conversation between the program and the server. Like other options, debug can be set at the time of object creation or can be set later within the program:

```
$smtpconn->debug(1);
```

The output from debug looks similar to this (your output will vary):

```
Net::SMTP>>> Net::SMTP(2.29)
Net::SMTP>>>   Net::Cmd(2.26)
Net::SMTP>>>     Exporter(5.58)
Net::SMTP>>>   IO::Socket::INET(1.27)
Net::SMTP>>>     IO::Socket(1.28)
Net::SMTP>>>       IO::Handle(1.24)
Net::SMTP=GLOB(0x82e1f58)<<< 220 dfw0.icgmedia.com ESMTP Postfix (Debian/GNU)
Net::SMTP=GLOB(0x82e1f58)>>> EHLO netserver.braingia.org
Net::SMTP=GLOB(0x82e1f58)<<< 250-dfw0.icgmedia.com
Net::SMTP=GLOB(0x82e1f58)<<< 250-PIPELINING
```

---

2. Some idiotic Internet providers block their clients from making connections to remote SMTP servers on port 25. This is purportedly done to prevent spam, but really only serves to break the end-to-end nature of the Internet. The port() option can help you get around these poorly managed Internet providers. Obviously, the true solution for these Internet providers would be to ensure that customers who send spam get disabled rather than breaking everyone else's Internet service!

```
Net::SMTP=GLOB(0x82e1f58)<<< 250-SIZE 15000000
Net::SMTP=GLOB(0x82e1f58)<<< 250-ETRN
Net::SMTP=GLOB(0x82e1f58)<<< 250-XVERP
Net::SMTP=GLOB(0x82e1f58)<<< 250 8BITMIME
```

In this example, you can see the calls to various other Perl modules, including Net::Cmd and IO::Socket. The actual POP3 conversation follows and shows that I don't have any mail waiting.

Sending a Message

Once you've established the connection, the next step is to send the e-mail. Recall that the example set the host and hello options upon creation of the connection object:

```
use Net::SMTP;
$smtpconn = Net::SMTP->new('mail.example.com', hello => 'mycomputer.example.com');
```

The SMTP protocol requires that certain commands be issued, and Net::SMTP contains methods to issue those commands. The first command, EHLO or HELO, is sent at connection automatically (see the discussion of the hello option of the new() constructor). Next comes the MAIL FROM command, followed by RCPT TO, and finally the DATA command. Here's a telnet session of a SMTP conversation (with the lines I typed in shown in bold):

```
telnet localhost 25
Trying 127.0.0.1...
Connected to localhost.
Escape character is '^]'.
220 dfw0.icgmedia.com ESMTP Postfix (Debian/GNU)
EHLO mycomputer.example.com
250-dfw0.icgmedia.com
250-PIPELINING
250-SIZE 15000000
250-ETRN
250-XVERP
250 8BITMIME
MAIL FROM: <perlbook@braingia.org>
250 Ok
RCPT TO: <suehring@braingia.net>
250 Ok
DATA
354 End data with <CR><LF>.<CR><LF>
Hello,

How would you like an e-mail sample?

.
250 Ok: queued as 7B797170DD
QUIT
221 Bye
Connection closed by foreign host.
```

The methods in Net::SMTP essentially mirror the functions from this telnet session excerpt. For example, the mail() method sends the MAIL FROM command, the to() method sends the RCPT TO command, the data() method sends the DATA command, and so on. Actually, the data() method has siblings that are used to send the body of the message and also to signal the end of the DATA command. You use the datasend() method to send the text of the message. Notice that a single dot (.) is used to signal the end of the DATA command in the telnet session example. The Net::SMTP dataend() method signals that same end. Here's an example that sends the same e-mail as the one shown in the telnet session example:

```
use Net::SMTP;
$smtpconn = Net::SMTP->new('mail.example.com', hello => 'mycomputer.example.com');
$smtpconn->mail('perlbook@braingia.org');
$smtpconn->to('suehring@braingia.net');

$smtpconn->data();
$smtpconn->datasend("Hello,\nHow would you like an e-mail sample?\n");
$smtpconn->dataend();

$smtpconn->quit;
```

The quit() method closes the connection. Although the connection would be closed at program exit, it's always a good idea to explicitly close the connection, if for no other reason than to save a small bit of resources.

■Note The reset() method effectively cancels the e-mail message, as long as the DATA command has not yet been sent.

Subject and Other Header Fields

The SMTP commands to send e-mail, including the MAIL FROM and RCPT TO commands, don't provide the same friendly From and To fields that most e-mail users are accustomed to. For this reason, it's a good idea to set these and others, such as Subject. You do this from within the DATA command, as shown in Listing 6-9.

Listing 6-9. *An SMTP Example*

```
use Net::SMTP;
$smtpconn = Net::SMTP->new('mail.example.com', hello => 'mycomputer.example.com');
$smtpconn->mail('perlbook@braingia.org');
$smtpconn->to('suehring@braingia.net');

$smtpconn->data();
$smtpconn->datasend("To: <suehring\@braingia.net>\n");
$smtpconn->datasend("From: Steve Suehring <perlbook\@braingia.org>\n");
```

```
$smtpconn->datasend("Subject: Test E-mail\n\n");
$smtpconn->datasend("Hello,\nHow would you like an e-mail sample?\n");
$smtpconn->dataend();

$smtpconn->quit;
```

Notice in the example that each line is terminated with a newline (\n) and that the final header line, Subject, actually contains an extra newline. This separates it from the body of the message.

Multiple Recipients

The easiest way to send e-mail to multiple recipients is through the recipient() method. The recipient() method accepts a list of e-mail addresses, which will then each receive a copy of the e-mail. For example, if you had recipient variables defined as $recipient1 and $recipient2, your call to the recipient() method would look like the code in Listing 6-10.

Listing 6-10. *Sending to Multiple Recipients with Net::SMTP*

```
use Net::SMTP;
$smtpconn = Net::SMTP->new('mail.example.com', hello => 'mycomputer.example.com');
$smtpconn->mail('perlbook@braingia.org');
$smtpconn->recipient($recipient1, $recipient2);

$smtpconn->data();
$smtpconn->datasend("To: <suehring\@braingia.net>\n");
$smtpconn->datasend("From: Steve Suehring <perlbook\@braingia.org>\n");
$smtpconn->datasend("Subject: Test E-mail\n\n");
$smtpconn->datasend("Hello,\nHow would you like an e-mail sample?\n");
$smtpconn->dataend();

$smtpconn->quit;
```

The recipient() method is basically the same as sending carbon copies and blind carbon copies, which you can also do with the cc() and bcc() methods, respectively. The methods expect an e-mail address as their argument. The example in Listing 6-11 sends a carbon copy to the e-mail address theboss@braingia.org.

Listing 6-11. *Using the CC method with Net::SMTP*

```
use Net::SMTP;
$smtpconn = Net::SMTP->new('mail.example.com', hello => 'mycomputer.example.com');
$smtpconn->mail('perlbook@braingia.org');
$smtpconn->to('suehring@braingia.net');
$smtpconn->cc('theboss@braingia.org');

$smtpconn->data();
$smtpconn->datasend("To: <suehring\@braingia.net>\n");
$smtpconn->datasend("From: Steve Suehring <perlbook\@braingia.org>\n");
```

```
$smtpconn->datasend("Subject: Test E-mail\n\n");
$smtpconn->datasend("Hello,\nHow would you like an e-mail sample?\n");
$smtpconn->dataend();

$smtpconn->quit;
```

■**Note** Net::SMTP is a more complex module than Net::POP3. Many additional methods are defined within the module. For example, etrn() initiates an Extended Turn (ETRN) transfer. For more information about the methods, see the Net::SMTP documentation at http://search.cpan.org/~gbarr/libnet-1.19/Net/SMTP.pm or perldoc Net::SMTP. Additionally, see the Mail::Mailer module for another way to send e-mail using Perl.

Checking DNS with Net::DNS

The Net::DNS module provides a group of Perl interfaces into advanced DNS methods used to both resolve and update DNS. Net::DNS gives the Perl programmer a much more advanced interface into DNS than other functions in Perl. Of course, this doesn't mean that you're limited to using Net::DNS for these functions. You could write your own interface into DNS, customized to your needs. However, Net::DNS does a lot of the heavy lifting and does it well. This section examines just some of the functions and tasks that you can accomplish with Net::DNS and its interfaces.

■**Tip** You can do simple DNS resolution in Perl through the gethostbyname(), gethostbyaddr(), and related functions. Use perldoc perlfunc for more information about these functions. You can go directly to the documentation for these functions using perldoc -f gethostbyname and perldoc -f gethostbyaddr.

The Net::DNS module is included with many Linux distributions or can be installed through the distribution's package-management system. You can also install Net::DNS from your favorite CPAN mirror.

■**Note** This section assumes some level of familiarity with DNS, along with its types of queries, responses, and records. For more information about DNS, I recommend *DNS and BIND, Fourth Edition*, by Paul Albitz and Cricket Liu (O'Reilly, 2001). The first few chapters of that book are essential for anyone new to DNS.

Performing a Simple DNS Lookup

Anyone who has ever tried to program anything working with DNS knows that there's nothing simple about a DNS lookup. DNS lookups with Net::DNS are provided through the Net::DNS::Resolver class. As with other object-oriented modules in Perl, you begin working with the Net::DNS module by calling the new() method.

```
use Net::DNS;
$resolver = Net::DNS::Resolver->new();
```

Net::DNS::Resolver uses various methods for performing lookups. A common method is query(), which sends a query:

```
$queryobject = $resolver->query('www.braingia.org');
```

The query() method does not use the search list, which is a list of domains that are appended to a given hostname. In Linux, the search list is located in /etc/resolv.conf. The search() method performs a query and includes the search list:

```
$queryobject = $resolver->search('www.braingia.org');
```

The object returned from the resolver's call to search or query is a hash containing a number of elements based on the DNS packet itself. These are based on the objects found in Net::DNS::Packet and include header, question, answer, authority, and additional sections. Of primary concern for a DNS query is the answer section (although other portions such as the authority section may be of interest from time to time). When working with the answer section of a query object, it's important to check the type of record received. For example, assuming that an A record will be returned can cause your application to break and will, if another type is returned, cause a warning from the Net::DNS module.

Listing 6-12 (Dnsexample1.pl) shows an example that queries for the IP address or addresses of a host. If the return is either an A record or a CNAME record, the output will be sent to STDOUT.

Listing 6-12. *Printing an A Record*

```perl
#!/usr/bin/perl -w

use Net::DNS;
use strict;

my $resolver = Net::DNS::Resolver->new();
die "Lookup failed: ", $resolver->errorstring unless \
    my $queryobject = $resolver->query('ord.braingia.org');

foreach my $record ($queryobject->answer) {
    if ($record->type eq "A") {
        print $record->address, "\n";
    }
    elsif ($record->type eq "CNAME") {
        print $record->cname, "\n";
    }
}
```

The example first creates a new resolver object, as you've already seen. Next, the query() method is called within a die() function. If the query fails for any reason—including that the DNS entry isn't found—the die() function will be invoked, and the error will displayed through a call to the errorstring() method. If execution continues, a foreach loop is invoked to iterate through the answer or answers from the resolver's query. Within the foreach loop, the record type is evaluated and the result printed for either an A record or a CNAME record.

When I run this program, the simple output looks like the record for a machine within my local network:

```
192.168.1.2
```

Searching for MX Records

You can use the mx() method is used to find the mail exchanger (MX) records and their corresponding preferences. The mx() method accepts a resolver and domain as arguments. You can also call it with just the domain for the MX lookup, but then you can't evaluate error conditions, so I recommend creating your own resolver object, as shown in Listing 6-13 (Dnsexample2.pl).

Listing 6-13. *Printing MX Records*

```perl
#!/usr/bin/perl -w

use Net::DNS;
use strict;

my $resolver = Net::DNS::Resolver->new();
die "Lookup failed: ", $resolver->errorstring unless my @mxrecords =
    mx($resolver, 'braingia.org');

foreach my $record (@mxrecords) {
    print "Exchanger is: ", $record->exchange, " with preference ",
        $record->preference, "\n";
}
```

This example first creates a resolver object, $resolver, and then makes a call to the mx() method with the resolver and the domain, braingia.org, as arguments. Notice again that this call to mx() falls within the context of die() to check for errors. Finally, the @mxrecords array is iterated through and the exchangers are printed to STDOUT. When run against my domain, braingia.org, the output is as follows:

```
Exchanger is: mail.braingia.org with preference 0
```

Looking for the Authoritative DNS Servers

Another common task when working with DNS from within a program is to find the authoritative DNS servers for a given host. This is accomplished through the resolver object. Recall that one of the types of information returned from a resolver call is the authority information. You can parse this data to determine the authoritative DNS servers for the domain, as shown in Listing 6-14 (Dnsexample3.pl).

Listing 6-14. *Printing the Authority Records*

```perl
#!/usr/bin/perl -w

use Net::DNS;
use strict;

my $host = "www.braingia.org";

my $resolver = Net::DNS::Resolver->new();
die "Lookup failed: ", $resolver->errorstring unless
    my $queryobject = $resolver->query($host);

my @authority = $queryobject->authority;
foreach my $serverhash (@authority) {
    foreach $key (keys %{$serverhash}) {
        print "Authoritative Server for $host:
            $serverhash->{$key}\n" if ($key eq "nsdname");
    }
}
```

This example is largely the same as Listing 6-12, up to the point of the query. There, it calls the $queryobject->authority() method, which returns a hash of the information returned from the server for the authoritative DNS servers, including the type of record, the time to live (TTL), and other information. This hash, called $serverhash in the example, is then iterated through with a foreach loop, where it searches for the key nsdname. When that key is found, the output is printed to STDOUT. When run against my domain, the output is as follows:

```
Authoritative Server for www.braingia.org: ns0.braingia.org
Authoritative Server for www.braingia.org: ns1.braingia.org
```

Sending a Ping with Net::Ping

The ping command is familiar ground for many. The ping command uses ICMP to send an echo request to another networked device, which then responds (if it can) with an echo reply. A Net::Ping module exists for working with ICMP packets from a Perl program. Net::Ping works with numerous protocols aside from ICMP, including the Transmission Control Protocol (TCP) and User Datagram Protocol (UDP). In fact, the default protocol for Net::Ping is TCP.

LIMITATIONS OF ICMP, NET::PING, AND HOST CHECKING

ICMP, the protocol used by the `ping` command, is disabled on some hosts or at the firewalls of some networks. This means that ICMP is not an entirely reliable predictor of host reachability. For example, sending a ping to a web site might fail, but the site itself is operational when viewed through a web browser.

`Net::Ping` uses TCP as the default protocol and requires that the program be run as root or setuid to root in order to use the ICMP protocol. This is a security risk, simply because the program must run as root or use setuid. The `ping` command itself is commonly setuid root, but security recommendations and security programs such as Bastille remove the setuid bit from ping to prevent an avenue for privilege escalation.

When performing service checks through an ICMP packet, or even by sending a TCP packet to an open port, the amount of information that can be gained is limited. For example, you could send a plain ping to a computer, which responds successfully, but that's no indicator of whether the computer is listening on its web port. Furthermore, you could send a TCP packet to port 80 (the typical HTTP port) and receive a successful TCP three-way handshake. However, that is no indication that the web server is actually serving content. For that, you need a more complex type of check, such as that performed by Nagios and similar software.

Net::Ping is less common than other Net:: modules on Linux systems. Therefore, there's a good chance that you might need to install the software from your local CPAN mirror. It's also important to note that the TCP and UDP checks used by Net::Ping are sent to the echo service port on the remote host. It's very uncommon for the echo port to actually be listening on remote hosts. Therefore, Net::Ping enables you to set the port on the remote server for the check.

■**Caution** Unlike other Net:: modules, Net::Ping is called with the Ping in mixed case. Other Net:: modules use all uppercase, as in Net::SMTP, Net::LDAP, Net::POP3, and so on. This case-sensitivity is important when importing the module into the namespace, since the Perl compiler wouldn't be able to find the module if you specify use Net::PING instead of use Net::Ping.

Creating a Ping Object

As you would expect by now, you work with Net::Ping first through its new() method. The new() method accepts a number of arguments, including the protocol, timeout, bytes to be sent, source device, and type of service. In practice, you'll use the protocol and timeout options the most often. The option order is as follows for the new() method:

```
Net::Ping->new(protocol, timeout, bytes, source_device, type_of_service);
```

For example, if you want to change the protocol from its default TCP, do so when creating the ping object. This example sets the protocol to ICMP:

```
$pingobj = Net::Ping->new('icmp');
```

Separate multiple arguments with commas when invoking new. For example, to set `timeout` to 10 seconds, explicitly set the protocol first, and then set the timeout:

```
$pingobj = Net::Ping->new('icmp', 10);
```

Sending an ICMP Echo Request

Using Net::Ping to send an ICMP echo request requires root privileges or that the Perl program be setuid root. I won't promote the use of setuid. Therefore, if you want to run an ICMP-based check with Net::Ping, the program will need to be run as root. I dislike this option as well, but I'm choosing the lesser of two evils.

Listing 6-15 (Pingex1.pl) sends a simple ICMP echo request to a host on the Internet and from there, reports on the response.

Listing 6-15. *A Simple Ping*

```perl
#!/usr/bin/perl -w

use Net::Ping;
use strict;

my $pingobj = Net::Ping->new('icmp');

my $host = "www.google.com";

my ($status,$time,$ip) = $pingobj->ping($host);
if ($status) {
        print "Host $host ($ip) responded in $time seconds\n";
} else {
        print "Host $host ($ip) unreachable\n";
}
```

■**Note** Don't forget that you need root privilege to run the program in Listing 6-15. If you see an error similar to `icmp ping requires root privilege`, that means you don't have root privilege!

This example first invokes the new() method, creating the ping object, called $pingobj. The call to new() also changes the protocol to ICMP. Next, the host is set, which is www.google.com in this example. The ping() method is called against the $pingobj with the argument of the host to be pinged.

When called in scalar context, the ping() method returns 1 for success or undef for a failure (an unsuccessful ping). When called in a list context, the ping() method returns the success flag (1 for success), the time that the operation took, and the IP address used.

When run, the program produces output like this:

```
Host www.google.com (64.233.167.104) responded in 0 seconds
```

The time returned by ping() is sent in integer format by default. This means that, many times, the time will be integer 0, since the ping operation took less than a second. To obtain more accurate times, use the Time::HiRes module, as described in the next section.

The final section of the example evaluates the $status variable. If the $status variable is 1, the ping was successful and the results are printed. If the $status variable is 0, the ping was unsuccessful and the corresponding result is also printed.

Getting More Accurate Times

As previously stated, the time returned by ping() is returned in integer seconds. This is fine if all you're looking for is success or failure of the ping operation as a whole. However, if you want to obtain more accurate times, you need to use the Time::HiRes module, available from CPAN. The code in Listing 6-16 (Pingex2.pl) is essentially the same as Listing 6-15, with two exceptions: the Time::HiRes module is brought into the namespace, and it includes a call to the hires() method on the ping object.

Listing 6-16. *A Ping Using Time::HiRes for More Accurate Times*

```perl
#!/usr/bin/perl -w

use Net::Ping;
use Time::HiRes;
use strict;

my $pingobj = Net::Ping->new('icmp');

my $host = "www.google.com";

$pingobj->hires();
my ($status,$time,$ip) = $pingobj->ping($host);
if ($status) {
        print "Host $host ($ip) responded in $time seconds\n";
} else {
        print "Host $host ($ip) unreachable\n";
}
```

When run, the program produces output similar to that shown here:

```
Host www.google.com (64.233.167.104) responded in 0.0691518783569336 seconds
```

Sending a TCP Check

As I mentioned earlier, the default protocol used by Net::Ping is TCP. However, the default port used by Net::Ping is the echo port. It's quite uncommon to find an Internet host running the echo service. Therefore, to check a host using TCP, you will probably need to change the port on which the TCP check will be sent. The port should be one that the remote port is listening on, which might be port 80 for HTTP, port 25 for SMTP, and so on. The /etc/services file shows common port number-to-name mappings.

The port change is invoked on the ping object:

```
$pingobj->{port_num} = "<port>";
```

For example, here's the syntax to change the port to 80 on the ping object called $pingobj:

```
$pingobj->{port_num} = "80";
```

Listing 6-17 (Pingex3.pl) shows a more complete example, building on the example shown in Listing 6-16. This example checks port 80 (HTTP) on Google's web site.

Listing 6-17. *Using TCP for a Different Type of Check*

```
#!/usr/bin/perl -w

use Net::Ping;
use Time::HiRes;
use strict;

#$pingobj = Net::Ping->new('icmp');
my $pingobj = Net::Ping->new();

my $host = "www.google.com";

$pingobj->hires();
$pingobj->{port_num} = "80";
my ($status,$time,$ip) = $pingobj->ping($host);
if ($status) {
    print "Host $host ($ip) responded in $time\n";
} else {
    print "Host $host ($ip) unreachable\n";
}
```

Again, it should be noted that this check merely looks to see whether port 80 is capable of completing the TCP three-way handshake. This check is not indicative of the host actually serving web content or content on the actual page, and you should not rely on it for such information. When run, the program produces output like this:

```
Host www.google.com (64.233.167.99) responded in 0.0651910305023193
```

Security Considerations with Net:: Modules

The modules introduced in this chapter don't have any specific security issues associated with them, other than those inherent in the protocols for which they operate and the usual security considerations that a programmer would have when working with a program that might use external data.

POP3 is inherently insecure. When POP3 sends the username and password, it does so in plain, clear text. This means that anyone who happens to be listening at any point in the network can see both your username and your password. In addition, the e-mail being sent between the server and your POP3 client (usually your computer) is not encrypted. This is less of a concern, since that same e-mail was already sent over the Internet unencrypted! POP3S, or POP3 over SSL, fixes both of these problems by sending the POP3 conversation over the Secure Sockets Layer. See the `Mail::POP3Client` documentation for more information about using SSL with POP3 through Perl.

SMTP also sends mail in clear text across the Internet. These concerns aren't specific to the Perl `Net::` modules. They apply whether you're using Perl or a proprietary e-mail software package.

Summary

This chapter examined the `Net::` tools for interacting with various types of servers and services on the Internet. First, it covered how to check e-mail using POP3 with `Net::POP3` and `Mail::Box::POP3`. Next, you learned how to send e-mail with `Net::SMTP`. Then you looked at how to query DNS for information. Finally, you learned how to use `Net::Ping` together with `Time::HiRes` to check on servers and services.

The next chapter will look at XML and RSS and their use with Perl.

## PART 3

XML and RSS

CHAPTER 7

■ ■ ■

SOAP-Based Web Services

SOAP has become a ubiquitous protocol for exchanging information on the Internet. SOAP is a means by which remote procedures or methods can be called as if they were local. When you call a SOAP method, you're asking for an application to perform some computation and return a result to your program. This is the same concept as a local method call; it's just that the SOAP call happens to be remote. These method calls sent using SOAP can be transported over a number of mechanisms, although this chapter will examine only the use of SOAP over HTTP.

SOAP provides a well-formed means to obtain information from a data source. In a SOAP request, you provide parameters as required by the receiving application. These parameters are then used by the server, which executes the query to the application's data source on behalf of the client and returns values to the client in a SOAP response. This information can then be parsed and used within the local Perl application.

This chapter begins with a brief primer on SOAP, and then describes how to use the Perl `SOAP::Lite` module to create a SOAP client and a SOAP listener.

A Quick SOAP Primer

SOAP is the acronym for Simple Object Access Protocol,[1] a protocol defined by the W3 Consortium (`http://www.w3.org/2002/ws/`). This section describes SOAP at a high level.

■Note I assume that you're either familiar with XML or can live without knowing all of those details. If you'd like to know more about XML, take a look at `http://www.w3schools.com/xml/default.asp`.

SOAP is client/server format, with one side sending the message and the other side parsing the XML content of the message. The application may take action based on the results of the message, either on the receiver or sender, or both.

SOAP is an XML format with three elements: envelope, header, and body. The SOAP header and SOAP body are both contained within the SOAP envelope. The SOAP header is

---

1. Some say the acronym for SOAP is really Service-Oriented Access Protocol or even Service-Oriented Architecture Protocol. I really don't care which you call it. I'd rather work with it.

actually optional, although it's almost always included. The SOAP body contains the heart of the SOAP message. Here's an example of a SOAP request:

```
<?xml version="1.0" encoding="UTF-8"?>
<SOAP-ENV:Envelope xmlns:xsi="http://www.w3.org/1999/XMLSchema-instance"
  xmlns:SOAP-ENC="http://schemas.xmlsoap.org/soap/encoding/"
  xmlns:SOAP-ENV="http://schemas.xmlsoap.org/soap/envelope/"
  xmlns:xsd="http://www.w3.org/1999/XMLSchema"
  SOAP-ENV:encodingStyle="http://schemas.xmlsoap.org/soap/encoding/">
    <SOAP-ENV:Body>
        <namesp1:NDFDgenByDay
        xmlns:namesp1="http://weather.gov/forecasts/xml/DWMLgen/wsdl/ndfdXML.wsdl">
            <latitude xsi:type="xsd:float">44.52</latitude>
            <longitude xsi:type="xsd:float">-89.58</longitude>
            <startDate xsi:type="xsd:string">2005-04-23</startDate>
            <numDays xsi:type="xsd:int">5</numDays>
            <format xsi:type="xsd:string">12 hourly</format>
        </namesp1:NDFDgenByDay>
    </SOAP-ENV:Body>
</SOAP-ENV:Envelope>
```

This example sends a request to the United States National Weather Service for forecast data that the site has available through SOAP. The entire message is encapsulated within the `<SOAP-ENV:Envelope>` section, which contains the SOAP body inside the `<SOAP-ENV:Body>` section. Naturally, since I already stated that the SOAP header is almost always included, I found an example that doesn't contain the SOAP header.

When connecting to a web service, you need to know the address of the service, including transport information. Since SOAP can be transported over so many different types of protocols (HTTP, e-mail, or some other protocol), the address information not only shows where the web service resides, but also how to communicate with it. In addition to the address information, the namespace of the web service must also be included. The namespace is used to further locate the web service on the server itself. Finally, the method or function to be called on the remote server, along with any parameters, are included in the SOAP call. In the sample SOAP request, I provide parameters as required by the receiving application.

The parameters required by a given SOAP service are usually defined in the service definition document known as the Web Service Definition Language (WSDL). The WSDL describes the interfaces for a given web service. Using the WSDL, the programmer can determine the names of the services offered, along with the required parameters and their data types. As you'll see in the next section, Perl's `SOAP::Lite` module can also use the WSDL to handle some of the heavy lifting for the programmer.

SOAP has become popular because it is built to use well-known protocols such as HTTP and XML. Several popular web sites have SOAP interfaces available. Table 7-1 lists a select few of these services, along with a short description of each.

Table 7-1. *Some Web Sites with SOAP Interfaces*

Site/Service	Description	Information URL
Amazon.com	Numerous web services to expose data on products at Amazon.com	`http://www.amazon.com/gp/aws/landing.html`
National Weather Service	Web services to expose forecasts and conditions based on latitude and longitude; available for U.S. locations	`http://weather.gov/xml/`
Google	Interfaces to query Google's directory and more	`http://www.google.com/apis/`

SOAP Meets Perl: SOAP::Lite

One package in Perl, `SOAP::Lite`, stands apart from other modules capable of talking SOAP. `SOAP::Lite` enables a developer to create both a SOAP client to send SOAP requests and a SOAP listener to receive SOAP requests. `SOAP::Lite` is a collection of a number of other SOAP- and XML-related packages in Perl, so importing `SOAP::Lite` into a program's namespace effectively makes numerous functions available to your program.

The `SOAP::Lite` package is available with many Linux distributions and also at your favorite CPAN mirror. Some of the classes available with `SOAP::Lite` include the following:

- `SOAP::Data`
- `SOAP::Deserializer`
- `SOAP::Header`
- `SOAP::Lite`
- `SOAP::Parser`
- `SOAP::Serializer`
- `SOAP::Server`
- `SOAP::Transport`

Importing and Debugging SOAP:Lite

First things first—you need to know how to import and, more important, how to debug the package. As with other packages, you first import `SOAP::Lite` into your program's namespace with the `use` pragma:

```
use SOAP::Lite;
```

When importing into the namespace, you can specify some debugging, or *tracing* as it's known to `SOAP::Lite`. This tracing can be helpful—no, more appropriately, this tracing can be a huge time- and headache-saver—when working with web services. Like other debugging, such as that for `Net::SMTP`, `SOAP::Lite` tracing can show method calls and other useful bits that can assist in troubleshooting a call to a web service. Multiple levels of tracing are available with `SOAP::Lite`. Some levels are applicable to the client only, the server only, or both. Table 7-2 lists some the events that are traceable with `SOAP::Lite`.

Table 7-2. *SOAP:Lite Traceable Events*

Event	Applies To	Description
transport	Client	Provides details of the request and response
result	Server	Shows the result of the method call
parameters	Server	Shows the parameters received for the method call
headers	Server	Shows the headers of the message as it was received
debug	Both	Shows details about the transport
objects	Both	Shows calls to new() and destroy()
trace	Both	Shows entry into various functions

In practice, you'll find that it's most helpful to enable all the debugging.[2] To enable trace debugging for all types of events, use this code:

```
use SOAP::Lite +trace;
```

SOAP::Lite also gives the developer the opportunity to enable all debugging, but then selectively disable certain types of events. For example, this code enables all debugging but then turns off the trace for objects:

```
use SOAP::Lite +trace => [ all -objects ];
```

SOAP::Lite also has an on_debug() method, which takes a reference to a subroutine as an argument. This means that you can perform more complex debugging by defining your own subroutine for the debugging to, for instance, send the output to a log file or elsewhere. Here's an example:

```
on_debug(sub {print STDOUT @_})
```

Setting Up the SOAP Object

The SOAP::Lite package contains a number of important methods for working with SOAP as a client. Some of these are used frequently when working with SOAP. Of course, since it's Perl, there are many ways to accomplish the same tasks, even within the same package! I'll highlight a few methods here, before jumping into some examples.

new(): Unlike many other packages, the new() method is not required with SOAP::Lite. I'm highlighting it here simply because of that fact.

proxy(): The proxy() method is used to set the location of the web service to call. This includes transport information such as http:. Recall that SOAP::Lite is a congregation of a number of other modules. Behind the scenes, the proxy() method calls SOAP::Transport, and the appropriate transport information will also be included. In other words, when you call the proxy() method with an http: transport, the SOAP::Transport::HTTP::Client

---

2. I've always found that, if I'm having trouble with a program and need to debug, I'd rather have too much information, at least at first.

module will actually be called for you. The proxy() method also accepts parameters, depending on the given transport. For example, the http: method might include a timeout parameter, and you could call it like so:

```
proxy("http://www.example.com", timeout => 30);
```

■**Note** For more information about the parameters available with a given transport, use perldoc for that transport. For example, to check the parameters for SOAP::Transport::HTTP, you would run perldoc SOAP::Transport::HTTP.

---

uri(): The uri() method sets the namespace for the web service. In future versions of SOAP::Lite, the uri() method will be phased out in favor of a method called ns(). For now, the uri() method works, but watch for new versions of SOAP::Lite to deprecate this method. The difference between the uri() (ns() in future versions) and proxy() is that proxy() defines the address of server or the global location of this web service, whereas uri() defines the location of the method locally to the server. The proxy tells your program where to find the SOAP server, and the URI tells the SOAP server where to find the method that you would like to call.

service(): The service() method is used to give the location of the WSDL document. You can invoke a web service in SOAP::Lite with a combination of the proxy() and uri() (or the new ns()) methods, or you can invoke the web service by calling the WSDL through the service() method. In either case, you also call the web service method from within the Perl code, supplying any arguments to the method call.

Listing 7-1 (Example1.pl) shows an example of a SOAP object setup using the proxy() and uri() methods.

Listing 7-1. *Setting Up a SOAP Object*

```perl
#!/usr/bin/perl -w

use SOAP::Lite;
use strict;

my $soap = SOAP::Lite
 -> proxy('http://weather.gov/forecasts/xml/SOAP_server/ndfdXMLserver.php')
 -> uri('http://weather.gov/forecasts/xml/DWMLgen/wsdl/ndfdXML.wsdl#NDFDgenByDay');
```

This next example sets up the same object, but goes through the WSDL to do so:

```perl
$soap = SOAP::Lite
 -> service('http://weather.gov/forecasts/xml/DWMLgen/wsdl/ndfdXML.wsdl');
```

Note that neither of these code snippets produces any output.

■Note The methods that I use frequently might be used sparingly by other developers. I encourage you to read the documentation on SOAP::Lite. Use perldoc SOAP::Lite once you install SOAP::Lite or examine the documentation at http://www.soaplite.com.

How you set up your SOAP object depends on your own preferences. I've seen programs use the WSDL exclusively with the service() method, and I've seen programs use the proxy() and uri() methods to set up the SOAP object. I would venture that the proxy() and uri() methods are more common. In addition, the service() method is slower, since the program must first retrieve the WSDL using an HTTP GET, parse the WSDL, and then create a SOAP request to the appropriate namespace using an HTTP POST. I prefer the proxy() and uri() methods.

Calling SOAP Methods

Recall that SOAP is a means to include functions executed on remote machines in your program as if they were local. When you call a SOAP method, you're asking a remote application to use its method by that name and return something to you. In the previous section, you saw how to set up a SOAP object by configuring the location for the service, as well as the namespace for the service. In this section, you'll see how to call a SOAP method.

Throughout this chapter, you'll see a call to a fictitious SOAP implementation called BookInfo.cgi. I've created a sample application to provide the back end for this application. If you would like to test any of the examples, you can implement this code (BookInfo.cgi), as shown in Listing 7-2.

Listing 7-2. *The Book Info SOAP Implementation*

```perl
#!/usr/bin/perl -w

use strict;
use SOAP::Transport::HTTP;

SOAP::Transport::HTTP::CGI
        -> dispatch_to('isbnsearch')
        -> handle;

package isbnsearch;

sub isbnsearch {
        my $class = shift;
        my $isbn = shift;
        if ($isbn eq "1590595319") {
                return "Beginning Perl Web Development\n";
        } elsif ($isbn eq "0672327716") {
                return "Linux Firewalls - Third Edition\n";
        } elsif ($isbn eq "0764549324") {
```

```
        return "MySQL Bible\n";
    } else {
        return "Steve hasn't worked on that book yet\n";
    }
}
```

Calling a SOAP method is actually rather easy. Once you get comfortable with the terminology of SOAP::Lite—such as proxy, URI, and such—the method call is essentially the same as you would find with any function or method call in Perl. You call the SOAP method and include any parameters required by the method. Consider this example:

```
$soap = SOAP::Lite
    -> proxy('http://www.example.com/BookInfo.cgi')
    -> uri('http://www.example.com/isbnsearch')
    -> isbnsearch("1590595319");
```

In this example, the proxy() and uri() methods are called, and the SOAP::Lite object is created, as you've seen before. Added to this example is the call to the function or method on the remote side, isbnsearch(). A single argument is sent with this method call: an ISBN.[3] The program produces no output.

Result

The call to the SOAP web service is all well and good, but it would be nice to actually see the response, too. The result() method is used to see the response. Adding that, along with a print statement, to the code example yields this:

```
$soap = SOAP::Lite
    -> proxy('http://www.example.com/BookInfo.cgi')
    -> uri('http://www.example.com/isbnsearch')
    -> isbnsearch("1590595319");

print $soap-> result;
```

The simple output, based on the sample BookInfo.cgi program, looks like this:

```
Beginning Perl Web Development
```

Of course, there's no reason why you couldn't write this with one command or line of code. Listing 7-3 (Printbookinfo.pl) shows a more complete example.

Listing 7-3. *Printing the Results of an ISBN Search*

```
#!/usr/bin/perl -w

use strict;
use SOAP::Lite;
```

---

3. An ISBN is a number used to identify a book. See http://www.isbn-international.org/en/whatis.html if you're curious.

```
my $soap;

print $soap = SOAP::Lite
    -> proxy('http://www.braingia.org/cgi-bin/BookInfo.cgi')
    -> uri('http://www.braingia.org/isbnsearch')
    -> isbnsearch("1590595319")
    -> result;
```

Notice the separate call to print is missing in Listing 7-3. This example is a quick way to print a result to STDOUT, but it doesn't allow for easy (and readable) error handling. I'll cover SOAP error handling in the next section.

Obviously, you'll likely want to do more with those results than merely print them to STDOUT. The results arrive in XML and can therefore be parsed with Perl's rich set of XML parser packages, including XML::Simple and XML::Parser, just to name a couple.

Autodispatch

Autodispatch refers to a mechanism whereby any method calls not located in the current namespace are automatically sent through a SOAP call. This means that you can call the method as you would any other function within a Perl program. Consider the code example just shown. Using autodispatch, that same code would look like this:

```
use SOAP::Lite +autodispatch =>
    proxy => 'http://www.example.com/BookInfo.cgi',
    uri => 'http://www.example.com/isbnsearch';

isbnsearch("1590595319");

print SOAP::Lite->self->call->result;
```

Since no $soap SOAP object was created, you must call the SOAP::Lite self object in order to view the result. The call() method of the self object contains the SOAP envelope; therefore, calling result() on the SOAP envelope object prints the result.

Handling SOAP Errors

I had originally written about SOAP errors being slippery in the opening paragraph for this section, but then thought better of it. As you would expect, errors do indeed occur with SOAP method calls. The errors could be at any level and completely unrelated to SOAP, like a server being down or my cable Internet service being temporarily unavailable again. When the errors occur at the SOAP level—say, in a method call—you can access the error within the SOAP object itself through the fault() method. By examining the fault() method, which will return undef unless there is a problem, you can determine whether the SOAP method call was successful.

Consider this code:

```
$soap = SOAP::Lite
    -> proxy('http://www.example.com/BookInfo.cgi')
    -> uri('http://www.example.com/isbnsearch')
    -> isbnsearch("1590595319");
```

```
if ($soap->fault) {
    print "Error found: ", $soap->faultcode,
      ": ", $soap->faultstring, " Detail: ",
      $soap->faultdetail;
} else {
    print $soap->result;
}
```

The output from this example will depend on whether you get an error and, if so, what that error is. Here's an example of the output:

```
Error found: SOAP-ENV:Client: Failed to access class (BookInfo.cgi) at
/usr/share/perl5/SOAP/Lite.pm line 2100.
```

Setting Types and Names

Perl, as a language, doesn't really care what type of value you store within a variable, a string "5150" and an integer 5150 aren't functionally different to Perl (although they are in the background). This isn't the case with most SOAP calls.

Luckily, SOAP::Lite attempts to automatically set the type based on the data value, and it does quite well at that. SOAP::Lite can guess that a value of 5150 is an integer and a value of "Distance" is a string type. However, sometimes SOAP::Lite doesn't guess correctly. In such cases, you can specify the type of data by working with the SOAP::Data class. For example, to explicitly set the data type of an element to a string, and then set the value to 5150, the code looks like this:

```
SOAP::Data->type( string => 5150 );
```

Using the BookInfo.cgi example, assume that the isbnsearch() method required a data type of a string. However, since an ISBN is all digits, SOAP::Lite naturally would guess that the data type is an integer. To correct that, you would set the type when making the call, as shown here:

```
$soap = SOAP::Lite
    -> proxy('http://www.example.com/BookInfo.cgi')
    -> uri('http://www.example.com/isbnsearch')
    -> isbnsearch(SOAP::Data->type( string => "1590595319"));
```

Unlike other method and function calls, some SOAP methods don't care as much about the ordering of arguments as they care about the name of those arguments. This means that it's important to ensure that the names of the arguments are set according to the names that the SOAP method is expecting. Not all SOAP methods are like this, and I usually recommend to first get the order correct before setting the names.

You set the names of the parameters in much the same way as you set parameter types:

```
$soap = SOAP::Lite
    -> proxy('http://www.example.com/BookInfo.cgi')
    -> uri('http://www.example.com/isbnsearch')
    -> isbnsearch(SOAP::Data->name("isbn" => "1590595319"));
```

And setting types and names is done like so:

```
$soap = SOAP::Lite
    -> proxy('http://www.example.com/BookInfo.cgi')
    -> uri('http://www.example.com/BookInfo.cgi#isbnsearch')
    -> isbnsearch(SOAP::Data->name("isbn" => "1590595319")->type(string));
```

Or, you could reverse that and set the type first:

```
$soap = SOAP::Lite
    -> proxy('http://www.example.com/BookInfo.cgi')
    -> uri('http://www.example.com/BookInfo.cgi#isbnsearch')
    -> isbnsearch(SOAP::Data->type( string => "1590595319")->name("isbn"));
```

Creating a SOAP Listener

Up to this point in the chapter, you've been reading almost exclusively about SOAP from the client side, which is only half of the equation. SOAP::Lite also has methods for running its own SOAP server to respond to requests as well. These methods are accessed through SOAP::Transport::HTTP class, although other transports are available. This section examines how to create a SOAP listener.

When creating a listener, three methods are of primary concern: new(), dispatch_to(), and handle(). The new() method sets the address and port for the server. These are the local address and port that the server will be listening on. If the port you choose is below 1024, you'll need to have root privileges in order to run the program. I strongly recommend against this, since there's no reason to run a service such as this as root and risk a security problem resulting in an attacker getting root privileges. In either case, you'll need to ensure that the server isn't listening on the port in question. You can check this by using the netstat shell command. For example, say you want to have the SOAP listener use port 18001. The following command checks to see if the server is already listening on port 18001:

```
netstat -an | grep 18001
```

If the command doesn't return any output, that means the port is available. On the other hand, if the command returns output such as the following, then the server is indeed listening:

```
tcp        0      0 0.0.0.0:18001           0.0.0.0:*               LISTEN
```

For testing purposes in this chapter, I'm going to set the listener to use only the localhost, so that the program won't actually be available on the network. This code sets the server to listen on the localhost and on port 18001:

```
$server = SOAP::Transport::HTTP::Daemon
    ->new(LocalAddr => 'localhost', LocalPort => '18001');
```

The dispatch_to() method specifies the method name that will actually do the processing on the server side. This can be a path, a module, a module::method combination, or just a method. The code to set the method, which in this example will be called doubleit, in combination with the call to the new() method, looks like this:

```
$server = SOAP::Transport::HTTP::Daemon
    ->new(LocalAddr => 'localhost', LocalPort => '18001')
    ->dispatch_to('doubleit');
```

Finally, the handle() method sets the server up to continue listening. Combining this with the previous method calls nearly completes the setup of the server:

```
$server = SOAP::Transport::HTTP::Daemon
    ->new(LocalAddr => 'localhost', LocalPort => '18001')
    ->dispatch_to('doubleit');
    ->handle();
```

Finally, you need to set up the method, doubleit. In this case, I implement the doubleit method through a module of its own. This is much more common than the alternative, which is to include the method within the server code itself. The code to implement that method is shown in Listing 7-4 (Doubleit.pm). It's simple code that takes a number as input and doubles it.

Listing 7-4. *Code to Implement the Server Package for the SOAP Call*

```
package doubleit;

sub doubler {
        my $class = shift;
        my $num = shift;
        return ($num*2);
}

return 1;
```

This file, which I saved as Doubleit.pm in my home directory, needs to be included within the server code so that program can include the methods available in doubleit within its namespace. The client will call the actual method (called doubler()). Listing 7-5 shows the full server code (Doublerserver.pl).

Listing 7-5. *Code to Implement the Server (Listener) for the SOAP Call*

```
#!/usr/bin/perl -w

use strict;
use SOAP::Transport::HTTP;
require ("doubleit.pm");

my $daemon = SOAP::Transport::HTTP::Daemon
        ->new(LocalPort => 18001)
        ->dispatch_to('doubleit')
        ->handle( );
```

A MORE ROBUST SERVER

The `SOAP::Lite` module provides an excellent choice for implementing a SOAP server. However, for high-volume sites, a more robust solution is preferable. Using a proven web server such as Apache and building a CGI-based SOAP handler provides a great solution that takes advantage of Apache's proven track record. There is also a package for implementing SOAP within a `mod_perl` environment. The package is called `Apache::SOAP`.

The `SOAP::Transport::HTTP` module from CPAN includes a class that enables a normal Apache server running `mod_cgi` to service SOAP requests. Many of the examples in this chapter are shown as they would run against a CGI-based SOAP server running on Apache. The sample program `BookInfo.cgi` was written (and is running) on a `mod_cgi` Apache server.

No special configuration is required on the Apache server side (other than that what is required to run CGI programs). For more information, see the Perl documentation for `SOAP::Transport::HTTP` and `SOAP::Transport::HTTP::CGI`. See the `BookInfo.cgi` example earlier in this chapter for a working implementation of a SOAP server with `Apache mod_cgi`.

In the next section, I'll show you how to call the web service server that you just created. For now, you can run the server by simply executing it from the command line:

```
./doublerserver.pl
```

Once run, the server will not fork into the background, so it will remain running until you press Ctrl+C. You can verify that the server is running with the `netstat` command shown earlier in this section. Now, you should indeed see that the server is listening.

Consuming a SOAP Web Service

In the previous section, you saw how to create a SOAP server that listens on a port of your choosing and implements a simple method call to double the number it receives as input. You've already seen how to implement SOAP calls as the client side of the protocol. This section wraps it all into one package by showing how to call the SOAP service you created in the previous section. In addition, I'll show you a more complex example that calls the National Weather Service SOAP service.

Calling Your SOAP Server

The SOAP server you created in the previous section has one method, `doubler()`, which accepts a number as an argument and returns the double of that number. Recall that you invoke a SOAP method by creating a SOAP object with the `proxy()` and `uri()` methods, then calling the SOAP service including any arguments, and then doing something with the result.

Listing 7-6 (`Calldouble.pl`) shows a client implementation to call the SOAP service created in the previous section.

Listing 7-6. *A Program to Call the Local SOAP Service*

```perl
#!/usr/bin/perl -w

use SOAP::Lite;
use strict;

my $soap = SOAP::Lite
    -> uri("http://localhost/doubleit")
    -> proxy("http://127.0.0.1:18001/");
my $originalnum = 2;
my $result = $soap->call('doubler', $originalnum);
die $result->faultstring if $result->fault;
print "result is: " . $result->result . "\n";
```

The example begins by importing the SOAP::Lite package in the namespace, and then it creates a SOAP object, called $soap. This object uses the http: transport to send to a proxy of 127.0.0.1:18001. The URI or namespace is set to http://localhost/doubleit.

The original number is set to 2 and the doubler() method is called, including the $originalnum as an argument. Next, the SOAP fault is evaluated to see if there was a problem, and if not, the result is printed. Here's the output:

```
result is: 4
```

If you receive an error such as the following when attempting to run this code, it likely means that the server isn't running:

```
500 Can't connect to 127.0.0.1:18001 (connect: Connection refused)
    at ./caller.pl line 9
```

Calling the National Weather Service SOAP Service

Earlier in the chapter, I showed a SOAP response from the National Weather Service and the proxy() and uri() methods for this service. Here they are again:

```perl
use SOAP::Lite;
use strict;

my $soap = SOAP::Lite
 -> proxy('http://weather.gov/forecasts/xml/SOAP_server/ndfdXMLserver.php')
 -> uri('http://weather.gov/forecasts/xml/DWMLgen/wsdl/ndfdXML.wsdl#NDFDgenByDay');
```

The SOAP service at the National Weather Service has two methods: NDFDgen() and NDFDgenByDay(). These are found at http://weather.gov/forecasts/xml/SOAP_server/ ndfdXMLserver.php and also within the WSDL. Obviously, you need to call one of these two methods.

The call to these methods is more complicated than the other calls shown in this chapter, as there are a number of parameters that must be sent and must be formatted correctly. Luckily, the SOAP services are well documented, which makes it easy to send the correct format.

The method that I'm using for this example is NDFDgenByDay(), which accepts five parameters as arguments, for the latitude, longitude, start date, number of days, and format. Of course,
this code assumes that the values are all set in the variables for latitude, longitude, and so on.
So, here they are (using the latitude and longitude for Stevens Point, Wisconsin):

```
my $latitude = "44.52";
my $longitude = "-89.58";
my $startdate = "2005-04-28";
my $numdays = "5";
my $format = "12 hourly";
```

The service does not require that the parameters be sent as a specific type. In other words,
SOAP::Lite's guesses, though incorrect in this case, work okay with this SOAP service. To set up
the method call for this service, use the SOAP::Data->name() method to set the name of each
parameter along with its corresponding value:

```
->NDFDgenByDay(SOAP::Data->name("latitude" => $latitude),
               SOAP::Data->name("longitude" => $longitude),
               SOAP::Data->name("startDate" => $startdate),
               SOAP::Data->name("numDays" => $numdays),
               SOAP::Data->name("format" => $format));
```

With the method call set up correctly, you merely need to print the result:

```
print $soap->result;
```

Tip You can use the National Weather Service's site to find the latitude and longitude for your location.
This service is available only in the United States. Also note that this service may have changed by the time
you're reading this. Visit http://weather.gov/xml/ for the most current information. There, you'll find
more information about the National Weather Service's XML initiative, including SOAP information.

Listing 7-7 (Callnws.pl) shows the complete code for calling the National Weather Service
SOAP service.

Listing 7-7. *Calling the National Weather Service SOAP Service*

```
#!/usr/bin/perl -w

use SOAP::Lite;
use strict;

#Be sure to change these unless you live in Stevens Point
#   and want an old forecast (since it doesn't work with past dates)
my $latitude = "44.52";
my $longitude = "-89.58";
my $startdate = "2005-04-28";
```

```
my $numdays = "5";
my $format = "12 hourly";

my $soap = SOAP::Lite
    -> proxy('http://weather.gov/forecasts/xml/SOAP_server/ndfdXMLserver.php')
    -> uri('http://weather.gov/forecasts/xml/DWMLgen/wsdl/ndfdXML.wsdl#NDFDgenByDay')
    ->NDFDgenByDay(SOAP::Data->name("latitude" => $latitude),
                   SOAP::Data->name("longitude" => $longitude),
                   SOAP::Data->name("startDate" => $startdate),
                   SOAP::Data->name("numDays" => $numdays),
                   SOAP::Data->name("format" => $format));

print $soap->result;
```

You will want to change the date to a date nearer to the date that you're reading this. The SOAP call won't work for dates in the past!

The result, as printed by the program, is shown in part here. (Note that I've broken some of the long lines in order to print them in the book.)

```
<?xml version='1.0' ?>
<dwml version='1.0' xmlns:xsd="http://www.w3.org/2001/XMLSchema"
                    xmlns:xsi="http://www.w3.org/2001/XMLSchema-instance"
                    xsi:noNamespaceSchemaLocation=
"http://www.nws.noaa.gov/forecasts/xml/DWMLgen/schema/DWML.xsd">
   <head>
      <product concise-name="dwmlByDay" operational-mode="developmental">
         <title>NOAAs National Weather Service Forecast by 12 Hour period</title>
         <field>meteorological</field>
         <category>forecast</category>
         <creation-date refresh-frequency='PT1H'>2005-04-30T05:46:16Z
         </creation-date>
      </product>
      <source>
         <more-information>http://www.nws.noaa.gov/forecasts/xml/</more-information>
         <production-center>Meteorological Development Laboratory <sub-center>
         Product Generation Branch</sub-center>
         </production-center>
         <disclaimer>http://www.nws.noaa.gov/disclaimer.html</disclaimer>
         <credit>http://weather.gov/</credit>
         <credit-logo>http://weather.gov/images/xml_logo.gif</credit-logo>
         <feedback>http://weather.gov/survey/nws-survey.php?code=xmlsoap</feedback>
      </source>
   </head>
   <data>
      <location>
         <location-key>point1</location-key>
         <point latitude="44.52" longitude="-89.58" />
      </location>
```

```
<time-layout time-coordinate="local" summarization="12hourly">
    <layout-key>k-p24h-n5-1</layout-key>
        <start-valid-time period-name="Later Today">2005-04-30T06:00:00-05:00
        </start-valid-time>
            <end-valid-time>2005-04-30T18:00:00-05:00</end-valid-time>
```

That's all there is to calling a SOAP web service: find the location, set it as the proxy, set the namespace with the uri() method, call the method according to its required parameters, and do something with the results.

Security Considerations with SOAP Web Services

Calling a SOAP web service usually means calling a remote method, likely located on a remote computer, possibly on a different network. Furthermore, this method call might traverse an untrusted network such as the Internet. For all of these reasons, you must be careful with the data received from a SOAP call. The return from a SOAP method call might contain malicious data if the remote server was compromised or if someone can spoof the remote server. Additionally, if the data being transferred is sensitive in nature, you should consider using SSL as the transport. From your program, all this really means is changing the transport from http: to https:.

When operating a SOAP server, you must be careful that the server itself doesn't become compromised. This means running the server as a nonprivileged user and using a firewall to limit any remote calls of the method or methods being served by the SOAP server. If the server does become compromised through the SOAP server, at least the user will have privileges of only a local user, as opposed to the root user. Additionally, if you're running a SOAP server that includes methods to send sensitive data, consider using a secure transport such as SSL to ensure that eavesdroppers can't view the data as it traverses the network.

Summary

In this chapter, you learned about SOAP web services through Perl. Specifically, you were introduced to SOAP itself with a brief introduction to the protocol. Next, you met SOAP::Lite and saw how to consume SOAP web services. You also saw how to create a SOAP listener with Perl. Finally, you looked at a real-world example of a SOAP service by calling the National Weather Service's SOAP forecast service.

In the next chapter, you'll be introduced to RSS and Perl.

## CHAPTER 8

Perl and RSS

RSS (an abbreviation for Rich Site Summary or RDF Site Summary) is used to syndicate content from a web site. RSS is helpful for gathering headlines and other news-related items from web sites or getting recent changes to a web page. It's common for an end user to use news aggregation software to consume RSS feeds. Web browsers such as Mozilla Firefox also enable RSS feeds to be used as bookmarks.

Various Perl modules handle RSS feeds. Some of the modules, such as XML::RSS, are general and designed to work with most any RSS feed; others are specific to a particular site's RSS feed. For example, XML::RSS::Headline::PerlJobs gets the headlines from jobs.perl.org, and XML::RSS::Headline::Fark gets headlines from the popular Fark web site.

This chapter looks at RSS from a Perl perspective. Specifically, you'll see how to consume and create RSS feeds using the XML::RSS module.

RSS: Versioning Fun

At the time of this writing, there are four versions of the RSS protocol: 0.90, 0.91, 1.0, and 2.0. Some aggregation software works with only certain versions of the protocol. The aggregators may support a limited subset of a newer version, or they may not support a newer version at all. Similarly, the Perl modules may or may not support every version of the RSS protocol. Some RSS modules handle the versions well, simply ignoring things that they don't implement, while others don't fail so gracefully. The best method for determining whether the module you're using works with a particular version of RSS is to read the documentation for that particular module.

For those not familiar with RSS, you can pull up an RSS feed through your web browser. You can point your browser at the example used throughout the chapter: http://www.spc.noaa.gov/products/spcwwrss.xml. You should be able to view it in a manner similar to Figure 8-1.

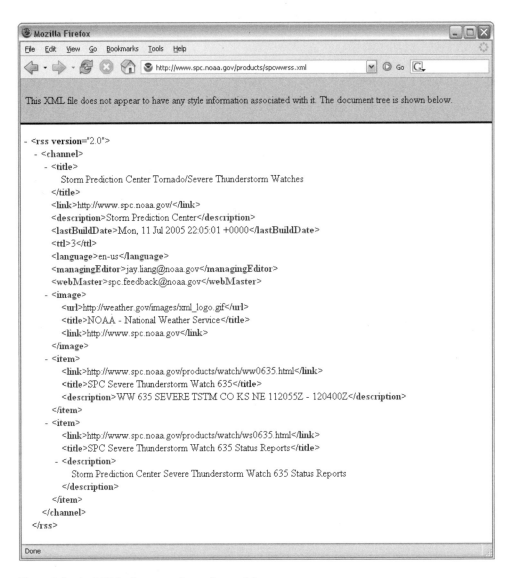

Figure 8-1. *An RSS feed as seen through a web browser*

Reading RSS with XML::RSS

The previous chapter described how to consume a SOAP-based web service from the United States National Weather Service. The National Weather Service has a division called the Storm Prediction Center (SPC), which handles the forecasting of severe or extreme weather events for the United States. The SPC home page is http://www.spc.noaa.gov/. Among the many products offered for current conditions and forecasting is an RSS feed of mesoscale discussions, convective outlooks, and watches. Here, you'll see how to consume the RSS feed for weather watches offered by the National Weather Service.

You'll use the XML::RSS module for reading an RSS feed. XML::RSS is available within many Linux distributions or from your favorite CPAN mirror. XML::RSS includes methods to both parse (read) and create (write) RSS feeds.

Parsing RSS Feeds

This section looks specifically at parsing an RSS feed for interesting items. While XML::RSS can work with RSS feeds, it does not include methods to retrieve the actual RSS from the Internet. For this functionality, you can turn to LWP::Simple, which was covered in Chapter 5.

Parsing an RSS feed can be broken into three basic steps:

1. Get the RSS.

2. Parse the RSS.

3. Do something with the RSS.

To accomplish the first task, LWP::Simple will retrieve the RSS feed and place it into a variable. XML::RSS can perform the second task. The third task is accomplished by you, doing whatever it is that you would like to do with the program, assisted by XML::RSS methods.

Here are the beginning bits of code for the program to be built in this section:

```
use strict;
use XML::RSS;
use LWP::Simple;
```

These lines of code import the modules into the program's namespace and also enable the strict pragma.

The URL for the SPC's Weather Watch RSS feed is http://www.spc.noaa.gov/products/spcwwrss.xml. Therefore, you can retrieve it by using the get() method of LWP::Simple, as shown here:

```
my $url = get("http://www.spc.noaa.gov/products/spcwwrss.xml");
```

The data from the RSS feed is saved into the $url variable for later use. If you would like to debug to ensure that the RSS was actually retrieved, you can use a simple print statement:

```
print $url;
```

For example, here's the output from that print statement:

```
<?xml version="1.0" encoding="UTF-8"?>
<rss version="2.0" xmlns:dc="http://purl.org/dc/elements/1.1/">
  <channel>
    <title>Storm Prediction Center Tornado/Severe Thunderstorm Watches</title>
    <link>http://www.spc.noaa.gov/</link>
    <description>Storm Prediction Center</description>
    <lastBuildDate>Mon, 11 Jul 2005 22:01:02 +0000</lastBuildDate>
    <ttl>3</ttl>
    <language>en-us</language>
    <managingEditor>jay.liang@noaa.gov</managingEditor>
    <webMaster>spc.feedback@noaa.gov</webMaster>
```

```
    <image>
      <url>http://weather.gov/images/xml_logo.gif</url>
      <title>NOAA - National Weather Service</title>
      <link>http://www.spc.noaa.gov</link>
    </image>

    <item>
      <link>http://www.spc.noaa.gov/products/watch/ww0635.html</link>
      <title>SPC Severe Thunderstorm Watch 635</title>
      <description>WW 635 SEVERE TSTM CO KS NE 112055Z - 120400Z</description>
    </item>
    <item>
      <link>http://www.spc.noaa.gov/products/watch/ws0635.html</link>
      <title>SPC Severe Thunderstorm Watch 635 Status Reports</title>
      <description>Storm Prediction Center Severe Thunderstorm Watch 635 Status
          Reports</description>
    </item>
  </channel>
</rss>
```

■**Note** Unless all you want to do is print the RSS to STDOUT, you would obviously use the `print` statement only for debugging. Otherwise, comment it out or remove it entirely.

The first order of business is to instantiate an RSS object, which I'll call $rss in this code. Next, you parse the RSS that was retrieved by LWP::Simple using the parse() method of XML::RSS.

```
my $rss = XML::RSS->new;
$rss->parse($url);
```

With the RSS parsed, it's now a matter of gleaning from the RSS whatever information is useful for your program using one of the XML::RSS methods, iterating through a hash of items, and so on. For example, you might use the channel() method, which enables you to print the title, the link the description, and other information about the RSS feed:

```
print $rss->channel('title'), "\n";
```

Each item within the RSS feed is placed into an array and can be referenced by iterating through the array, as shown in this example:

```
foreach my $item (@{$rss->{'items'}}) {
      print "Title: $item->{'title'}\n";
      print "Desc: $item->{'description'}\n";
      print "Link: $item->{'link'}\n";
}
```

In the example, each item is placed into the scalar variable $item, and then attributes of this scalar variable are called, as you see by the print statements to output the title, description, and link. The entire program is shown in Listing 8-1.

Listing 8-1. *An Initial RSS Example*

```perl
#!/usr/bin/perl

use strict;
use XML::RSS;
use LWP::Simple;

my $url = get("http://www.spc.noaa.gov/products/spcwwrss.xml");

# Debugging - Comment out when not debugging #
#print $url;

my $rss = XML::RSS->new;
$rss->parse($url);

print $rss->channel('title'), "\n";
foreach my $item (@{$rss->{'items'}}) {
        print "Title: $item->{'title'}\n";
        print "Desc: $item->{'description'}\n";
        print "Link: $item->{'link'}\n";
}
```

When executed, the program produces this output:

```
Storm Prediction Center Tornado/Severe Thunderstorm Watches
Title: SPC Severe Thunderstorm Watch 587
Desc: WW 587 SEVERE TSTM KS NE 031245Z - 031800Z
Link: http://www.spc.noaa.gov/products/watch/ww0587.html
Title: SPC Severe Thunderstorm Watch 587 Status Reports
Desc: Storm Prediction Center Severe Thunderstorm Watch 587 Status Reports
Link: http://www.spc.noaa.gov/products/watch/ws0587.html
```

Be aware that some sites monitor the number of RSS retrievals performed from a specific IP address within a certain time period. This is because of abuse by some people who retrieve the RSS looking for updates too frequently. For example, some people have been known to configure their RSS aggregator to request the RSS feed every few seconds. While one user doing this wouldn't likely cause a performance degradation, if 1,000 users requested constant updates, that would quickly lead to a distributed denial of service. Therefore, be careful when debugging the script that you don't request the RSS feed too many times and get blocked in the process! In the next section, you'll see a method for developing your script so that it doesn't cause the site operator to lose sleep.

Debugging RSS Scripts

While you're developing a script to retrieve an RSS feed, it's not uncommon to run that script multiple times within a short period. As I just mentioned, this can, on certain sites, cause your IP address to get blocked for abusive RSS requests. The site operator who owns the RSS feed likely won't be able to tell the difference between someone debugging a script and someone requesting constant RSS updates.

Here's how I solve the problem: When developing the script, I use LWP::Simple to retrieve the RSS and print the resulting RSS to STDOUT using the print statement shown in the preceding section. Then I save the output to a file by using a simple shell redirect.

For example, assume you created a script to retrieve an RSS feed called get_rss.pl. That script looks like this:

```perl
#!/usr/bin/perl

use strict;
use XML::RSS;
use LWP::Simple;

my $url = get("http://www.spc.noaa.gov/products/spcwwrss.xml");

print $url;
```

You run the script, and the output is printed to STDOUT. Redirect that output to a file:

```
./get_rss.pl > spc_rssfeed.xml
```

With the RSS contained in the file, you'll be able to use the XML::RSS parsefile() method to parse the RSS feed, rather than requesting the RSS from the site again. Recall the example shown in the previous section. Instead of using the get() method, you comment that out and use the parsefile() method, along with an argument of the filename containing the RSS feed, as shown in Listing 8-2.

Listing 8-2. *Debugging an RSS Feed Script*

```perl
#!/usr/bin/perl

use strict;
use XML::RSS;
use LWP::Simple;

#my $url = get("http://www.spc.noaa.gov/products/spcwwrss.xml");

# Debugging - Comment out when not debugging #
#print $url;

my $rss = XML::RSS->new;
$rss->parsefile("spc_rssfeed.xml");
```

```perl
print $rss->channel('title'), "\n";
foreach my $item (@{$rss->{'items'}}) {
        print "Title: $item->{'title'}\n";
        print "Desc: $item->{'description'}\n";
        print "Link: $item->{'link'}\n";
}
```

Once the script has been developed and debugged, you uncomment the get() method and change the parsefile() method to the parse() method. This extra bit of work makes the site operator of the RSS feed happy and can prevent you from getting blocked.

Writing RSS with XML::RSS

Along with parsing an RSS feed, XML::RSS can also write RSS. Some of the same methods used for parsing an RSS feed with XML::RSS are used in creating one, and others are simply reversed; instead of reading with the methods, you write with them.

As an example, let's see how to build an RSS feed using repackaged data from the National Weather Service's Weather Watch RSS. I live in Wisconsin. Therefore, I'm interested in weather events in and around the state of Wisconsin. It would be nice to be able to ignore watches for other states and produce an RSS file that contains only items relevant to my area. (Fortunately, there are no weather watches for my area on the day that I'm writing this chapter. Therefore, I'll also be checking in Kansas, since I know there's a weather watch there, and I'll also include the states of Minnesota, and Iowa.)

When creating an RSS feed with XML::RSS, you can set the RSS version. If not specified, the default version is 1.0. Since this program will repackage data from the SPC's RSS feed, the opening bits of the program are much the same as the previous examples:

```perl
use strict;
use XML::RSS;
use LWP::Simple;
my $url = get("http://www.spc.noaa.gov/products/spcwwrss.xml");
my $rss = XML::RSS->new;
$rss->parse($url);
```

The existing XML::RSS object, $rss, is used to parse the incoming RSS feed. Therefore, you need a new XML::RSS object to create the new feed. I'll call this new object $rsswriter:

```perl
my $rsswriter = XML::RSS->new;
```

Since no version is specified, version 1.0 will be used. However, if you wanted to specify the version, the statement would look like this for a version 0.91 feed:

```perl
my $rsswriter = XML::RSS->new(version => '0.91');
```

Instead of reading the channel information as in the previous example, this time, you're creating your own RSS channel.

```
$rsswriter->channel(
    title => "My Watch Summary",
    link => "http://www.braingia.org/",
    description => "Weather Watches for KS, IA, MN, and WI"
);
```

As in the previous examples, you iterate over each item of the incoming RSS feed. Instead of printing all of the items to STDOUT, this time, each one is examined to see if the description contains one of the four states that you're interested in for this example. If one of those states is listed within the incoming item's description, the add_item() method is called on the $rsswriter object:

```
foreach my $item (@{$rss->{'items'}}) {
    if ($item->{'description'} =~ /KS|WI|IA|MN/) {
        $rsswriter->add_item(
            title => $item->{'title'},
            description => $item->{'description'},
            link => $item->{'link'}
        );
    }
}
```

Once each item in the incoming feed has been examined, it's time to write the RSS feed. You can do this by using the save() method or by printing the feed with the as_string() method. I chose to save the RSS feed to a file called mywatchsummary.xml:

```
$rsswriter->save("mywatchsummary.xml");
```

If you would rather print the RSS to STDOUT, use a print statement with the as_string() method:

```
print $rsswriter->as_string;
```

Regardless of which method you use, the resulting file or output looks like this:

```
<?xml version="1.0" encoding="UTF-8"?>

<rdf:RDF
 xmlns:rdf="http://www.w3.org/1999/02/22-rdf-syntax-ns#"
 xmlns="http://purl.org/rss/1.0/"
 xmlns:taxo="http://purl.org/rss/1.0/modules/taxonomy/"
 xmlns:dc="http://purl.org/dc/elements/1.1/"
 xmlns:syn="http://purl.org/rss/1.0/modules/syndication/"
 xmlns:admin="http://webns.net/mvcb/"
>

<channel rdf:about="http://www.braingia.org/">
<title>Watch Summary for Western Great Lakes</title>
<link>http://www.braingia.org/</link>
```

```
<description>Weather Watches for IA, MN, and WI</description>
<items>
 <rdf:Seq>
  <rdf:li rdf:resource="http://www.spc.noaa.gov/products/watch/ww0587.html" />
 </rdf:Seq>
</items>
</channel>


<item rdf:about="http://www.spc.noaa.gov/products/watch/ww0587.html">
<title>SPC Severe Thunderstorm Watch 587</title>
<link>http://www.spc.noaa.gov/products/watch/ww0587.html</link>
<description>WW 587 SEVERE TSTM KS NE 031245Z - 031800Z</description>
</item>


</rdf:RDF>
```

If you wanted to, you could also use the output attribute to convert between RSS versions. For example, the previously shown output is version 1.0. However, using the output attribute of the XML::RSS object, $rsswriter, you can change this to a different version on the fly. For example, the code to change the version just prior to printing the output looks like this:

```
$rsswriter->{'output'} = '0.91';
print $rsswriter->as_string;
```

The resulting output would show the change:

```
<?xml version="1.0" encoding="UTF-8"?>


<!DOCTYPE rss PUBLIC "-//Netscape Communications//DTD RSS 0.91//EN"
          "http://my.netscape.com/publish/formats/rss-0.91.dtd">


<rss version="0.91">


<channel>
<title>My Watch Summary</title>
<link>http://www.braingia.org/</link>
<description>Weather Watches for KS, IA, MN, and WI</description>


<item>
<title>SPC Severe Thunderstorm Watch 587</title>
<link>http://www.spc.noaa.gov/products/watch/ww0587.html</link>
<description>WW 587 SEVERE TSTM KS NE 031245Z - 031800Z</description>
</item>


</channel>
```

The final program is shown in Listing 8-3.

Listing 8-3. *Retrieving Weather Watches with RSS*

```perl
#!/usr/bin/perl

use strict;
use XML::RSS;
use LWP::Simple;

my $url = get("http://www.spc.noaa.gov/products/spcwwrss.xml");

my $rss = XML::RSS->new;
$rss->parse($url);

my $rsswriter = XML::RSS->new;

$rsswriter->channel(
    title => "My Watch Summary",
    link => "http://www.braingia.org/",
    description => "Weather Watches for KS, IA, MN, and WI"
);

foreach my $item (@{$rss->{'items'}}) {
    if ($item->{'description'} =~ /KS|WI|IA|MN/) {
        $rsswriter->add_item(
            title => $item->{'title'},
            description => $item->{'description'},
            link => $item->{'link'}
        );
    }
}

$rsswriter->save("mywatchsummary.xml");
```

The XML:RSS module contains other methods and attributes that you may find helpful for your own RSS writing projects. Look over the perldoc for XML::RSS for more information about these methods and attributes.

Security Considerations with RSS

Creation of your own RSS feeds doesn't pose any great security risk in itself. Of course, you don't want to release any sensitive information through an RSS feed, just as you wouldn't want to allow access to certain data through a web page or CGI program.

Consuming an RSS feed carries with it the same risks inherent in any external data source. You should be sure that all data external to your program is safe for use within the program. If an RSS feed contains malicious data, using it within your program puts the program and the system at risk.

Summary

This chapter dealt with RSS feeds through Perl, covering both creation and consumption of RSS feeds. Specifically, you saw how to parse and write RSS using the `XML::RSS` module. Other modules for parsing and writing RSS with Perl, such as `XML::RSS::Feed`, are available.

When parsing an RSS feed, you create a new RSS object to parse an RSS file. Retrieval of the RSS file is left for another module. In this chapter, you saw how to use `LWP::Simple` to retrieve an RSS feed from an Internet site, but you can use any means to get an RSS feed into the parser, including using a local file. A local file is recommended when developing and debugging the RSS feed, so that the site operator doesn't misinterpret the repeated retrieval requests.

Many of the same methods are used for both parsing and writing an RSS feed. You can choose and change the version for writing RSS by specifying it at instantiation time or with the `output` attribute.

This and the previous chapter have both touched on XML-related services in one form or another and provided a good introduction into XML applications in the real world. In the next chapter, you'll finally look at straight XML parsing with Perl.

■■■

## CHAPTER 9

XML Parsing with Perl

You have some data in XML. Maybe that data is from a SOAP web service, maybe it's from an RSS feed, or maybe it's from another source. Now you want to read the XML and extract the data from it. As is the theme with Perl, you have multiple ways to accomplish this task.

XML parsing with Perl has a storied history. Early modules were quirky, while others were incomplete.

Parsing simple XML with Perl is, well, simple. Parsing complex XML with Perl can be quite difficult. The important thing to remember is that XML is just a way to represent data. That data happens to be in an XML document. The program that you write to parse XML will first need to read the XML, and then use the results as it would any other data input.

This chapter looks at XML parsing with Perl. It first reviews the main parsing methods, and then describes using two modules: `XML::Simple` and `XML:SAX`. Finally, it examines tree-based parsing.

XML Parsing Methods

Recall that there's always more than one way to do the same thing with Perl. XML parsing is no different. And, of course, there's no rule that says that you must use an XML parser at all. It's quite possible for you to write your own XML parser, just as it would be possible to write your own module for anything in Perl, rather than using an already existing module.

Primarily, two methods exist for parsing an XML document:

Stream parsing: Stream-based parsers process XML as it is read into the parser. As new elements are encountered (which are called *tokens*), they are processed by the parser and sent into your program through a process of events. This means that the program must process each piece of data as it is encountered by the stream-based parser. Stream-based parsers have lower memory requirements than their tree-based counterparts, simply because they don't store any data; rather, they send data along into the rest of the program as it is found. Of course, the lower memory requirements are gained at the expense of complexity when compared to tree-based parsers.

Tree parsing: Tree-based parsers load entire XML structures into memory for later processing. This means that the entire document is parsed prior to your program needing to handle it. In turn, this leads to less complex programs when compared to stream-based parsing. The extra simplicity comes at the cost of higher memory requirements. Naturally, on a modern computer with a small document to parse, the memory required will be minimal.

At their core, all XML parsers are stream parsers. It's just that some build a tree structure on top of the stream automatically for you. XML::Parser is an example of an early (although still useful) stream parser in Perl. XML::SAX, or the Simple API for XML, is another stream-based implementation, which will be covered later in this chapter.

XML Parsing Considerations

The following are some important general reminders and caveats for working with XML in Perl:

- When you build a program to parse XML, it really exists only for that XML. This means that the program to parse the XML will invariably be largely one-time-use code.

- There are many Perl modules for parsing XML and assisting with XML work. Regardless of which module you use, it is expected that the XML used as input will be well-formed. The XML parsing modules will likely produce wonky results—if they produce any results at all—when presented with poorly formed XML.

- Not all XML modules can handle all aspects of XML such as namespaces, entities, and declarations, or at best, they don't all handle those objects the same way. It's important to make sure the output is correct, rather than just *looks* correct. A small and subtle change to the XML input could break the program if a module is being used incorrectly.

- Spacing and character encodings are important items to consider when parsing XML. It's possible for white space or unfamiliar or unexpected character encodings to cause unexpected results.

Parsing XML with XML::Simple

XML::Simple is an example of a tree-based XML parser, which is, well, simpler to use than other XML parsers. XML::Simple has just two subroutines: XMLin() and XMLout(). XMLin() is used to read an XML structure into an in-memory hash. The source of this XML is usually a string or file. From the XMLin() subroutine comes a reference to a hash. XMLout() creates XML when passed a reference to a hash that contains an encoded document.

Consider this bit of XML:

```
<?xml version="1.0"?>
<customer-data>
<customer>
    <first_name>Frank</first_name>
    <last_name>Sanbeans</last_name>
    <dob>3/10</dob>
    <email>frank@example.com</email>
</customer>
<customer>
    <first_name>Sandy</first_name>
    <last_name>Sanbeans</last_name>
    <dob>4/15</dob>
    <email>sandy@example.com</email>
</customer>
</customer-data>
```

This XML is saved in a file titled example1.xml. The code to parse this XML structure is as follows:

```perl
#!/usr/bin/perl

use strict;
use XML::Simple;

my $xml = XMLin('./example1.xml',forcearray => 1);

foreach my $customer (@{$xml->{customer}}) {
    print "Name: $customer->{first_name}->[0] ";
    print "$customer->{last_name}->[0]\n";
    print "Birthday: $customer->{dob}->[0]\n";
    print "E-mail Address: $customer->{email}->[0]\n";
}
```

The code begins with the familiar use strict pragma, and then imports XML::Simple into the namespace:

```perl
use XML::Simple;
```

The XMLin() subroutine is called using the name of the file and setting the forcearray option. The XMLin() subroutine returns an array reference, which is what the forcearray => 1 option does:

```perl
my $xml = XMLin('./example1.xml',forcearray => 1);
```

Next, the array reference is dereferenced into its components. In the sample XML, each element is broken into a customer element at its base with a number of other elements below. Each of these elements is called and printed in turn within the foreach loop:

```perl
foreach my $customer (@{$xml->{customer}}) {
    print "Name: $customer->{first_name}->[0] ";
    print "$customer->{last_name}->[0]\n";
    print "Birthday: $customer->{dob}->[0]\n";
    print "E-mail Address: $customer->{email}->[0]\n";
}
```

This program is rather simple and does nothing more than print out each element listed for both customers in the file. Obviously, you could expand this to perform additional functions within the foreach loop. The output looks like this:

```
Name: Frank Sanbeans
Birthday: 3/10
E-mail Address: frank@example.com
Name: Sandy Sanbeans
Birthday: 4/15
E-mail Address: sandy@example.com
```

The code shown uses the forcearray option, which isn't really necessary. The XML being parsed in this example consists of solely single values—each customer record has one and only one value for date of birth, e-mail address, and so on. Another method to parse this particular XML looks like this:

```
#!/usr/bin/perl

use strict;
use XML::Simple;

my $xml = XMLin('./example1.xml');

foreach my $customer (@{$xml->{customer}}) {
    print "Name: $customer->{first_name} $customer->{last_name}\n";
    print "Birthday: $customer->{dob}\n";
    print "E-mail Address: $customer->{email}\n";
}
```

The difference between this and the previously shown code is subtle. Missing from this example is the reference to the first element in the array ->[0]. When parsing XML with multivalued elements, accessing those elements with forcearray makes access to the elements much easier, as you'll see a bit later in the "XML::Simple Options" section.

Data::Dumper

An even simpler, though arguably less useful method, for parsing an XML file with XML::Simple is to use Data::Dumper. You can use the Data::Dumper module to quickly print out the XML as it is being read and processed by the XMLin() subroutine. Doing so helps during debugging and in other cases, such as working with databases. Rather than using the foreach loop in the previous example, you could use Data::Dumper to print the contents of the XML, as shown in this example:

```
#!/usr/bin/perl

use strict;
use XML::Simple;
use Data::Dumper;

my $xml = XMLin('./example1.xml',forcearray => 1);

print Dumper($xml);
```

Compare the output from the earlier example with the output from the Data::Dumper version of the program:

```
$VAR1 = {
          'customer' => [
                          {
                            'email' => [
                                         'frank@example.com'
                                       ],
```

```
                        'dob' => [
                                   '3/10'
                                 ],
                        'last_name' => [
                                         'Sanbeans'
                                       ],
                        'first_name' => [
                                          'Frank'
                                        ]
                  },
                  {
                        'email' => [
                                     'sandy@example.com'
                                   ],
                        'dob' => [
                                   '4/15'
                                 ],
                        'last_name' => [
                                         'Sanbeans'
                                       ],
                        'first_name' => [
                                          'Sandy'
                                        ]
                  }
              ]
      };
```

Notice that each element in the Data::Dumper version is placed into its own array. This was the result of enabling the forcearray option. Contrast that output with a call to XMLin() with forcearray disabled:

```
$VAR1 = {
          'customer' => [
                          {
                            'email' => 'frank@example.com',
                            'dob' => '3/10',
                            'last_name' => 'Sanbeans',
                            'first_name' => 'Frank'
                          },
                          {
                            'email' => 'sandy@example.com',
                            'dob' => '4/15',
                            'last_name' => 'Sanbeans',
                            'first_name' => 'Sandy'
                          }
                        ]
      };
```

XML::Simple Options

Some XML::Simple options are more important than others. This section examines two frequently used XML::Simple options: forcearray and KeyAttr. For a full listing and explanation of all of the XML::Simple options, see perldoc XML::Simple.

Forcearray

You already saw the forcearray option in an example, but that example didn't really need to have forcearray enabled. Consider this XML:

```
<?xml version="1.0"?>
<customer-data>
<customer>
    <first_name>Frank</first_name>
    <last_name>Sanbeans</last_name>
    <dob>3/10</dob>
    <email>frank@example.com</email>
    <vehicle>Volvo S60</vehicle>
    <vehicle>Honda Accord</vehicle>
</customer>
<customer>
    <first_name>Sandy</first_name>
    <last_name>Sanbeans</last_name>
    <dob>4/15</dob>
    <email>sandy@example.com</email>
    <vehicle>McLaren MP4-20</vehicle>
    <vehicle>Chevrolet S-10</vehicle>
</customer>
</customer-data>
```

The following is code to parse this XML. Notice its similarities to the first example shown in the chapter.

```perl
#!/usr/bin/perl

use strict;
use XML::Simple;

my $xml = XMLin('./xml_example2',forcearray=>1);

foreach my $customer (@{$xml->{customer}}) {
    print "Name: $customer->{first_name}->[0] ";
    print "$customer->{last_name}->[0]\n";
    print "Birthday: $customer->{dob}->[0]\n";
    print "E-mail Address: $customer->{email}->[0]\n";
    print "Vehicle(s): @{$customer->{vehicle}}\n";
}
```

The code reads in the XML with the forcearray option enabled. Each value is then accessed through its dereferenced array index. The exception is the <vehicle> element, which may be multivalued. The <vehicle> element is printed by using an array reference to that specific element.

Since four of the five elements in this XML data structure can have only one value, you may want to specify which elements should go into an array, instead of rolling every element into an array. Instead of merely accepting 1 for enabled and 0 for disabled, the forcearray option can accept a comma-separated list of elements that should be rolled into an array. Continuing with the previous example, using forcearray just for the <vehicle> element looks like this:

```perl
#!/usr/bin/perl

use strict;
use XML::Simple;

my $xml = XMLin('./xml_example2',forcearray=> [ 'vehicle' ]);

foreach my $customer (@{$xml->{customer}}) {
    print "Name: $customer->{first_name} ";
    print "$customer->{last_name}\n";
    print "Birthday: $customer->{dob}\n";
    print "E-mail Address: $customer->{email}\n";
    print "Vehicle(s): @{$customer->{vehicle}}\n";
}
```

Notice in this example that the array index ->[0] is now gone for the original four elements, since those are no longer rolled into an array by XML::Simple.

KeyAttr

The KeyAttr option is used to control how elements are rolled into arrays and hashes. Recall an earlier example showing an XML structure as displayed with Data::Dumper. Changing the key attribute to be the <email> element reveals this output:

```perl
$VAR1 = {
          'customer' => {
                  'frank@example.com' => {
                                         'dob' => '3/10',
                                         'first_name' => 'Frank',
                                         'last_name' => 'Sanbeans'
                                        },
                  'sandy@example.com' => {
                                         'dob' => '4/15',
                                         'first_name' => 'Sandy',
                                         'last_name' => 'Sanbeans'
                                        }
                        }
        };
```

The code that produced this output is similar to the earlier Data::Dumper example. Notice the use of the KeyAttr option in the call to the XMLin() subroutine.

```perl
#!/usr/bin/perl

use strict;
use XML::Simple;
use Data::Dumper;

my $xml = XMLin('./example1.xml',forcearray=> [ 'vehicle' ],KeyAttr=>[
'email' ] TheSansMonoConNormal
);
print Dumper($xml);
```

■Note Take a look through the perldoc for XML::Simple. The documentation for this module is quite good and actually helps to sort out the options into categories such as important, handy, advanced, and others.

Parsing XML with XML::SAX

XML::SAX is a stream-based parser. When XML is parsed by XML::SAX, each new element encountered signals an event to the parser. XML::SAX hands off the processing for that event to the appropriate method. It's your responsibility to write handlers for events as they are passed by XML::SAX. For example, XML::SAX will encounter the beginning of an XML tag. When it does so, it passes the information along in an event stream to the parser. This parser implements a number of handlers to work with that event. The data from the event is usually placed inside a hash, but that depends on the type of event.

There are parsers already written for XML::SAX. Two such handlers are XML::LibXML::SAX::Parser and XML::SAX::PurePerl. XML::LibXML::SAX::Parser requires the libxml2 library and is written in C. As you might guess by the name, XML::SAX::PurePerl is written entirely in Perl. These two handlers, along with others for XML::SAX, may be already installed on your system. In practice, you'll find that you'll be writing your own parser more often than not.

This program prints a list of the available parsers on your system:

```perl
#!/usr/bin/perl

use XML::SAX;
use strict;

my @parsers = @{XML::SAX->parsers()};

foreach my $parser (@parsers) {
    print "--> ", $parser->{ Name }, "\n";
}
```

On my Debian (Sarge) system, the output looks like this:

```
--> XML::SAX::PurePerl
--> XML::LibXML::SAX::Parser
--> XML::LibXML::SAX
--> XML::SAX::Expat
```

A parser is chosen through the XML::SAX::ParserFactory interface. However, in practice, programmers frequently leave it up to XML::SAX to decide which parser to use, with the default being decided by the order in which the parsers were installed. Though this may sound blatantly obvious, parsers implement functions to parse XML. The parser methods include parse_uri(), parse_file(), and so on.

It's important to realize the difference, from an XML::SAX standpoint, between a parser and a handler. A *parser* is usually software in the form of a Perl module that is installed with XML::SAX or can be installed from CPAN. A *handler*, on the other hand, is software that you write as part of the XML parsing programming task. The parser is created or instantiated by the XML::SAX::ParserFactory and is passed an argument telling it which handler will be used. The handler then implements interfaces for events handed to it from the parser. Note that a parser can be passed numerous arguments in addition to the name of the handler to use.

XML::SAX Parser Methods

As previously stated, a parser implements several methods for parsing XML. For most of the methods, you pass the XML as an argument, as well as other options for parsing. The parser methods are as follows:

- parse([options]): This is a generic method that can accept optional options in list, *name=>value* pairs, or hash format.

- parse_uri(uri [, options]): This is a commonly used method to parse XML as denoted by the URI.

- parse_file(filestream [, options]): This method parses a filestream such as a file-handle. Do not confuse this method with an argument of a plain file rather than a stream.

- parse_string(string [, options]): This method parses the XML contained in the string passed to it.

SAX2 Handler Interfaces

The handler that you create will need to implement code to handle events as they are passed in by the parser. XML::SAX provides access to events to ensure that the SAX2 specification is met. XML::SAX and related parsers also work with namespaces.

Logically, XML::SAX events and handlers can be grouped into categories. Many of the more common handlers fall into the category of content handlers. Content handlers work with the actual content of the document itself, and so content handlers are where you'll spend a large amount of time coding. Another important category of handlers includes the error handlers that enable you to create custom error handling code. Other handlers include lexical handlers that work with CDATA sections, comments, DTDs, and entities. The following sections look at content and error event handlers.

Content Event Handlers

This following are some of the event handlers that you'll encounter when working through the content of the XML:

- `start_document(document)`: The `start_document()` method is sent with an empty `document` parameter.

- `end_document(document)`: The `end_document()` method can be called at the end of the XML input or when an error occurs. Whatever this method returns—whether it's an error condition or normal condition—it will be used as the return value by the `parse()` method.

- `start_element(element)`: The `start_element()` method is called when a new `start` tag is found. The method is passed a hash parameter, `element`, containing the following:

  - `Name`: The name of the element, including any namespace prefix.

  - `Attributes`: Contains a hash of attributes, if any. Be careful not to confuse the attributes with other XML data. The attributes are themselves a hash. The attributes hash contains `Name` (full name, including prefix), `Value` (value of the attribute, trimmed to remove spaces), `NamespaceURI` (URI) for the namespace, `Prefix` (portion of the full name before the local portion), and `LocalName` (portion of the full name that is local).

  - `NamespaceURI`: The namespace for the element.

  - `Prefix`: The prefix for the name.

  - `LocalName`: The portion of the full name that is local.

- `end_element(element)`: The `end_element()` method is called when a new `end` tag is found. The method is passed a hash parameter, `element`, containing the following:

  - `Name`: The name of the element, including any namespace prefix.

  - `NamespaceURI`: The URI for the namespace.

  - `Prefix`: The portion of the full name before the local portion.

  - `LocalName`: The portion of the full name that is local.

- `characters(data)`: The `characters()` method is used for any character data (plain text) in the XML. This method is most frequently used to obtain the actual values contained within the XML, but there's no guarantee that this method will be called for only those values. In other words, it could be called for any other character data encountered in the XML. The `data` parameter is a hash containing the string of characters.

Other content handlers include `processing_instruction`, `skipped_entity`, `ignorable_whitespace`, and `set_document_locator`, among others. See the `perldoc` on `XML::SAX` for more information about these and other content event handlers that you may want to code into your handler.

Error Event Handlers

Three error event handlers exist:

- `warning()`: A warning is an error that doesn't stop the parser but is notable nonetheless. You can choose to forego implementing this handler; in which case, the parser will simply ignore the warning.

- `error()`: An error is a serious event, but the parser will continue. An invalid XML document is an example of an error.

- `fatal_error()`: The most serious of the error events, as the name implies, this type of event can cause processing of XML to stop, though the parser may choose to continue.

Each handler accepts a single argument: the exception.

A Basic Parser and Handler

Now that you have an idea of the theory of parsing XML with XML::SAX, as well as a look at some of the more important events to be implemented by your handler, it's time to get busy with coding your first parser. This section will show you how to code a parsing routine using XML::SAX by creating your own handler for some content events. First, recall the XML from earlier in the chapter. This XML will be used throughout this section:

```
<?xml version="1.0"?>
<customer-data>
<customer>
    <first_name>Frank</first_name>
    <last_name>Sanbeans</last_name>
    <dob>3/10</dob>
    <email>frank@example.com</email>
    <vehicle>Volvo S60</vehicle>
    <vehicle>Honda Accord</vehicle>
</customer>
<customer>
    <first_name>Sandy</first_name>
    <last_name>Sanbeans</last_name>
    <dob>4/15</dob>
    <email>sandy@example.com</email>
    <vehicle>McLaren MP4-20</vehicle>
    <vehicle>Chevrolet S-10</vehicle>
</customer>
</customer-data>
```

Two elements involved in parsing with XML::SAX: the parser, or main program code, and the handler code. The first task is to create the main program code, which will import XML::SAX into the namespace and set up the parser, as well as perform any other functions that you might want the program to perform outside the XML-specific items. Then you write the handler code, which will largely be specific to the XML being parsed.

Coding the Main Program

You use the use pragma to import XML::SAX into the namespace. However, an additional use pragma is also necessary in order to import your yet-to-be-coded handler package.

```
use XML::SAX;
use MyHandler;
use strict;
```

Since this handler package is something that you will create, you can name it as you wish (assuming a valid name, of course). Don't fret the details of the handler package yet; you'll be coding it shortly.

Next, create a parser object and pass it a reference to the handler that you'll be creating:

```
my $parser = XML::SAX::ParserFactory->parser( Handler => MyHandler->new);
```

One of the parser methods is called next. For this example, assume that the XML is stored in a file called example1.xml in the current directory:

```
$parser->parse_uri("example1.xml");
```

That's all there is to the code for the main program. Save the main program as xml-custom.pl and make it executable (chmod 700 xml-custom.pl).

This code is rather simple. The key to the code is within the handler package, MyHandler, which you'll create as a separate file. This program, as it stands now, will produce an error if you attempt to execute it, since the handler package doesn't exist yet.

Creating the Handler Package

With the main program coded, the parser will be invoked and will attempt to pass events to the specified handler. Create a separate file, called MyHandler.pm, to hold the code for the custom handler. The handler package is coded as shown in Listing 9-1.

Listing 9-1. *A Handler for Parsing XML*

```
package MyHandler;
use base qw(XML::SAX::Base);

sub start_document {
    my $self = shift;
    my $document = shift;
}

sub start_element {
    my $self = shift;
    my $element = shift;
```

```
        print $element->{LocalName}, " = ";
}
sub characters {
        my $self = shift;
        my $char = shift;
        print $char->{Data};
}
1;
```

The first task within the code is to declare it as a package:

```
package MySAXHandler;
```

From there, the XML::SAX::Base methods are imported into the namespace. This enables the handler package to take advantage of the XML::SAX framework:

```
use base qw(XML::SAX::Base);
```

Three subroutines follow: start_document(), start_element(), and characters(). Each of these is invoked by the parser as it works through the XML input. The start_document() routine is mostly a placeholder in this application. start_element() is important for parsing XML data. In this simple example, however, it does nothing more than print the name of each XML element, such as customer-data, customer, first-name, last-name, and so on, followed by an equal sign in the output. characters() is where the actual data of the XML is printed as output.

Running the Parser

You've created both the main program and the custom handler package. You can now run the xml-custom.pl program to parse the XML. It should produce this output:

```
customer-data =
customer =
    first_name = Frank
    last_name = Sanbeans
    dob = 3/10
    email = frank@example.com

customer =
    first_name = Sandy
    last_name = Sanbeans
    dob = 4/15
    email = sandy@example.com
```

A common error when parsing XML is to have XML that is not well-formed. Make sure the XML is well-formed by taking advantage of the Data::Dumper package to print the XML quickly. Additionally, make sure that the names are correct for the handler package that you created. For example, importing a misnamed handler package or calling it incorrectly in the main program or from within the handler code itself will cause errors.

Including Attributes

Attributes are important within XML parlance. They are parsed as part of the start_element()
subroutine, and their use may not be blatantly obvious at first glance. This is because, as you'll
recall, the attributes are sent as a hash within the elements hash. Here's the sample XML from
earlier, this time including attributes to indicate that the email element is a required field:

```
<?xml version="1.0"?>
<customer-data>
<customer required="email">
    <first_name>Frank</first_name>
    <last_name>Sanbeans</last_name>
    <dob>3/10</dob>
    <email>frank@example.com</email>
    <vehicle>Volvo S60</vehicle>
    <vehicle>Honda Accord</vehicle>
</customer>
<customer required="email">
    <first_name>Sandy</first_name>
    <last_name>Sanbeans</last_name>
    <dob>4/15</dob>
    <email>sandy@example.com</email>
    <vehicle>McLaren MP4-20</vehicle>
    <vehicle>Chevrolet S-10</vehicle>
</customer>
</customer-data>
```

For brevity's sake, consider the code for the handler package MyHandler to be the same,
with the exception of the start_element() subroutine, which now looks like this:

```
sub start_element {
    my $self = shift;
    my $element = shift;

        foreach my $key (keys %{ $element->{Attributes}}) {
                my $attrib = $element->{Attributes}->{$key};
                print $attrib->{Name}, " = ", $attrib->{Value}, "\n";
        }
        print $element->{LocalName}, " = ";
}
```

Again, the remainder of the code for MyHandler.pm (Listing 9-1) is exactly the same as the
earlier example. Now there's a foreach loop to iterate through the keys to the attributes hash
and then print them. The output is as follows. Notice the addition of the required = email line:

```
customer-data =
required = email
customer =
    first_name = Frank
    last_name = Sanbeans
```

```
        dob = 3/10
        email = frank@example.com
        vehicle = Volvo S60
        vehicle = Honda Accord

required = email
customer =
        first_name = Sandy
        last_name = Sanbeans
        dob = 4/15
        email = sandy@example.com
        vehicle = McLaren MP4-20
        vehicle = Chevrolet S-10
```

You've now seen how to parse XML using XML::SAX by creating your own handler for XML::SAX parser events. However, the examples here have only scratched the surface of XML parsing with XML::SAX. It is a very powerful specification and package with Perl. I invite you to spend some time reading the XML::SAX and XML::SAX::Base documentation and experimenting with the code and with more complex examples to parse XML in Perl with this excellent module.

Using Tree-Based Parsing

The chapter began with a look at XML::Simple for parsing simple XML. You then read about parsing of XML with XML::SAX, a framework around which very complex XML parsing can be done. Tree-based parsing, or simply tree parsing, is yet another process for parsing XML. This method delivers the entire XML structure to your program as one logical entity, as opposed to the delivery in chunks that you get with a stream processor. As noted earlier in the chapter, tree parsers are almost always stream-based parsers at heart, but they hold the data until the end of the parsing.

Needing to pass the entire structure at once almost always means that tree parsers have higher memory requirements than their stream-based counterparts. Since XML structures can be quite complex, it's not uncommon to receive an Out of Memory error when using a tree parser on complex and/or lengthy XML.

Tree parsers include XML::Parser, which can be used both as a tree and a stream parser, XML::Grove, XML::TreeBuilder, XML::Twig, and XML::SimpleObject, just to name a few. The parser that you saw earlier in the chapter, XML::Simple, is yet another tree parser.

Each XML parser has its own features and invariably its own syntax as well. XML::Twig, for example, is interesting in that it can hold part of the XML tree, thus saving memory. XML::Twig also provides a simple means for converting XML into HTML or into other formats. The following example prints XML using the indented option with XML::Twig:

```
#!/usr/bin/perl

use strict;
use XML::Twig;
```

```
my $tree = XML::Twig->new(pretty_print => 'indented');
$tree->parsefile("example1.xml");

$tree->print;
```

When executed, the output looks as follows:

```
<customer-data>
  <customer>
    <first_name>Frank</first_name>
    <last_name>Sanbeans</last_name>
    <dob>3/10</dob>
    <email>frank@example.com</email>
  </customer>
  <customer>
    <first_name>Sandy</first_name>
    <last_name>Sanbeans</last_name>
    <dob>4/15</dob>
    <email>sandy@example.com</email>
  </customer>
</customer-data>
```

As previously stated, each tree parser has different features and strengths. The modules are still under development and constantly being enhanced.

Security Considerations with XML Parsing

Like other similar tasks, parsing XML with Perl has no inherent risks other than the introduction of untrusted data into the application. It's important with XML parsing, as with other tasks that use external data, to make sure that the data that's coming in is what you expect for the particular application you're coding. Always assume that the data is incorrect or tainted until you've proven otherwise by checking the data against the smallest subset of known good data.

Summary

This chapter examined XML parsing with Perl. The chapter began with an overview of the parsing methods, and then reviewed some of the considerations for parsing XML with Perl, including making sure that the XML is well-formed and other tips. You examined XML::Simple as a tree parser for simple XML structures. Then you saw how XML:SAX handles event- or stream-based XML parsing. Finally, the chapter gave an overview of other tree parsers.

This chapter wraps up this part on XML and RSS. The next part of the book looks at using the mod_perl module to enhance the performance of your programs.

PART 4

■ ■ ■

Performance Enhancement with mod_perl

## CHAPTER 10

Apache and mod_perl

When Perl programs are executed through Apache, they are sent through an Apache module called mod_cgi. The mod_cgi module works well—very well, in fact—for countless web sites. However, because of the way in which Perl programs are executed by mod_cgi, using it has some performance drawbacks.

On the other hand, the Apache module called mod_perl enables higher performance for Perl programs operating on the web server. It does this by embedding the Perl interpreter directly into the Apache binary itself. However, far from being merely a performance boost for Perl scripts, mod_perl gives the developer access to the Apache request object itself which, in turn, means that entire Apache modules can be written in Perl.

This chapter looks at how Apache handles requests, where mod_cgi and mod_perl fit in, and finally how to install and configure mod_perl. The Apache 1.3 series will be the basis for this chapter, since that version is so widely deployed.

How Apache Handles Requests

Chapter 5 gave an overview of the HTTP protocol. Recall that HTTP is a request/response protocol, where the client, usually a web browser, sends a request to a web server for a resource on that server. The web server then responds with that resource.

Learning how Apache—by far, the most popular web server out there—handles requests can be quite helpful for writing advanced web applications. If you have any desire to write an Apache module in Perl with the help of mod_perl, learning the Apache request model is essential.

■**Note** It would be somewhat more than an overstep to write a section of a chapter of a book on Perl and encompass all that is the Apache web server. Here, I briefly touch on a few points regarding how Apache handles requests and how CGI programs are handled in Apache. For more information about how Apache works, see *Pro Apache, Third Edition*, by Peter Wainwright (Apress, 2004).

Apache is a long-running background server process, meaning that once you start it, it stays around in the background until you stop it. To run this way, Apache must be stable and not prone to dying unexpectedly. One of the ways that Apache accomplishes this feat is by creating child processes to actually go off and respond to the requests. This way, if one of the children encounters something that might cause a crash, Apache can simply kill the child process and respawn another. In addition, the child processes handle only a certain number of requests (which you can configure) before they automatically die and a new one is respawned.

When Apache starts, it goes through the initialization process, which includes looking for and parsing any command-line arguments given, parsing configuration files, and opening its log files. Apache normally starts as the root user so that it can bind to a privileged port,[1] usually TCP port 80. Once initial configuration is done, Apache starts initializing various modules, as indicated through its configuration files. Finally, or as finally as one can get with a long-running process, Apache will begin the process of child initialization.

Apache's Child Processes

Recall that the final step in the Apache startup process is to spawn or fork one or more child processes. When a child is spawned, it goes into a wait-service-wait loop, where the child waits for a request, services the request, and then goes back into a listening state until its next request is received. Where the main Apache process runs as root, these child processes run as an unprivileged user and group. Doing so greatly increases the security of the server. If an attacker is able to break in through Apache itself, he will have the privileges of that user, rather than the privileges of the root account!

■**Caution** Just because Apache child processes run as an unprivileged user doesn't mean that the server is secure. Even if an attacker gains access to the system through this unprivileged user, he might be able to escalate his privileges through a number of attack vectors.

As a child receives a request, the request falls through a number of Apache procedures before a response is sent. Some of these procedures provide entry points into the Apache API. Using the Apache API, a module writer can affect the handling of the request at a much lower level than merely responding to the request at the CGI level after it has been passed by the Apache child process. In other words, using the Apache API, a programmer could send special headers back as part of the response, in a much more efficient way than writing a CGI script to accomplish the task.

The main processing for Apache requests is handled in the `http_request.c` source code file. In this file, a number of procedures are defined, including `process_request`, which calls `process_request_internal`. The `process_request_internal` procedure contains the heart of Apache request handling. The Apache handling procedures are described in Table 10-1.

---

1. The privileged ports are historically those below 1024. These ports work with protocols for well-known services such as HTTP, SMTP, POP3, HTTPS, and numerous others. The ports can usually be bound only by the root user. The reason for this is part legacy and part good security. Since those ports serve well-known protocols, it was felt that the best way to ensure that those ports were running "trusted" services was to specify that they could be bound only by the system administrator, root. If the port is below 1024, the client can assume that the service was started by the system administrator and is therefore not just some random service started by a rogue user (at least, that's the theory).

Table 10-1. *Apache Request Procedures*

Procedure	Description
location_walk	Apache looks at the configuration file for any location directives based on the URI as passed in the request.
translate_name	Apache takes the name from the URI and converts it to a name in relation to the local filesystem. This has nothing to do with translation between languages, but rather is how Apache converts a URI to a local file.
directory_walk	Now that Apache has converted the URI to a local resource, it examines the configuration file for any directory directives that might apply to this particular resource.
file_walk	Apache examines the configuration file to find any file directives that might apply to the requested resource.
location_walk	Apache does another round of location walking in the configuration file to see if the translate_name procedure has changed the location, thus making the location directive now apply.
header_parse	The header of the request is parsed.
check_access	A number of authorization checks are done, with check_access being the first. It checks for access based on the IP of the request.
check_user_id	This procedure looks at authorization based on the identity of the remote user.
check_auth	This procedure looks at the username and password pair.
find_types	This procedure works with MIME types of the requested resource. At this stage, Apache chooses the correct content handler for the requested resource.
run_fixups	This procedure is somewhat misnamed. During this phase of the Apache request/response cycle, the response header is written and the content may also be sent to the client. This phase can work in conjunction with the invoke_handler procedure, called next.
invoke_handler	During this phase, if another module is necessary for fulfilling the request, it is called. This handler may also write the response header and send the content.
finalize_request_protocol	This phase performs some cleanup actions on the request but shouldn't be confused with any cleanup for the Apache child processes.
logging	Though not a procedure name, logging may be performed at any step in the process if an error is encountered or when the request is processed.

■**Note** The procedures described in Table 10-1 are used in the Apache 1.3 series, specifically from 1.3.33, for anyone keeping score at home. The procedures and the handling of requests are largely the same in Apache 2.

An Apache module, whether written in C or in Perl with the help of mod_perl, can implement these procedures to work with the Apache requests as they go through their various stages. For example, you might write a custom module for authentication, for logging, and so on. You'll see how to do this in Chapter 11.

Forking

Apache works by forking child processes that go off and handle the actual requests from clients. The Apache configuration file controls how these children work, including the number of child processes to fork, the number to keep around, and how long they should be kept around. Some Apache configuration directives are important in this regard. The following are some of those configuration directives:

- maxrequestsperchild: This directive sets the number of requests that a given child will handle before dying and being replaced by another child. If the web server is serving buggy and/or poorly written programs that have problems like memory leaks, adjusting this value (setting it lower) will help to control that memory leak. However, the trade-off is that Apache will need to spawn another child process each time one dies (in accordance with minspareservers). The spawning of new child processes is not without overhead of its own. In practice, you don't want to set the maxrequestsperchild value so low that Apache needs to fire up replacement child processes during busy times. The true solution is to fix whatever buggy and leaky programs are causing Apache to use extra memory during a child's lifetime.

- maxclients: This directive sets the limit for the number of requests that can be serviced at any given time. By default, Apache sets a hard limit on this directive, making the maximum value 256. You can increase this setting by changing the value in the httpd.h header file and recompiling Apache. This directive is key for surviving a heavy load spike.

- listenbacklog: This directive sets the length of the queue for pending requests. The default for this, 511, is normally high enough.

- minspareservers: This directive is used to configure the minimum number of idle children to have awaiting a request. Keeping a child server around will prevent Apache from needing to spawn another child process if all the children are busy. The default is 5.

- maxspareservers: This directive is used to set the maximum number of child processes to have awaiting a request. The parent process will kill off idle child processes to preserve system resources. The default is 10.

- startservers: This directive sets the number of child processes to spawn when starting Apache. The default is 5. Setting this value too high will cause a slowdown in the Apache startup process.

■Caution Keep in mind that the configuration parameters described here directly affect the performance of the Apache server. Setting these too low or too high can result in significantly decreased performance. I'm reluctant to give recommendations for these settings, since a large number of factors are involved in determining the optimum settings.

SURVIVING THE SLASHDOT EFFECT

The Slashdot web site (http://www.slashdot.org) is an extremely popular web site for technology news. Stories are submitted by the public, and the Slashdot moderators post selected stories on the public web site. The stories frequently contain links to other web sites. The load generated by the large spike in traffic frequently causes those sites to become nonresponsive or start spewing errors. The power of Slashdot to shine its spotlight onto a site and then watching that site go down has come to be known as the "Slashdot effect."

I've been the lucky recipient of the Slashdot effect through blog entries on my site. However, contrary to the experiences of other sites, I was happy to see that my configuration survived and, in fact, thrived on the extra attention. The server hardware isn't high-end; in fact, it is just a Pentium Celeron server with only 512MB RAM and a single 40GB IDE hard drive. The server also handles SMTP e-mail and DNS for a few domains. Even with the smaller resources being shared among multiple services, the server worked well. The reason that the server did so well was the operating system and web server choices.

The server is Debian with Apache 1.3. Inside the configuration, I changed one directive from its default, maxclients. The Debian maintainers chose good defaults for the rest of the settings, thus making the job of handling a large volume much easier. I set maxclients to 450, which is still below the Debian maximum of 512 (many vendors set this hard limit at 256).

If you find yourself with an increased web server load, you don't need to run out and get more hardware, buy expensive load-balancing devices, and make other costly changes. Look at the server you have and the configuration on it. Increasing maxclients is an easy and effective way to handle the increased load. You might also consider adjusting the minspareservers and listenbacklog directives, though I didn't need to adjust those for my server.

You've now seen a glimpse into how Apache handles requests and some of the directives available to configure Apache. A CGI program is a special type of content and is handled through an Apache module. The next section examines CGI program handling through mod_cgi and mod_perl.

mod_cgi vs. mod_perl

By default, the mod_cgi module is used to handle CGI content in Apache. The MIME type of the file, as well as its location, define whether or not mod_cgi will be invoked to handle the request. The location must fall within a directory defined as ScriptAlias. The scripts written so far in this book were written to run with mod_cgi.

When mod_cgi executes a CGI script, Apache forks a new process containing the interpreter for the CGI program. Since this is a book on Perl, it means that the Perl interpreter is loaded each time a CGI program is executed. The CGI program itself is compiled on each execution as well. Any database connections and other necessities are also created for each execution. Naturally, this forking, loading the interpreter, and compiling the program have a cost. On busy systems, the resource cost of running a CGI program can make the application unacceptably slow.

Where mod_cgi must load the Perl interpreter with each invocation of the CGI script, mod_perl embeds the Perl interpreter directly into the Apache child process. This means that the Perl interpreter is loaded only once for each child process, rather than once for each execution of the CGI program. mod_perl uses a couple of methods to execute Perl scripts. One of these methods compiles the program only once, when it is first used. The result is that the CGI program runs much, much faster—sometimes up to 100 times faster.

■**Note** Don't let my emphasis on mod_perl make you think that it is the only way to speed up execution of a CGI script with Apache. Far from it. mod_perl is just one method for speeding up execution of CGI programs. Another method is by using the FastCGI module. To find out more about FastCGI, visit http://www.fastcgi.com/.

Benefits of mod_perl

The obvious first benefit gained with mod_perl is faster execution of CGI scripts written in Perl. Since the Perl interpreter is loaded into the Apache child process, a new process doesn't need to be spawned for each execution.

In addition to the benefit of faster execution times for CGI programs, mod_perl also enables developers to write Apache modules entirely in Perl, as opposed to the more traditional C language for Apache modules. This essentially means that you can access any part of the Apache request-handling process and write your own handler for it using Perl. The "Beyond CGI Programming with mod_perl" section, coming up soon, provides more details on using mod_perl this way.

Another benefit of mod_perl is configuration access. Using mod_perl, you can configure the Apache server itself, in essence creating dynamic configuration files. Other Apache modules, such as mod_vhost_alias, perform this same function, but it is available through mod_perl as well.

Drawbacks of mod_perl

With all of the benefits of mod_perl, one might wonder why Apache isn't using mod_perl as its default handler for CGI programs. I'll examine the reasons in this section, as well as some other drawbacks to mod_perl. None of this discussion is meant to deter you from working with mod_perl or using it as much as possible. However, you should be aware of these issues.

Obviously, when the Perl interpreter gets embedded into each Apache child process, the Apache process itself is much larger. This means that each child will have a larger memory footprint than it would without mod_perl. This has real ramifications on busy servers or those with small amounts of spare resources. Using mod_perl, you may find that adjustments need to be made to the startservers configuration directive or the minspareservers configuration directive to account for the additional resource load imposed by mod_perl.

Programs compiled only once share the same global variables. For some CGI scripts, this creates a problem. Since the global variables aren't reinitialized, they may hold unknown values, which are then used again within the program. This means that many such programs need to be rewritten to work with mod_perl. However, to mitigate this, two mod_perl packages—Apache::Registry and Apache::PerlRun—execute the scripts in fundamentally different ways, as described shortly.

Beyond CGI Programming with mod_perl

mod_perl is much more than merely another way to execute CGI programs. Using mod_perl, you can access any portion of the Apache request process. This is accomplished through a series of handlers. Here are just a few of the things that you can do with a mod_perl handler:

- Perform authentication

- Create content

- Parse configuration files

- Read request headers

- Set response headers

- Work with MIME types

- Perform logging

Handlers for other areas can be used as well. This is all accomplished through the mod_perl API, which exposes a number of subroutines, some of which include the following:

- `PerlAuthenHandler`

- `PerlAuthzHandler`

- `PerlHandler`

- `PerlPostReadRequestHandler`

- `PerlHeaderParserHandler`

- `PerlTransHandler`

- `PerlTypeHandler`

- `PerlLogHandler`

Again, these are just a few of the possibilities with a handler coded through the mod_perl API. The Apache request header is important to understanding some of the functionality available with mod_perl. The Apache request object is used by mod_perl to enable access to the request. Chapter 11 will detail many of these interfaces. For now, the point is that mod_perl means much more than enhancing the performance of CGI programs.

Apache::Registry vs. Apache::PerlRun

You can use two packages within mod_perl to execute scripts:

- Apache::Registry maintains persistence between runs of the script by caching the script. The first time the script is accessed, the variables are initialized, and filehandles and database handles are created. If the script doesn't properly reinitialize the variables and close file and database handles, chaos can ensue.

- Apache::PerlRun, on the other hand, compiles the program at each request, which naturally means that variables and other objects in the namespace are cleared at each run.

Since the programs and all of the modules they use are loaded only once, Apache::Registry is the better performer of the two. However, Apache::PerlRun can be used to quickly port existing or misbehaving scripts over to mod_perl. While the performance gain isn't as great with Apache::PerlRun, there is still some benefit, since the Perl interpreter is embedded in the Apache process. Note that if a script is modified, Apache::Registry will recompile the script; Apache doesn't need to be restarted in order for the change to be picked up.

To demonstrate how namespace pollution can be important when you run scripts under Apache::Registry, consider this example:

```
use CGI;
$query = CGI->new();

if ($required_name) {
    print header;
    print "name is $required_name\n";
    #do something else
}
else {
    $required_name = $query->param("name");
#die
}
```

With mod_cgi, since the script is initialized every time, the variable $required_name will always start out undefined. However, with mod_perl's Apache::Registry, once $required_name is defined, it won't be undefined or reinitialized, and therefore will always execute the code within the conditional. Code such as this might be found in a CGI program that carries values forward from page to page, such as a shopping cart or other wizard-style CGI program.

Let's see what happens with this CGI script. On the first run, I input my name, as shown in Figure 10-1, and then click Submit Query.

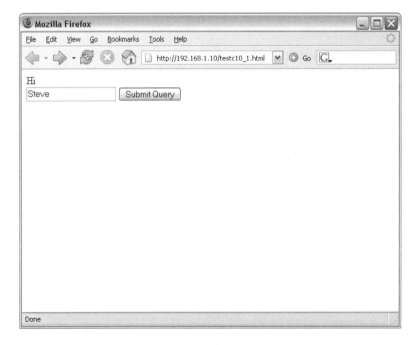

Figure 10-1. *Submitting a form that uses a CGI built for mod_cgi*

The output from this first run is shown in Figure 10-2. Everything looks okay.

Figure 10-2. *All appears normal, as shown by this output.*

Figure 10-3 shows another run of the program, this time with a different name as input.

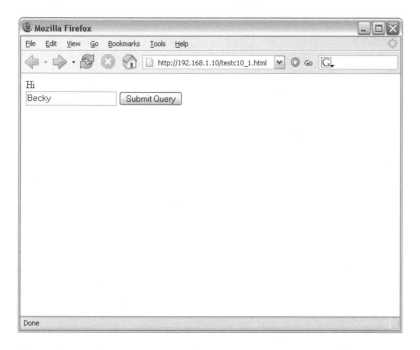

Figure 10-3. *Submitting the same form again, this time with a different name*

After clicking Submit Query, the name originally submitted, Steve, still shows up in the output page, as shown in Figure 10-4.

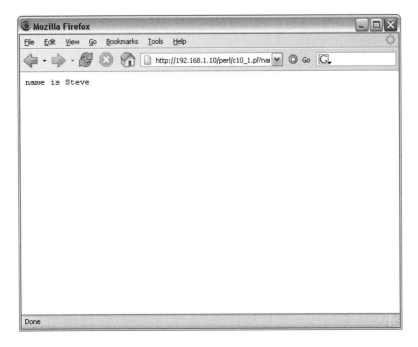

Figure 10-4. *The name originally used for input still shows up in the output with this program under mod_perl.*

Obviously, something is wrong with this script when run with Apache::Registry under mod_perl. This code would run fine, however, with Apache::PerlRun.

Even though the code would work with Apache::PerlRun, the better solution would be to fix the code so that variables are reinitialized on each execution of the script. The scripts would then run under Apache::Registry. For example, the code example previously given can be fixed as follows:

```perl
use strict;
use CGI;
my $query = CGI->new();
my $required_name;

if ($required_name) {
    print header;
    print "name is $required_name\n";
    #do something else
}
else {
    my $required_name = $query->param("name");
    print "name is $required_name\n";

}
```

Another way to fix it is like this:

```
use strict;
use CGI;
use vars qw($query $required_name);

$query = CGI->new();
$required_name = $query->param("name");

if ($required_name) {
    print header;
    print "name is $required_name\n";
    #do something
}
else {
    #die
}
```

Now that you have some idea of the advantages of mod_perl and its packages for executing scripts, you're ready to start working with it. The first step is installing the module.

mod_perl Installation

mod_perl is included as a package with many distributions of Linux. For many installations, the stock version from the distributions package will work fine. In some distributions, mod_perl is actually installed with the default web server, although it might need to be activated.

■**Note** The information for packaged installation changes quite rapidly. It could be the case that by the time you're reading this, mod_perl will be automatically installed and activated on your distribution. Check the documentation for your distribution to find out exactly how to install and activate mod_perl, if necessary.

If your distribution's packages don't provide the functionality that you need, the only other option is to compile from source.[2] This section looks at how to perform a basic compile of Apache with mod_perl. This section assumes that you do not currently have Apache installed, or if you do, that it will be removed before installing mod_perl. If you have existing configuration files for Apache, be sure to save those to a safe location, so that they aren't overwritten by the source install.

Getting the Code

Before you can compile the code, you need to get the code (that nugget of information alone made the entire book worthwhile for the reader, I'm sure). The code for mod_perl also requires the source code for Apache, so that the Perl interpreter can be embedded into Apache.

---

2. I suppose you could also download the source for the distribution's package, make changes, and recompile that version, but I'll leave that as an exercise for the reader.

You can download mod_perl's source code from http://perl.apache.org/, and you can get the source code for the Apache web server from http://httpd.apache.org/. Download the latest mod_perl in the 1.0 series and the latest Apache in the 1.3 series. Although the Apache 2.0 and mod_perl 2.0 series are available, the 1.*N* branch of each of these applications is much more widely deployed in production environments. Over the next three to five years, this situation will likely change, as is inevitable in the world of software.

Unpacking the Code

In these examples, I've downloaded the source code to my home directory, /home/suehring. Within that directory are the two tarred files containing the source code: mod_perl-1.0-current.tar.gz and apache_1.N.NN.tar.gz.

Unpack the Apache source:

```
tar -zxvf apache_1.3.33.tar.gz
```

Unpack the mod_perl source:

```
tar -zxvf mod_perl-1.0-current.tar.gz
```

Looking for Prerequisites

Building Apache and mod_perl requires some supporting software to be available. Most systems will have this software already loaded. However, if you haven't compiled software on the system before and no other software has been built as part of an installation, there's a chance that one or more of these prerequisites might not be installed.

Every Linux distribution I've ever used has the software available through the normal package-management tools. Therefore, if you find that you're missing a prerequisite, consult your distribution's documentation for installation of that prerequisite. It will likely be an easy process, since the prerequisites for building mod_perl are quite common.

The following three commands are recommended by the mod_perl documentation to determine the status of the prerequisites:

```
make -v
gcc -v
perl -v
```

I would hope by this point in the book that the Perl command will be successful! If any of these return something like Command not found, you'll need to install the prerequisite before proceeding.

Building and Installing mod_perl

Compiling Apache customized for a particular installation is a complex process. Locations for files, static linking, which modules to install, and other considerations make Apache one of the more complicated configurations of all Linux software. It would be quite difficult to select a certain set or subset of options to satisfy every need. The Apache documentation (http://httpd.apache.org/) is a good starting point for those wishing to learn about Apache's configuration options. In addition, the INSTALL documentation that comes with the Apache source is another great resource. For the purposes of this chapter, I'm going to show you how to build Apache with mod_perl with all options enabled.

Note Best practice system administration says, and I agree, that enabling all options is a bad idea on production systems. More applications and options mean a greater footprint in terms of both resources and security. The difference in resources between everything and a minimum set of functions isn't incredibly large with Apache and mod_perl, especially with modern hardware. However, more code almost always means more chances for bugs that could crop up at the most inopportune time. From a security standpoint, if something doesn't exist, it can't be exploited. When everything is compiled in, a security exploit for a piece of the code would make the program vulnerable. For these reasons, I recommend spending time learning exactly which Apache modules you need and disabling those you don't need.

With both the Apache and mod_perl sources unzipped, change into the mod_perl source directory:

```
cd mod_perl-1.NN
```

For example, to change into the mod_perl directory for version 1.29, this command would get you there:

```
cd mod_perl-1.29
```

mod_perl uses Perl to create the Makefile and uses some command-line arguments and switches to configure the compile process. Chief among those command-line arguments is the location of the Apache source code. Since you unpacked the Apache source to the directory one level up from the mod_perl source directory, however, mod_perl will be able to find it.

From within the mod_perl source directory, type the following:

```
perl Makefile.PL EVERYTHING=1 USE_APACI=1
```

The Makefile.pl script will now run. Pay particular attention to any warnings and follow their instructions. Here is an example:

```
************ WARNING *************

  Your Perl is configured to link against libgdbm,
  but libgdbm.so was not found.
  You could just symlink it to /usr/lib/libgdbm.so.1.7.3


************ WARNING *************
```

The script will ask a couple questions about how to build the software:

```
Will configure via APACI
Configure mod_perl with ../apache_1.3.33/src ? [y]
Shall I build httpd in ../apache_1.3.33/src for you? [y]
```

The script will create a Makefile checking for other prerequisites such as the Perl development files. If you installed Perl as a package with your distribution (this is usually the case), you might need to install the Perl development package as well. I recommend installing this package from your distribution, rather than downloading a new version of Perl and compiling it from source.

When the script is finished running, you'll see lines like the following towards the end of the output:

```
Writing Makefile for Apache::Table
Writing Makefile for Apache::URI
Writing Makefile for Apache::Util
Writing Makefile for mod_perl
```

Unfortunately, this doesn't guarantee that everything went well. There could be an error hidden in the output. Scrolling back through the output might help you locate any problems. Sometimes, the process will stop entirely, as shown here:

```
======== Error Output for sanity check ========
cd ..; cc  -DLINUX=22 -DHAVE_SET_DUMPABLE -DMOD_PERL -DUSE_PERL_SSI
-D_REENTRANT  -DTHREADS_HAVE_PIDS -DDEBIAN -fno-strict-aliasing
-I/usr/local/include -D_LARGEFILE_SOURCE -D_FILE_OFFSET_BITS=64
-DUSE_HSREGEX -DNO_DL_NEEDED -D_REENTRANT -DTHREADS_HAVE_PIDS -DDEBIAN
-fno-strict-aliasing -I/usr/local/include -D_LARGEFILE_SOURCE
-D_FILE_OFFSET_BITS=64 `./apaci` -I. -I/usr/lib/perl/5.8/CORE     -o
helpers/dummy helpers/dummy.c    -lm -lcrypt -Wl,-E -L/usr/local/lib
/usr/lib/perl/5.8/auto/DynaLoader/DynaLoader.a
-L/usr/lib/perl/5.8/CORE -lperl -ldl -lm -lpthread -lc -lcrypt
/usr/bin/ld: cannot find -lperl
collect2: ld returned 1 exit status
make: *** [dummy] Error 1
============== End of Error Report =============
```

Aborting!

Examining the output shown in the example reveals that I didn't have the Perl development libraries installed on the newly installed Debian Sarge computer. This is specifically shown in the following output:

```
/usr/bin/ld: cannot find -lperl
```

After installing the Perl development libraries (included with most distributions), I can restart the build.

Once the Makefile.pl script runs successfully, type the following:

```
make
```

The software will now be compiled. When that's complete, test the build by typing this:

```
make test
```

You might be tempted to skip this testing step, but I don't recommend doing so. The tests don't take terribly long, and if they're successful, you'll know that the compile isn't the problem if something goes wrong when you attempt to start Apache with mod_perl. When the test script is completed, you'll see output similar to this:

```
All tests successful, 6 tests skipped.
Files=34, Tests=402,  7 wallclock secs ( 5.14 cusr +  0.74 csys =  5.88 CPU)
kill `cat t/logs/httpd.pid`
rm -f t/logs/httpd.pid
rm -f t/logs/error_log
```

To install mod_perl, use the su - command to switch to the root user, and then type the following:

```
make install
```

This will install the mod_perl software, but you still need to install Apache. Do this by changing to the Apache source directory. If you've followed these instructions so far, the Apache source is in the directory just above the mod_perl source directory. From within the mod_perl source code directory, enter this command:

```
cd ../apache-<version>
```

Now, install the software by typing this:

```
make install
```

The last few lines of the Apache install output will show where the configuration file is located, as well as information about the apachectl script:

```
+----------------------------------------------------------+
| You now have successfully built and installed the        |
| Apache 1.3 HTTP server. To verify that Apache actually    |
| works correctly you now should first check the           |
| (initially created or preserved) configuration files     |
|                                                          |
|   /usr/local/apache/conf/httpd.conf                      |
|                                                          |
| and then you should be able to immediately fire up       |
| Apache the first time by running:                        |
|                                                          |
|   /usr/local/apache/bin/apachectl start                  |
|                                                          |
| Thanks for using Apache.       The Apache Group          |
|                                http://www.apache.org/    |
+----------------------------------------------------------+
```

You can now start Apache with the following command:

```
/usr/local/apache/bin/apachectl start
```

Point your web browser to the IP address of the server, paying particular attention to the port, as it might have been set to 8080 by default.

You should also see a line such as the following in /usr/local/apache/logs/error_log:

```
[Tue Jun 14 20:09:23 2005] [notice] Apache/1.3.33 (Unix) mod_perl/1.29 configured
-- resuming normal operations
```

If Apache doesn't start, examine that Apache error log for more information.

Choosing Compile Options

When you're installing mod_perl from source, configuration options abound. This section looks at some of the configuration options for mod_perl and Apache.

Since mod_perl causes the Perl interpreter to be compiled into the Apache binary, the Apache binary must be recompiled. Anyone who has ever compiled Apache knows that there are seemingly endless compile-time options for configuring Apache. One such option is the Apache Autoconf Interface (APACI), which makes the configuration easier because it enables you to change Apache compile-time options without needing to edit source configuration files.

Another popular option for Apache is Dynamic Shared Object (DSO) support. DSO support enables Apache modules to be loaded dynamically, rather than compiled into the Apache binary. Finally, Apache Extension (APXS) support enables development of modules outside the Apache source directory. This can add greater flexibility, especially for module development.

Recall the options that were passed to the Makefile.pl script:

```
perl Makefile.PL EVERYTHING=1 USE_APACI=1
```

As you can see from those options, the APACI option was indeed enabled, as was an option called EVERYTHING, which was specified within the earlier instructions for building and installing mod_perl.

An option that didn't need to be explicitly defined was the one to locate the Apache source code tree. By default, the Makefile.pl script looks in the directory above its current directory for an Apache source code tree. Since the Apache source was unzipped to the parent directory, the Makefile was able to find it. However, if you need to specify the location for the Apache source, you can do that with the APACHE_SRC option:

```
APACHE_SRC=/home/suehring/apache-1.3/src
```

Other options include DO_HTTPD, which causes the source path specified to be the only path used, and PREP_HTTPD, which causes the Apache source to be prepared but not built. This means that you must manually go into the Apache source tree and run make and make install to build and install Apache, as you did in the preceding instructions to build mod_perl and Apache.

The APACHE_PREFIX option is another important compile-time option. Using APACHE_PREFIX, you set the location for the Apache binaries and related items to be installed once they are built.

If you wish to build Apache with SSL support, use the SSL_BASE option. The SSL_BASE option points Apache to the include and lib directories of the SSL installation.

Numerous other options are available at compile-time for mod_perl. See the INSTALL document included with mod_perl for the most current list and documentation on these options.

Configuring for mod_perl

Even though Apache is running, you need to do some configuration before mod_perl will work. At this point, the Apache server is capable of serving static pages and not much else.

The Apache configuration file for the installation that you just completed is located in /usr/local/apache/conf/ and is called httpd.conf. (Usually, a few other configuration files are also located in that directory, but is the important one for this section.) Modify the httpd.conf file to work with mod_perl. For example, if you had a directory of scripts to be served by mod_perl located in /home/suehring/perl/, you would place the following lines at the end of the Apache configuration file:

```
Alias /perl/ /home/suehring/perl/
PerlModule Apache::Registry
<Location /perl/>
    SetHandler perl-script
    PerlHandler Apache::Registry
    Options +ExecCGI
    PerlSendHeader On
    Allow from all
</Location>
```

These options are very basic and will set up an environment where you can begin to code with mod_perl.

From mod_cgi to mod_perl

Recall what you've learned already in this book. CGI programs written in Perl normally use the mod_cgi Apache module to be interpreted and served through a web server. Developing a basic CGI program to be served through mod_cgi might look like this:

```
#!/usr/bin/perl

use CGI qw/:standard/;
use strict;

my $cgi = new CGI;


print header;
print start_html(-title => 'Basic Program');
print "Hello World";

print end_html;

exit;
```

This simple program, written as it is, doesn't require any modification to run with mod_perl. Moving the program to a directory configured to execute mod_perl programs, such as /home/suehring/perl/ in the example, will enable it to run through mod_perl. With a program of this size, however, you probably won't notice the benefits of mod_perl.

However, when porting already written Perl programs from mod_cgi to mod_perl, you may sometimes find that those programs won't behave as expected, or maybe they won't work at all. In such cases, the best option is to fix the program itself, rather than implement a workaround at the server level. Using the strict pragma will go a long way toward ensuring that a program will run under mod_perl's Apache::Registry. If a program runs with use strict enabled, chances are good that it will run correctly in mod_perl.

For times when a program absolutely won't run with Apache::Registry, you can enable Apache::PerlRun instead of Apache::Registry. As noted earlier in this chapter, Apache::PerlRun does not cache scripts as Apache::Registry does. Programs are executed every time they are run. As such, namespaces are cleared with every run, thus resolving many of the problems that cause the programs to run incorrectly under Apache::Registry. Obviously, since the programs are not cached under Apache::PerlRun, the performance is not as good as it is with Apache::Registry.

Modifying the Apache configuration for Apache::PerlRun is easy. Only two lines need to be changed, namely the lines that refer to Apache::Registry:

```
Alias /perl/ /home/suehring/perl/
PerlModule Apache::PerlRun
<Location /perl/>
    SetHandler perl-script
    PerlHandler Apache::PerlRun
    Options +ExecCGI
    PerlSendHeader On
    Allow from all
</Location>
```

Security Considerations with mod_perl

mod_perl introduces a certain set of security issues into the mix of securing a web server. When using mod_perl, the namespaces are shared within Apache's memory. It is possible for attackers to gain access to areas of the memory that they shouldn't be able to reach. This is especially the case on shared hosting servers.

Securing Apache is an expansive subject area best left to a book on Apache. If you're running a web server, I do recommend running it within a chroot environment to limit the damage from a successful attack. (For more information about chroot, see http://www.braingia.org/projects/.)

Summary

This chapter introduced the mod_perl Apache module. mod_perl enables high-performance execution of Perl programs in Apache and is meant to replace the normal mod_cgi Apache module for executing Perl programs and CGI scripts. mod_perl gains access to the entire Apache request object and can therefore be used for much more than just executing CGI programs. For example, mod_perl enables the developer to write Apache modules in Perl rather than in the traditional C language.

This chapter began with a look at how Apache handles requests and continued into the installation and configuration of mod_perl. The next chapter covers development in mod_perl.

■ ■ ■

## CHAPTER 11

Development with mod_perl

The previous chapter showed how to install mod_perl with Apache in order to achieve better performance from web applications created in Perl. Recall that mod_perl embeds the Perl interpreter into the Apache process, thus making the execution of Perl programs much faster than when you use the normal mod_cgi module. But mod_perl is much more than a way to get CGI programs to run faster. mod_perl also enables programs to access many parts of the request/ response cycle and manipulate those in order to not only increase performance, but fundamentally change the way that the server itself operates.

In this chapter, you'll learn how to build programs that run under mod_perl and take advantage of its features. As this book was wrapping up, mod_perl version 2.0 was officially released. As with the choice to cover the Apache 1.3 series, I chose to cover the mod_perl 1.0 series due to the sheer number of mod_perl 1.0 series installations available today.

Thinking in mod_perl

Ideally, every CGI script that you've already written will work "out of the box" with mod_perl. If you've incorporated the use strict pragma throughout your CGI programs, then you're a good way toward having them work in mod_perl. However, in practice, it's rare to have complex programs written for mod_cgi work in mod_perl without at least some debugging. This section begins with a look at some initial considerations for converting programs from mod_cgi to mod_perl, followed by a more detailed look at the Apache::Registry and Apache::PerlRun modules.

Note In the world of mod_perl version 2.0, Apache::Registry has been renamed to Modperl::Registry.

Initial Considerations

Recall from Chapter 10 that mod_perl can be used to create handlers for any phase during the Apache request process. The actual serving of the content—what you might consider the web page—is done during this process. During the request process, one of the handlers, PerlHandler, is invoked. Through PerlHandler, you specify exactly how you would like mod_perl to serve the content.

Recall also that there are two Perl modules primarily used for `PerlHandler`: `Apache::Registry` and `Apache::PerlRun`. `Apache::Registry` is the better performing of the two modules. `Apache::PerlRun` is the module most often used during the transition phase between mod_cgi-based programs and mod_perl-based programs.

Warnings and Taint Checking

It's common to use the `-w` option to enable warnings for Perl programs, as well as to enable taint checking with `-T`. This is usually accomplished on the shebang line, like this:

```
#!/usr/bin/perl -wT
```

However, many programs written for mod_perl don't use a shebang line. Therefore, there are two directives to enable warnings and taint mode. These are placed in the Apache configuration file should you choose to use them:

```
PerlWarn On
PerlTaintCheck On
```

Variable Scoping and Environment Variables

Think locally and not globally when coding for mod_perl. Global variables inevitably lead to unpredictable results when executing programs through mod_perl. If you have not thought about and coded for variable scoping, there's a chance that your programs won't work correctly every time when executing through a mod_perl server.

Environment variables, such as those found in %ENV and used by many CGI programs, are sent by default with mod_perl. In some cases, you might want to turn off this behavior. Use `PerlSetupEnv` within your Apache configuration file to disable this:

```
PerlSetupEnv Off
```

You can also set specific environment variables using `PerlSetEnv`. For example, if you have a CGI program that relies on an environment variable to be set, place the correct directive in the Apache configuration file:

```
PerlSetEnv DATASOURCE /home/suehring/customers
```

If the Apache process itself already has an environment variable that you merely want to take advantage of, use the `PerlPassEnv` directive in your Apache configuration file. For example, assume that the httpd parent process has an environment variable of `DATASOURCE` already set. You could access that variable with this statement:

```
PerlPassEnv DATASOURCE
```

Apache::Registry vs. Apache::PerlRun, Revisited

Remember the example in Chapter 10 that showed a script that didn't clean up its namespace very well. The broken version of that script is shown here again, so you don't have to flip back to refresh your memory:

```
use CGI;
$query = CGI->new();

if ($required_name) {
    print header;
    print "name is $required_name\n";
    #do something else
}
else {
    $required_name = $query->param("name");
}
```

Under Apache::Registry, the better performing of the two modules, the variable $required_name wouldn't be null except on the very first execution of the program. On subsequent executions, that variable, having already been assigned a value, would always be set and thus would never get a new value. If you modified the program, Apache::Registry would indeed notice the change though.

Using Apache::PerlRun, namespaces are flushed after each run of the program, thus assisting in the transition from mod_cgi to mod_perl. This means that variables such as $required_name that aren't properly initialized are cleared, just as they would be under mod_cgi. Figure 11-1 shows the same script now run under mod_perl with Apache::PerlRun.

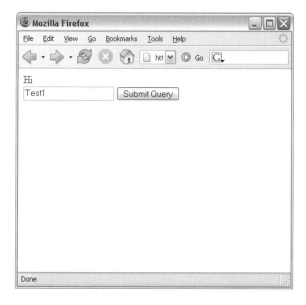

Figure 11-1. *The sample script run under Apache::PerlRun*

When submitted, the program works as expected, as illustrated in Figure 11-2.

Figure 11-2. *The name Test1 is used for the first run of the program.*

Figure 11-3 shows what happens when the program is run a second time, this time using the name Test2.

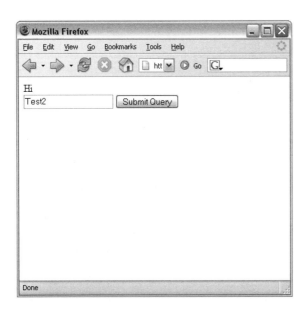

Figure 11-3. *The name Test2 is used for the next run of the program.*

When submitted, you can see from Figure 11-4 that the name is now Test2, indicating that the namespace was cleared as expected by Apache::PerlRun.

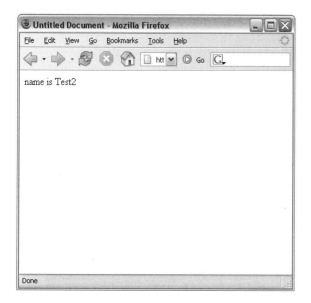

Figure 11-4. *The correct name is used by the program on the second run.*

Missing from the example shown in this section is the use strict pragma. Had use strict been used for the sample script, an error would have been raised, because $required_name wasn't declared prior to its first use.

Although the example shown here seems contrived, in reality, it's all too common, especially with legacy CGI programs.

Apache::PerlRun

Using Apache::PerlRun should be considered to be a quick-and-dirty workaround or hack into the world of mod_perl. It shouldn't be considered the end solution for running a CGI program with mod_perl. Rather, Apache::PerlRun should be an interim approach while the program is revised to clean up its namespaces.

Enabling Apache::PerlRun is a matter of setting the PerlHandler to Apache::PerlRun within the Apache configuration file. Replace the following:

```
PerlHandler Apache::Registry
```

with this:

```
PerlHandler Apache::PerlRun
```

Another area where namespace pollution shows up is with shared CGI programs and older common library files. If your program uses an older library, there is a chance that it won't properly initialize its namespace. When this happens, your first option will likely be to invoke Apache::PerlRun.

PerlRunOnce

Sometimes, even `Apache::PerlRun` by itself won't fix the problems. In such instances, you can also invoke `PerlRunOnce` option. With `PerlRunOnce` enabled, the process responsible for executing the Perl program is spawned only for the lifetime of that execution and dies thereafter. If you believe that this would cause nontrivial performance degradation, you are correct.

You set the `PerlRunOnce` option from within the Apache configuration, specifically within the `mod_perl` section. Recall the sample configuration for Apache and `mod_perl` from Chapter 10, now modified to use `Apache::PerlRun`:

```
<Location /perl/>
    SetHandler perl-script
    PerlHandler Apache::PerlRun
    Options +ExecCGI
    PerlSendHeader On
    Allow from all
</Location>
```

To enable `PerlRunOnce`, you use the `PerlSetVar` option:

```
PerlSetVar PerlRunOnce On
```

The configuration now looks like this:

```
<Location /perl/>
    SetHandler perl-script
    PerlHandler Apache::PerlRun
    PerlSetVar PerlRunOnce On
    Options +ExecCGI
    PerlSendHeader On
    Allow from all
</Location>
```

Apache::Registry

`Apache::Registry` is the better performing module of the two modules discussed here for serving content through `PerlHandler` configuration directive. Examples shown throughout the remainder of this chapter will assume the use of `Apache::Registry`.

Each program executed through `Apache::Registry` is done so by each Apache child, which compiles the program only once. This initial compile may result in the very first load of a program taking incrementally longer before the subsequent runs take advantage of that precompile.

The Apache configuration to `mod_perl` with `Apache::Registry` is typically as follows (replace `/home/suehring/perl` with the appropriate location for your installation):

```
Alias /perl/ /home/suehring/perl/
<Location /perl/>
    SetHandler perl-script
    PerlHandler Apache::Registry
```

```
    Options +ExecCGI
    PerlSendHeader On
    Allow from all
</Location>
```

Preloading Perl Modules

Another area for optimization using mod_perl is to preload Perl modules, rather than loading them with each program. For example, the CGI module or the DBI module could be loaded by Apache, thus giving even better performance for programs that use those modules.

Preloading Apache::DBI

As you learned in Chapter 3, the DBI provides database access through Perl. You can preload the DBI, and even the database-dependent bits through the DBD, to enhance performance. However, in the case of the DBI, you employ another method for initialization, using a specialized module called Apache::DBI. You load this module by using the following line in the Apache configuration file:

```
PerlModule Apache::DBI
```

With that line in the Apache configuration file, the Apache::DBI module will be preloaded and will overload the DBI namespace, enabling your programs to forego the use DBI pragma and also providing just that much more speed to the program.

Resurrecting an example from Chapter 3, Listing 11-1 (Newdb.cgi) shows that the same code can be used, but notice that the use DBI pragma is now missing from the program.

Listing 11-1. *Preloading the DBI*

```
use strict;
use CGI qw/:standard/;

my $username = "dbuser";
my $password = "dbpass";
my $dsn = "dbi:mysql:mysql:192.168.1.10";
my $dbh = DBI->connect($dsn,$username,$password)
  or die "Cannot connect to database: $DBI::errstr";

my $sth = $dbh->prepare("SELECT host,user FROM mysql.user");

$sth->execute()
    or die "Cannot execute sth: $DBI::errstr";
print header,
start_html('MySQL Hosts and Users'),
        table({-border=>1}),
    Tr({-align=>'CENTER',-valign=>'TOP'},
```

```
    [
       th(['User','Host'])
]);

while (my ($hostname,$username) = $sth->fetchrow_array()) {
        if ($username eq "") {
                $username = "<b>undef</b>";
        }
        print Tr({-align=>'CENTER',-valign=>'TOP'},
                [td(["$hostname","$username"])
                ]);
}

print end_html;

$dbh->disconnect();
```

As before, the code results in an HTML table, as shown in Figure 11-5.

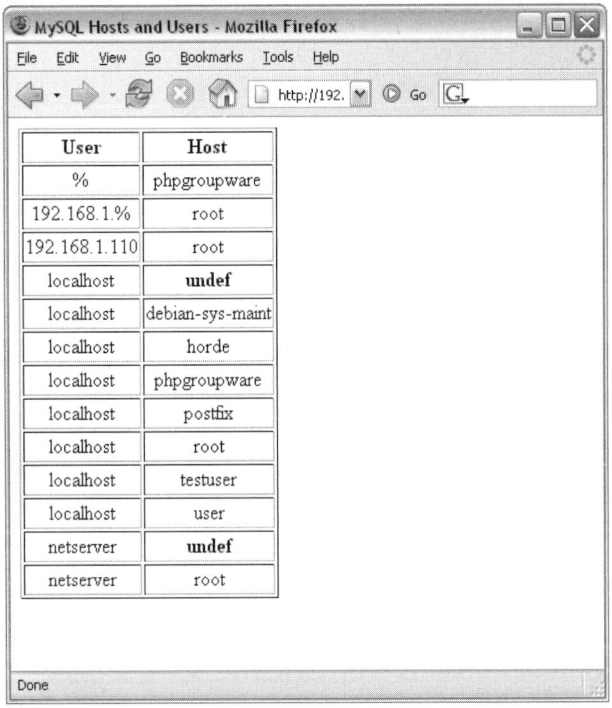

Figure 11-5. *Code to enumerate MySQL hosts and users run through Apache::DBI*

For more information about Apache::DBI, including some caveats on its use, see perldoc Apache::DBI.

Preloading Other Modules and Methods

You can also preload other modules and preload your own handlers from within the Apache httpd.conf configuration file. It's also common on dedicated mod_perl servers (as opposed to shared servers) to create a separate file with the use() statements and other handlers and modules. For example, you might create a file called mod_perlenv.pl containing the following:

```
#!/usr/bin/perl

use Apache::DBI;
use Apache::Registry;
use My::Package;

1;
```

You could then include this file from the httpd.conf configuration file with the PerlRequire directive:

```
PerlRequire mod_perlenv.pl
```

Although this type of configuration isn't required, it's a small thing you can do to try to eke out that much more performance from mod_perl.

Working with the Apache Request Object

As you learned in Chapter 10, central to programming in mod_perl is the Apache request object. The Apache request object gives you access to the various portions of the request/response lifecycle.

■**Note** See the src/include/httpd.h file included with the Apache source code for more information about the request/response lifecycle.

You access the Apache request object through the request() method of the Apache::Request class. The Apache::Request class, and many of the classes used throughout this chapter, are found in the libapreq module available on CPAN.

You'll commonly see Apache::Request referred to as $r in documentation, and I see no reason to change that convention here. Instantiation of the request object is commonly done like this:

```
my $r = Apache->request();
```

As stated previously, the request object is central to programming with mod_perl. Therefore, the request object is the first argument passed into mod_perl handlers. This, in turn, makes it possible to also grab the object off the stack:

```
my $r = shift;
```

You can use the Apache request object to retrieve, inspect, and modify request and response headers. These headers are defined by the HTTP standard, which is codified in RFC 2616 (see http://www.rfc-editor.org/).

You can both retrieve incoming headers (the request) and set outgoing headers (the response). Setting a response header is required for CGI programming and is usually done by the CGI module or by a simple print statement. Remember from way back in Chapter 1, where one of the first CGI examples shown sent a Content-Type header as the first line of output:

```
print "Content-Type: text/html\n\n";
```

The Apache request object has a method for accomplishing this same task:

```
my $r = shift;
$r->send_http_header('text/html');
```

Of course, you can send this header with the CGI module, too:

```
use CGI qw/:standard/;
print header;
```

Note that you can use another method, content_type(), to set the Content-Type within the Apache response, as well as set other response headers with the Apache request object, as you'll see in the "Accessing the Response" section later in this chapter. First things first though. In order to send a response, you first must receive a request.

Accessing the Request

The Apache request object gives you access to the actual request itself for the incoming request from the client. This includes the method used for the request such as GET, POST, and so on, as well as the path and HTTP version information.

Consider the code to print the incoming client request shown in Listing 11-2 (Printrequest.cgi).

Listing 11-2. *Printing the Request*

```
use strict;

my $r = shift;

$r->send_http_header('text/plain');
print $r->the_request();
```

When viewed through a browser, the output shows the incoming request, as shown in Figure 11-6.

Figure 11-6. *The incoming client request as viewed through the Apache request object*

Using Methods to Retrieve Request Values

The request, through the_request() method just shown, is further broken down into the relevant parts through other methods. Listing 11-3 (Printrequestbits.cgi) prints the relevant items from the request.

Listing 11-3. *Printing Some Relevant Items from the Request*

```
use strict;

my $r = shift;

$r->send_http_header('text/plain');

print "Method: ", $r->method, "\n";
print "URI: ", $r->uri, "\n";
print "Path: ", $r->path_info, "\n";
print "Hostname: ", $r->hostname, "\n";
print "Protocol: ", $r->protocol, "\n";
print "File: ", $r->filename, "\n";
```

The output from this program is shown in Figure 11-7.

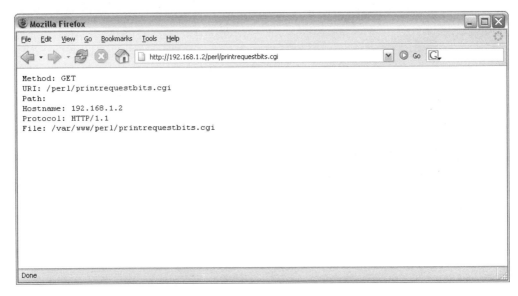

Figure 11-7. *The relevant bits of the request*

Missing from this example is the query string that can be included in a request. The query string is the portion of the URI that follows the path. Consider this example:

```
http://www.example.com/cgi-bin/order.cgi?name=Steve&value=ID
```

Here, the query string is as follows:

```
?customerid=5150&action=order
```

The items on the query string (after the ?) lend themselves to the *name=value* structure native in a hash. You can use the args() method to access the query string. It's no surprise that there are many ways to work with these *name=value* pairs. The first and most basic simply accesses the args() method directly, as shown in Listing 11-4 (`Printquery.cgi`).

Listing 11-4. *Printing the Query String*

```
use strict;

my $r = shift;

$r->send_http_header('text/plain');

print "Query String: ", $r->args, "\n";
```

Examining the output from this program, illustrated in Figure 11-8, shows that the *name=value* pairs have been essentially concatenated by the call to $r->args.

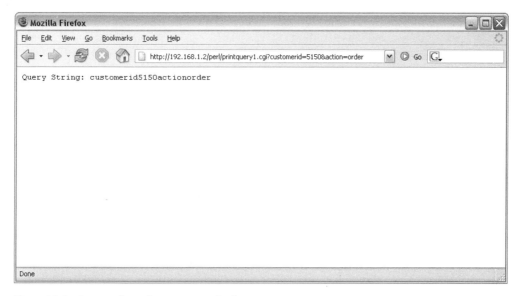

Figure 11-8. *Output from the args() method*

Another way to call the args() method is to cast it into a scalar, as shown in Listing 11-5 (Printquery2.cgi).

Listing 11-5. *Casting args() into a Scalar*

```
use strict;

my $r = shift;

$r->send_http_header('text/plain');

print "Query String: ", scalar $r->args, "\n";
```

This example produces output as it was received, including ampersands and equal signs, as illustrated in Figure 11-9.

Figure 11-9. *Another way to produce output from the args() method*

Yet another way to accomplish the task at hand is to place the output from the args() method into a hash, and then iterate through the hash, as shown in Listing 11-6 (Printquery3.cgi).

Listing 11-6. *Iterating Through the Arguments*

```
use strict;

my $r = shift;

$r->send_http_header('text/plain');

my %args = $r->args;

foreach my $arg (keys %args) {
    print "$arg = $args{$arg}\n";
}
```

This example has the effect of producing traditional *name=value* pairs that are easier to work with inside the program. This cleaner output is shown in Figure 11-10.

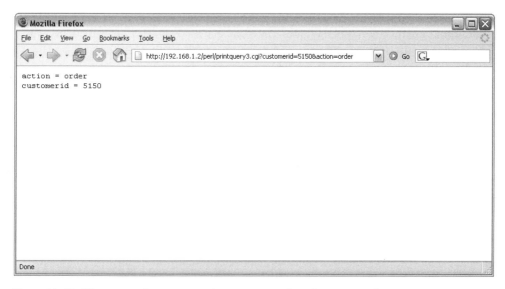

Figure 11-10. *The output from yet another way to retrieve the query string*

Using the args() method as shown in the previous examples works well in most instances. However, for multivalued objects, the normal ways to access this hash can't be used effectively. For instance, consider what would happen to the *name=value* nature of a CGI program called like this:

```
http://www.example.com/cgi-bin/order.cgi?action=order&action=final
```

Notice that there are two values for the action in the query string. The output in Figure 11-11 shows what happens when this query string is encountered by code similar to that shown in Listing 11-5.

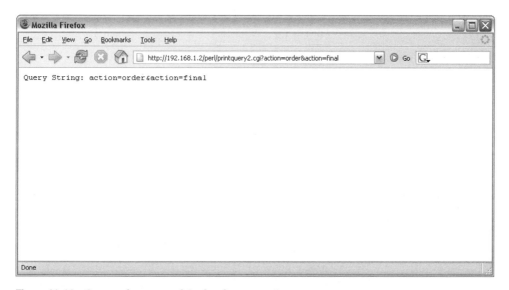

Figure 11-11. *Output from a multivalued query string*

Compare this output with that shown in Figure 11-12. This output was produced by placing the output from the args() method into a hash, as shown in Listing 11-6. Notice that only the final value for the action parameter is actually sent to output.

Figure 11-12. *Output from a multivalued query string*

Although you can iterate through multivalued parameters, if your CGI program will be using multivalued parameters, I recommend using the CGI.pm's methods for accessing these values, rather than coding around the args() method.

So far, these methods retrieve values from GET requests. For POST requests, use the content() method, as shown in Listing 11-7 (Post.cgi).

Listing 11-7. *Using the content() Method*

```
use strict;

my $r = shift;

$r->send_http_header('text/plain');

my %data = $r->content;

foreach my $name (keys %data) {
    print "$name = $data{$name}\n";
}
```

This code looks and is largely similar to Listing 11-6, which retrieved arguments using the args() method. Mainly, the variable names have been changed to protect the innocent. The only substantive difference is to the method used: content() in this case.

The Apache::Request class provides the most flexible method for working with form data through the param() method, as in the example in Listing 11-8 (Param.cgi).

Listing 11-8. *Using the param() Method to Look at Parameters*

```
use Apache::Request;

my $r = Apache::Request->new(shift);

$r->send_http_header('text/plain');

foreach my $param ($r->param) {
        print "Param: $param = " , $r->param($param), "\n";
}
```

The param() method works like CGI.pm, but is implemented in the C programming language as opposed to Perl. The param() method works with both GET and POST data.

▪**Note** The examples in this section also demonstrate how to work with HTML form fields through mod_perl. They show how to parse the parameters from the GET or POST request.

Other methods related to the incoming request include header_only(), for determining whether or not the incoming request was a HEAD type request, and proxyreq(), for determining whether or not the request is a proxy request. Both of these methods return true if they are positive, meaning that the method will return true if it's a HEAD request or if it's a proxy request, respectively.

Accessing Request Headers

So far, you've seen the actual request and methods for working with the request. As noted earlier, the client may also send headers related to the request.

You can access request headers through the headers_in() method, which contains a set of *name=value* pairs. The headers_in() method is part of the Apache::Table class, which also contains other class methods, including the following:

- err_headers_out()

- headers_out()

- info()

- notes()

- subprocess_env()

Each of the class methods of Apache::Table has its own set of methods, including the following:

- add()
- clear()
- do()
- get()
- merge()
- new()
- set()
- unset()

Since *name=value* pairs are sent from the headers_in() method, the output naturally lends itself to being represented in a hash. Listing 11-9 (Headersin.cgi) prints the output from the headers_in() method.

Listing 11-9. *The headers_in() Method to See Name=Value Pairs*

```
use strict;

my $r = shift;

$r->send_http_header('text/plain');

my %headers = $r->headers_in();

foreach my $header (keys %headers) {
    print "$header = $headers{$header}\n";
}
```

The output is shown in Figure 11-13.

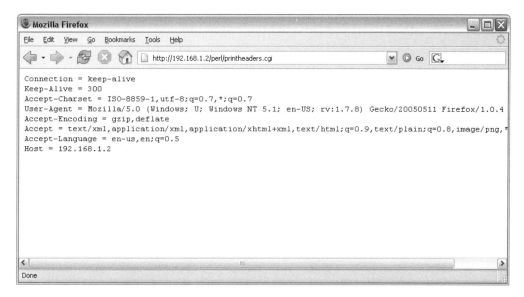

```
Connection = keep-alive
Keep-Alive = 300
Accept-Charset = ISO-8859-1,utf-8;q=0.7,*;q=0.7
User-Agent = Mozilla/5.0 (Windows; U; Windows NT 5.1; en-US; rv:1.7.8) Gecko/20050511 Firefox/1.0.4
Accept-Encoding = gzip,deflate
Accept = text/xml,application/xml,application/xhtml+xml,text/html;q=0.9,text/plain;q=0.8,image/png,
Accept-Language = en-us,en;q=0.5
Host = 192.168.1.2
```

Figure 11-13. *The headers for a request retrieved using the headers_in() method*

You could access individual headers by calling them within the hash. For example, Listing 11-10 (Printuseragent.cgi) shows the code to see the user agent used for the request.

Listing 11-10. *Looking at the User Agent*

```
use strict;

my $r = shift;

$r->send_http_header('text/plain');

my %headers = $r->headers_in();

print "The User-Agent is: $headers{'User-Agent'}\n";
```

The output from this program is shown in Figure 11-14.

Figure 11-14. *Printing the user agent based on output from the headers_in() method*

Accessing the Response

Using the Apache request object, you can set headers in the response, as well as to send server status codes.

Setting a Response Header

Earlier, you saw an example to send the Content-Type response header. As a refresher, that code looks like this:

```
my $r = shift;
$r->send_http_header('text/html');
```

The method used, send_http_header(), is fine for the examples that were shown insofar as it sets the Content-Type and sends the header on its way. However, if you need to set other headers in the response, then calling send_http_header will preclude that from happening. Rather, if you need to set the Content-Type and set other headers in the response, you should use the content_type() method, and then use the send_http_header() method, as in this example:

```
my $r = shift
$r->content_type('text/html');
$r->send_http_header();
```

By using the content_type() method and send_http_header() methods separately in this way, you can set other headers prior to sending them to the client. You can set other headers within the response using the methods described in Table 11-1.

Table 11-1. *Methods for Response Headers*

Method	Description
content_type()	Sets the MIME type as will be sent by the Content-Type header
set_content_length()	Sets the Content-Length header
set_last_modified()	Sets the Last-Modified header
no_cache()	Sets the No_Cache header

To set nonstandard headers, you can use another method, header_out(), as in this example:

```
my $r = shift;

$r->header_out("X-Server" => "My Apache Server v4");
$r->send_http_header;
```

Setting Response Status

Response codes are likely familiar to any web user. From a 404 Not Found to a 500 Internal Server Error or a 200 OK, these response codes communicate the status of the response back to the requesting client. The Apache::Constants class makes these response codes available to you. The response codes available through Apache::Constants use a relatively friendly name. Some of the more common names are described in Table 11-2.

Table 11-2. *Apache::Constants for Server Status Messages*

Apache::Constants Name	Status Code
REDIRECT	302 Found
NOT_FOUND	404 Not Found
SERVER_ERROR	500 Internal Server Error
OK	200 OK
AUTH_REQUIRED	401 Unauthorized

This code sends a 404 Not Found error to the client:

```
use Apache::Constants qw/:common/;

my $r = shift;

$r->status(NOT_FOUND);
```

This is a simple example. Of interest here is that the Apache::Constants class is loaded into the namespace. Notice that only the common set of status codes were imported into the namespace. Rarely will a program call for status codes from Apache::Constants that are not within the common namespace. You can also import only the status codes that you need for a given task. For example, in the previous example, it would be better to just import NOT_FOUND into the program's namespace, as shown here:

```
use Apache::Constants (NOT_FOUND);

my $r = shift;

$r->status(NOT_FOUND);
```

■**Note** You can also use methods for specific error headers. See the documentation for Apache::Table and mod_perl for more information about these headers.

Working with Cookies

As you know, cookies are another object that can be sent in the HTTP header. You can use the Apache::Cookie class, part of libapreq, to set and retrieve cookies the mod_perl way.

Jump in the wayback machine to Chapter 1, which covered cookies in detail. There, you learned all about the values for cookies and how to set them with CGI.pm. Unlike CGI.pm, Apache::Cookie is written in C. This section looks at writing and reading cookies using Apache::Cookie.

Writing Cookies

Cookies are written or sent to the client by instantiating a new Apache::Cookie object. The Apache::Cookie class contains methods that correspond to the various elements of a cookie, such as name, value, path, secure, expires, and so on. You can set these values when instantiating the object through the new() method or via calls to their respective method. Table 11-3 lists the methods, as well as the name of the corresponding parameter if you're using them when instantiating the object.

Table 11-3. *Apache::Cookie Methods and Parameters*

Method	Parameter	Description
name()	-name	The cookie name
value()	-value	The cookie's value
expires()	-expires	The cookie's expiration
domain()	-domain	The domain from which the cookie can be read
path()	-path	The path for the cookie
secure()	-secure	Whether or not the cookie must be read over an SSL transport

The cookies are sent to the browser with the bake() method. Listing 11-11 (Cookiewriter.cgi) shows an example that sets a cookie called testcookie using the Apache::Cookie class.

Listing 11-11. *Sending a Cookie with Apache::Cookie*

```
use Apache::Cookie;

use strict;

my $r = shift;

my $cookie = Apache::Cookie->new($r,
        -name => "testcookie",
        -value => "testvalue",
        -path => "/",
);

$cookie->bake();

$r->send_http_header();
```

The values for the cookie in the example are set via the new() method, and the bake() method is called to actually send the cookie to the client. The cookie arriving at the browser is shown in Figure 11-15.

Figure 11-15. *The cookie set with Apache::Cookie*

You can also set or change the parameter values for cookies by calling each individual method prior to calling bake(). For example, the program in Listing 11-12 (Securecookie.cgi) sets the secure flag on the cookie after it has already been instantiated with the new() method.

Listing 11-12. *Sending a Secure Cookie*

```
use Apache::Cookie;

use strict;

my $r = shift;
```

```perl
my $cookie = Apache::Cookie->new($r,
        -name => "securecookie",
        -value => "securevalue",
        -path => "/",
);

$cookie->secure('1');

$cookie->bake();

$r->send_http_header();
```

Notice that, in addition to the purely superficial name of the cookie itself changing, the secure method() is also called in this code:

```perl
$cookie->secure('1');
```

When sent to the browser, this will mean that the cookie can be read only over an encrypted channel such as over SSL. The cookie alert dialog box is shown in Figure 11-16. Notice the "Send For: Encrypted connections only" wording in this cookie.

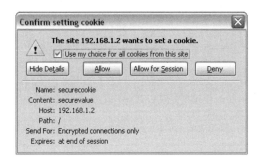

Figure 11-16. *A dialog box indicating that a cookie with the secure flag was sent*

Reading Cookies

You can also use Apache::Cookie to read cookies that are sent by the client. You can use either the parse() method or the fetch() method to retrieve the cookies.

The parse() method operates in three modes: the method can retrieve all cookies as a hash reference, as a hash, or individually. Listing 11-13 (Cookiereader.cgi) shows an example of retrieving cookies using Apache::Cookie's parse() method as a hash.

Listing 11-13. *Retrieving a Cookie with Apache::Cookie*

```perl
use Apache::Cookie;

use strict;

my $r = shift;
```

```perl
my %cookies = Apache::Cookie->new($r)->parse;

$r->send_http_header('text/plain');

foreach my $cookie (keys %cookies) {
        print "Name: ", $cookies{$cookie}->name, "\n";
        print "Value: ", $cookies{$cookie}->value, "\n";
}
```

The results of this code, when called through a browser, are shown in Figure 11-17.

Figure 11-17. *Retrieving cookies using Apache::Cookie and printing the names and values of the cookies*

■**Note** Make sure you actually set a cookie before trying to retrieve the cookie with the code in Listing 11-13. It only took me about ten minutes to figure out that I hadn't set a cookie, which is why my code wasn't producing any output.

Uploading Files

Uploading files is another area where there is also a suitable CGI.pm function for accomplishing the task. However, using Apache::Request and Apache::Upload can yield better performance.

The main interface for uploading files with Apache::Upload is the upload() method. This method can be called in a scalar context, and it will return a single upload object. If called in a list context, the `upload()` method will return objects corresponding to the number of files uploaded.

`Apache::Upload` contains a number of methods for working with uploaded files. For more information about working with file uploads through `Apache::Upload`, see the Perl documentation for `Apache::Upload`.

Working with the Apache Server

Like the HTTP request, the behavior of the Apache server itself can be examined and controlled using mod_perl. The `Apache::Server` object enables things like child creation and log control through a mod_perl interface. This section looks at the `Apache::Server` object.

Using `Apache::Server` is similar to `Apache::Request` in that you'll typically create an instance of the server local to your program, with something like this:

```
my $r = shift;
my $server = $r->server;
```

More commonly, you'll see the Apache server object placed into a variable called $s, like this:

```
my $s = $r->server;
```

The server object in this example is created from the current request object; you can see that the $r request object is created first. This means that the server object will be related to whatever server section is actually serving the request within the Apache configuration. You could also call `Apache::Server` directly, which would then give you an object related to the properties that aren't specific to the current request.

■**Caution** Any changes made to the Apache server through the Apache server object will last for the lifetime of the child Apache process.

Getting Information About the Server

Through the Apache server object, you can find out a lot about the Apache server itself, all from within a Perl program. As an example, Listing 11-14 (`Showserver.cgi`) prints out some information about the server using various methods available with `Apache::Server`.

Listing 11-14. *Printing Information About the Apache Server*

```
use strict;

my $r = shift;

my $s = $r->server;

$r->send_http_header('text/plain');
```

```
print "UID: ", $s->uid, "\n";
print "GID: ", $s->gid, "\n";
print "Port: ", $s->port, "\n";
print "Timeout: ", $s->timeout, "\n";
print "ErrorLog: ", $s->error_fname, "\n";
print "ServerName: ", $s->server_hostname, "\n";
```

When viewed through a browser, the output looks similar to that in Figure 11-18.

Figure 11-18. *Output from a program to get information about the server*

■**Note** Here's some trivia: The server name in Figure 11-18, ord, is named after the O'Hare Airport in Chicago.

For more information about the methods available with Apache::Server, see the Perl documentation for Apache::Server.

Controlling Logging

Another interface to work with the Apache server is through Apache::Log. Using Apache::Log, you can write to the Apache error log.

Within the error log are eight levels of errors, corresponding to the logging levels available on a Linux system, such as warn, info, debug, error, and so on. Each of these logging levels has its own method within Apache::Log. In other words, by calling the individual method, you can control which logging level will be used. The logging level methods are as follows:

- emerg()

- alert()

- crit()

- error()

- warn()

- notice()

- info()

- debug()

A log object is instantiated through a current request within a mod_perl program:

```
my $log = $r->server->log;
```

There's really not much to writing a log entry. Instantiate a request object, then instantiate a log object, and then write to the log. Listing 11-15 (Logger.cgi) shows an example.

Listing 11-15. *Printing to the Error Log with Apache::Log*

```
use Apache::Log;

use strict;

my $r = shift;

my $log = $r->server->log;

$log->error("Moo");
```

When executed, this code produces an entry in the error log like this:

```
[Sat Jun 11 20:12:23 2005] [error] Moo
```

As previously stated, Apache::Log can write at any of the eight logging levels, so instead of calling the error() method, you could make that a warning instead:

```
use Apache::Log;

use strict;

my $r = shift;

my $log = $r->server->log;

$log->warn("Moo");
```

This would produced a warning in the error log:

```
[Sat Jun 11 20:14:32 2005] [warn] Moo
```

■**Note** If you're not receiving an error message in your log file, check the `LogLevel` directive in your Apache configuration.

Listing 11-16 (`Logua.cgi`) shows another example that incorporates a log message with an earlier example to look at the user agent. This code will print a warning in the error log if the site is visited by an Internet Explorer user.

Listing 11-16. *Logging Based on the User Agent*

```
use Apache::Log;

use strict;

my $r = shift;
my $log = $r->server->log;

$r->send_http_header('text/plain');

my %headers = $r->headers_in();

if ($headers{'User-Agent'} =~ m/MSIE/) {
    $log->warn("Someone is actually still using IE");
}
```

When visited by a browser with the string `MSIE` in `UserAgent`, the warning is printed in the error log:

```
[Sat Jun 11 20:22:16 2005] [warn] Someone is actually still using IE
```

Security Considerations with mod_perl, Revisited

As noted in Chapter 10, using `mod_perl` introduces its own set of security risks. Since the Perl interpreter is embedded into the Apache process, and since namespaces can be shared, there is potential for data to be read and possibly altered within and between programs running with `mod_perl`. Keeping namespaces clean by using local variable scope and using the `use strict` pragma go a long way toward mitigating this risk. This is less of a concern on a server that isn't shared.

In addition, consider exactly what you're doing with mod_perl programs when working with the Apache request/response lifecycle and the Apache server itself. All of these things can introduce risk into programs if they are executed maliciously. For instance, writing to log files from a mod_perl program could result in an attacker filling up a disk with spurious log entries.

Finally, mod_perl inherits all of the risks present in CGI programs, such as possible attacks if input from forms isn't properly sanitized. Refer to the earlier chapters on CGI programming (Chapters 1 through 4) for more information about those security considerations.

Summary

This chapter examined development with mod_perl. You learned about variable scoping with mod_perl, Apache::Registry, and the Apache request object. To appreciate the full power of mod_perl, I highly recommend working with it to perform more advanced programming and to increase the performance of your programs. The benefits of mod_perl for high-performance web sites are immense.

Looking ahead, the next chapter will shift gears once again and discuss templating with Perl. By using templates, you can increase your web design productivity. As you'll see, Perl offers more than a few options for templating.

PART 5

Creating Web Templates

CHAPTER 12

■■■

The Template Toolkit

Although templates don't seem quite as fun as, say, programming a SOAP interface into the United States National Weather Service, they are actually quite interesting and they are definitely timesavers. I have yet to meet a Perl programmer who doesn't like saving time; let the computer do the work.

In this chapter, you'll examine the Template Toolkit in detail, and then concentrate on using the Template Toolkit to create and maintain a web site. But first, let's briefly look at why Perl is ideal for use with templates.

Perl and Templates

Perl lends itself to the task of creation and completion of templates on many levels. Whether it's plain text substitutions in plain text documents, PDFs, or HTML, Perl is an excellent language for working with templates, for the same reasons Perl is great for almost any task:

- Perl is lightweight. There's not much overhead required to create powerful programs.

- Perl is easy to learn. You don't have to work through idiotic and arcane syntax to make Perl programs do what you want them to.

- Perl is widely supported. You can run Perl programs on many platforms and architectures.

These and a whole host of other reasons give Perl an advantage for templates and beyond.

I currently use the Perl templating software Mason for my web site. Using Mason, I'm able to define a common header and footer for the site and have pages constructed on-the-fly using those items. Mason works with `mod_perl` and integrates tightly into the process of serving web page. Mason will be covered in detail in Chapter 13.

Converting a site to Mason can be a little involved, and there are other well-implemented Perl packages for templating available. You'll look at one such package, the Template Toolkit, next in this chapter. The Template Toolkit is easy to learn and offers a good way to get your feet wet with templating, to find out if you want to convert your site to Mason (or if you *need* to convert it to Mason!).

Template Toolkit Introduction

The Template Toolkit is powerful template processing software for Perl that's actually a combination of a number of packages. Far from being a one-hit wonder, the Template Toolkit is a great multitasker (how's that for mixing metaphors) that is able to work with HTML as well as other formats, such as XML and even PDF.

In this section, you'll learn about templating with Perl through the Template Toolkit.

Template Toolkit Example

Templates are objects (think: documents) that enable copying or reuse of textual patterns containing a mix of dynamic, changing text, surrounded by static and unchanging text. You can think of a template as a classic form letter—for example, "Dear [Your Name Here], You have just won a million dollars!" A marketing company develops the main body of text, "You have just won a million dollars," and plugs that into a document. The company then feeds the document through some template-processing software to substitute the "[Your Name Here]" part with someone's actual name. The final version would (or should) read, "Dear Steve Suehring, You have just won a million dollars!"

This isn't very far off from the Template Toolkit syntax. Changing the form letter to typical Template Toolkit syntax and filling it out a little more might look like this:

```
Dear [% recipient %],

You have just won a million dollars!  To retrieve your million dollars,
send your bank account information to [% scammer_address %].  I will
require you to give me [% scam_amount %] so that I can get the funds.

Yours,

[% scammer_name %]
```

This text is saved to a file called templateexample.txt. Creating the end result letter with the Template Toolkit looks like this:

```
tpage --define recipient=Steve \
> --define scammer_name=Dan \
> --define scammer_address=dan@example.com \
> --define scam_amount=\$500 \
> templateexample.txt
```

The final letter is as follows:

```
Dear Steve,

You have just won a million dollars!  To retrieve your million dollars,
send your bank account information to dan@example.com.  I will
require you to give me $500 so that I can get the funds.

Yours,

Dan
```

The command tpage processes templates with the Template Toolkit on a file-by-file basis. This is in addition to the ttree command that processes templates on a per-directory basis. Both commands are covered in detail later.

The command shown to process the template first defines four variables: recipient, scammer_name, scammer_address, and scam_amount. Notice that the order of these definitions is not tied to the order in which they appear in the document, as scammer_name was used last in the document but defined second. The command then indicates which template to process—templateexample.txt, in this case.

When executed, the command prints to STDOUT. This could easily be shell redirected into a new file I'll call letter.txt:

```
tpage --define recipient=Steve \
> --define scammer_name=Dan \
> --define scammer_address=dan@example.com \
> --define scam_amount=\$500 templateexample.txt > letter.txt
```

You've now seen a rudimentary example of what the Template Toolkit can do. The benefits you can reap from the Template Toolkit are directly related to the number of templates you can create for processing.

Considering specifically web site creation and maintenance, pages frequently have a common or usually common header and footer. Using the Template Toolkit, it's possible to create that common header and footer, and feed the raw pages through ttree to create the site.

Beyond tpage and ttree, the Template Toolkit can plug directly into Apache through mod_perl with the help of the Apache::Template module. Using Apache::Template, it's possible to create pages on-the-fly with the Template Toolkit. Apache::Template won't be covered in much detail in this chapter but another on-the-fly web page creation module (Mason) will be covered in the next chapter.

Using the Template Toolkit

The Template Toolkit is a large and powerful application set. You can use the toolkit through several interfaces, including two programs (tpage and ttree), a Perl module, and an Apache module. This section begins by examining the interfaces that you'll use to process templates through the Template Toolkit.

tpage

As you've seen already, the tpage program can be used to process a template where the name of the template is used as an argument. The output is sent to STDOUT. You can also send the output through a redirect to send it into a file, as was shown previously as well.

When using tpage to process a file, it's common to use the --define option to define variables for substitution. This example was shown earlier and is repeated here for your reference:

```
tpage --define recipient=Steve \
> --define scammer_name=Dan \
> --define scammer_address=dan@example.com \
> --define scam_amount=\$500 templateexample.txt > letter.txt
```

You can also call tpage without any arguments to use it in interactive mode. When using tpage in interactive mode, you're required to enter both the variables and the text. A ^D indicates the end of input and the beginning of processing. From the command prompt, you type **tpage**, as in this example:

```
tpage
[% server = 'www'
    ip = '127.0.0.1'
%]
We noticed that your server, [% server %], at IP [% ip %],
    is currently down.
```

When you're ready to process the template, press Ctrl+D (^D) to begin processing. Here's the output you'll see:

```
We noticed that your server, www, at IP 127.0.0.1,
    is currently down.
```

ttree

When updating a web site with the Template Toolkit, you'll frequently use the ttree program. ttree operates on entire directories of files and offers much greater flexibility to the developer attempting to maintain a large web site through templates. ttree offers a huge number of options, compared with tpage, as shown in Listing 12-1.

Listing 12-1. *Options Available with ttree*

```
ttree 2.78 (Template Toolkit version 2.14)

usage: ttree [options] [files]

Options:
    -a        (--all)        Process all files, regardless of modification
    -r        (--recurse)    Recurse into sub-directories
    -p        (--preserve)   Preserve file ownership and permission
    -n        (--nothing)    Do nothing, just print summary (enables -v)
    -v        (--verbose)    Verbose mode
    -h        (--help)       This help
    -s DIR    (--src=DIR)    Source directory
    -d DIR    (--dest=DIR)   Destination directory
    -c DIR    (--cfg=DIR)    Location of configuration files
    -l DIR    (--lib=DIR)    Library directory (INCLUDE_PATH)  (multiple)
    -f FILE   (--file=FILE)  Read named configuration file     (multiple)

File search specifications (all may appear multiple times):
    --ignore=REGEX          Ignore files matching REGEX
    --copy=REGEX            Copy files matching REGEX
    --accept=REGEX          Process only files matching REGEX
```

```
File Dependencies Options:
    --depend foo=bar,baz      Specify that 'foo' depends on 'bar' and 'baz'.
    --depend_file FILE        Read file dependencies from FILE.
    --depend_debug            Enable debugging for dependencies


File suffix rewriting (may appear multiple times)
    --suffix old=new          Change any '.old' suffix to '.new'

Additional options to set Template Toolkit configuration items:
    --define var=value        Define template variable
    --interpolate             Interpolate '$var' references in text
    --anycase                 Accept directive keywords in any case.
    --pre_chomp               Chomp leading whitespace
    --post_chomp              Chomp trailing whitespace
    --trim                    Trim blank lines around template blocks
    --eval_perl               Evaluate [% PERL %] ... [% END %] code blocks
    --load_perl               Load regular Perl modules via USE directive
    --absolute                Enable the ABSOLUTE option
    --relative                Enable the RELATIVE option
    --pre_process=TEMPLATE    Process TEMPLATE before each main template
    --post_process=TEMPLATE   Process TEMPLATE after each main template
    --process=TEMPLATE        Process TEMPLATE instead of main template
    --wrapper=TEMPLATE        Process TEMPLATE wrapper around main template
    --default=TEMPLATE        Use TEMPLATE as default
    --error=TEMPLATE          Use TEMPLATE to handle errors
    --debug=STRING            Set TT DEBUG option to STRING
    --start_tag=STRING        STRING defines start of directive tag
    --end_tag=STRING          STRING defined end of directive tag
    --tag_style=STYLE         Use pre-defined tag STYLE
    --plugin_base=PACKAGE     Base PACKAGE for plugins
    --compile_ext=STRING      File extension for compiled template files
    --compile_dir=DIR         Directory for compiled template files
    --perl5lib=DIR            Specify additional Perl library directories
    --template_module=MODULE Specify alternate Template module

See 'perldoc ttree' for further information.
```

Like tpage, ttree can have its execution controlled by combining these options on the command line. However, when working with ttree, it's common to use a configuration file to hold information about the project, its file locations, and the behavior for ttree. Configuration files are typically created on a per-project basis and then either included on the command line for ttree or placed in the ttree run control file.

Controlling the execution of ttree is a run control (rc) file called .ttreerc, which is located in your home directory by default. The first time that you run ttree, you are presented with a prompt to create a sample configuration file:

```
Do you want me to create a sample '.ttreerc' file for you?
(file: /home/suehring/.ttreerc)   [y/n]:
```

I recommend entering a **y** to indicate that ttree should create the run control file. The default run control file contains some interesting bits of information, as shown in Listing 12-2.

Listing 12-2. *Default Run Control File*

```
#-------------------------------------------------------------------------
# sample .ttreerc file created automatically by ttree version 2.78
#
# This file originally written to /home/suehring/.ttreerc
#
# For more information on the contents of this configuration file, see
#
#      perldoc ttree
#      ttree -h
#
#-------------------------------------------------------------------------

# The most flexible way to use ttree is to create a separate directory
# for configuration files and simply use the .ttreerc to tell ttree where
# it is.
#
#      cfg = /path/to/ttree/config/directory
# print summary of what's going on
verbose

# recurse into any sub-directories and process files
recurse

# regexen of things that aren't templates and should be ignored
ignore = \b(CVS|RCS)\b
ignore = ^#

# ditto for things that should be copied rather than processed.
copy = \.png$
copy = \.gif$

# by default, everything not ignored or copied is accepted; add 'accept'
# lines if you want to filter further. e.g.
#
#      accept = \.html$
#      accept = \.tt2$

# options to rewrite files suffixes (htm => html, tt2 => html)
#
#      suffix htm=html
#      suffix tt2=html
```

```
# options to define dependencies between templates
#
#    depend *=header,footer,menu
#    depend index.html=mainpage,sidebar
#    depend menu=menuitem,menubar
#
#-----------------------------------------------------------------------
# The following options usually relate to a particular project so
# you'll probably want to put them in a separate configuration file
# in the directory specified by the 'cfg' option and then invoke tree
# using '-f' to tell it which configuration you want to use.
# However, there's nothing to stop you from adding default 'src',
# 'dest' or 'lib' options in the .ttreerc.  The 'src' and 'dest' options
# can be re-defined in another configuration file, but be aware that 'lib'
# options accumulate so any 'lib' options defined in the .ttreerc will
# be applied every time you run ttree.
#-----------------------------------------------------------------------
# # directory containing source page templates
# src = /path/to/your/source/page/templates
#
# # directory where output files should be written
# dest = /path/to/your/html/output/directory
#
# # additional directories of library templates
# lib = /first/path/to/your/library/templates
# lib = /second/path/to/your/library/templates
```

The items in this run control file are also used in a configuration file. Therefore, if you maintain only one site, you can leave the .ttreerc file as is. However, if you maintain more than one site with the Template Toolkit, you'll likely want to create a minimal .ttreerc file and call individual ttree configuration files based on each project. You should do this because each ttree configuration file will hold information about files to ignore, directories to find the template files and to place the output files, and so on. Specifying the configuration file for ttree to use as part of its command line looks like this:

```
ttree -f /path/to/project-ttree.cfg
```

A Quick Look at ttree Options

When using ttree to create and manage a web site, it's common to use certain directives and options. Some of those options are placed in the default .ttreerc file shown previously. This section looks briefly at a few of those options before they are discussed in detail later.

Since ttree operates on templates within a directory, you need to tell it where to find the source template files. Related to that, you also need to tell ttree where to place the destination or output files. The -s and -d command-line options specify the source and destination directories, respectively:

```
ttree -s sourcedir -d destdir
```

Headers and footers are the common text that appears on many web sites at the top and bottom of pages. A header might include a common menu or navigation components, while the footer might include a copyright notice and contact information. Rather than including this text inside of each file to be processed by `ttree`, they can be included using the `pre_process` and `post_process` options:

```
ttree -s sourcedir -d destdir --pre_process=headerfile --post-process=footerfile
```

When processing templates with headers and footers, the `pre_processed` headers frequently need to use variables. For example, a web page header template would usually need to define a title to go within the `<title></title>` markup. To have these defined on a per-page basis, developers frequently use the `META` directive within an individual template file to define a variable that is accessible to all pages being processed, even those that are `pre_processed`. The `META` directive will be shown later in the chapter during a full example of `ttree`. For now, know that if you're using a common header and footer, and you need to have variables available within the `pre_processed` header, you will need to define it using `META`:

```
[% META variable = "Value" %]
```

The Template Module and Apache::Template

In addition to the `tpage` and `ttree` commands that come with the Template Toolkit, you can also use the Template Toolkit as a module within Perl programs by importing it into the namespace with the familiar `use` pragma:

```
use Template;
```

You can use the Template Toolkit along with the `Apache::Template` module on a `mod_perl`-enabled Apache server to process templates on-the-fly and serve them through the Apache server. `Apache::Template` is available from your favorite CPAN mirror.

Using `Apache::Template` and the `Template` module within a Perl program will not be covered further in this chapter.

Template Toolkit Syntax

The Template Toolkit is a powerful and mature template-processing package. That power and maturity is particularly evident in the syntax, which includes the use of variables, directives, filters, and other properties of the processing language. In this section, you'll look at some of the primary syntactical items in the Template Toolkit.

■Note When processing templates through the Template Toolkit, items within the tags ([% and %]) will be processed by the Toolkit as being part of the directive. Other text won't be processed at all. You can change this behavior with chomping options PRE_CHOMP and POST_CHOMP, as well as the INTERPOLATE option. INTERPOLATE is interesting because it causes the text outside of the tags to be processed looking for variables with a $ prefix.

Chomping

A side effect of the Template Toolkit is that white space is ignored—even the extra white space created by template directive blocks. This is usually fine for HTML processing, but it can cause headaches for web designers at times. For example, consider the following code:

```
Welcome,
[% month = october %]
Thank you for visiting.
```

This would be processed with the extra newline character left intact and output as follows:

```
Welcome,

Thank you for visiting.
```

The Template Toolkit enables you to control the "chomping" of white space by using the - flag from within a directive or the PRE_CHOMP and POST_CHOMP options. A - directly following the start tag causes newlines and white space preceding the directive to be removed. A - directly before the end tag causes newlines and white space after the directive to be removed. Consider this example:

```
Welcome,
[%- month = october %]
Thank you for visiting.
```

With the - directly following the start tag, the processing would essentially look like this:

```
Welcome,[%- month = october %]
Thank you for visiting.
```

which in turn results in output such as the following:

```
Welcome,
Thank you for visiting.
```

On the other hand, when you place the - directly preceding the end tag like this:

```
Welcome,
[% month = october -%]
Thank you for visiting.
```

the processing will essentially look like this:

```
Welcome,
[%- month = october %]Thank you for visiting.
```

and the output will look like this:

```
Welcome,
Thank you for visiting.
```

The PRE_CHOMP and POST_CHOMP configuration directives can control this behavior at the file or directory level when stored inside of the configuration file. When set to 1, these directives cause behavior as shown in the examples just shown. When set to 2, the newlines and white space are collapsed into a single space rather than being removed entirely.

A + effectively toggles the behavior of the chomping, and it is used within individual directives to control the chomping for that directive alone. In other words, if you enable both PRE_CHOMP and POST_CHOMP in your configuration file, but you want to disable them for a certain tag, you would use the following syntax:

```
Welcome,
[%+ month=october +%]
Thank you for visiting.
```

Other behaviors for chomping are also available. You can find out more about chomping in the perldoc for Template::Manual::Config.

Interpolation

Using the INTERPOLATE option causes variables indicated with a $ to be interpolated within the plain text of the template to be processed. Braces must be used when the Template Toolkit cannot discern the variable name. For example, this code does not need braces:

```
Welcome,
It is now $month
```

However, this code needs braces:

```
Welcome,
Contact us at $email@$domain.com
```

In the preceding example, the process doesn't know whether $email@$domain.com is all one variable, or really how to handle it at all. Placing braces around the variables makes it clear to the processor exactly what it should interpolate:

```
Welcome,
Contact us at {$email}@{$domain}.com
```

■**Note** When INTERPOLATE is enabled, you must escape any true $ characters that you want to use in your code. For example, using $1.99 to indicate a price will confuse the processor; you should write this as \$1.99.

Comments

Comments in code help you to remember why you did what you did when you did it. Chances are that at some point you'll go back to look at a piece of code and scratch your head, wondering what exactly that piece of code does. You can use comments inside of templates as well. As in Perl, comments in a template are denoted by a hash sign (#). When used inside a template directive, a comment effectively disables processing of the line upon which it appears, as in this example:

```
[% # This line is not processed, but the next line is
   PROCESS header
%]
```

Notice that there is a space between the start tag and the comment indicator in the preceding example. Concatenating the start tag and the comment character affects how the comment works. If the start tag and the comment character are connected, the entire template directive will be ignored, for example:

```
[%# This entire directive will be ignored.
   PROCESS header
%]
```

This is a very subtle but important difference in comment processing between instances where there is a space within the start tag and where the space is missing.

Tag Styles

Whether you're using tpage or ttree, you can specify the type of tags to indicate the beginning and end of an interpreted section. Recall that the default is [% and %]. The TAGS directive is used to change this behavior, and you have several tag options. For example, this code changes the default tags to the tag convention used in the PHP programming language:

```
[% TAGS php %]
```

The tags to indicate pieces of code to be processed are now <? and ?>.
Table 12-1 shows the different tag styles available.

Table 12-1. *Tags Available with the Template Toolkit*

Tag Name	Start and End Tag
asp	<% and %>
html	<!-- and -->
mason	<% and >
metatext	%% and %%
php	<? and ?>
star	[* and *]
template	[% and %]
template1	[% or %% and %] or %%

Beyond the predefined tag styles, you can create custom tag styles. For example, the following code changes the tag style to (- and -).

```
[% TAGS (- -) %]
```

You can change the tag style as a configuration option as well. In practice, you'll likely change the tag style from within a configuration file, using the TAG_STYLE, START_TAG, and END_TAG options, for a sitewide project as opposed to changing it from within an individual template file.

Variables

Variables store information for use in processing the template. You can name variables with alphanumeric characters and underscores. As with Perl, you can use scalars, arrays, and hashes as variables in the Template Toolkit, and you can also use subroutines as variables (dynamic variables).

In this section, you'll look at defining and setting variables (both static and dynamic), and you'll see an example of working with variables.

Defining and Setting Variables

At their most basic, variables are defined and set with the SET directive. However, it's rare to actually use the SET directive; most times you'll use simple assignment. The following code:

```
[% album = 5150 %]
```

is functionally equivalent to this:

```
[% SET album = 5150 %]
```

The GET directive retrieves the value previously set inside of a variable. Like SET, values can also be retrieved implicitly. This code retrieves the value for the album variable:

```
[% album %]
```

Setting longer strings can be accomplished by putting the values in quotes:

```
[% artist = "Van Halen" %]
```

This value can be split over multiple lines:

```
[% artist = "Van
            Halen"
%]
```

You can also set multiple values within the same directive:

```
[% album = 5150
    artist = "Van Halen"
%]
```

Notice that these lines are not terminated by semicolons; this is the convention when setting variables. However, when retrieving values, the lines must be terminated by semicolons:

```
[% album;
    artist;
%]
```

List variables are set by including the list of values within brackets, [and]:

```
[% months = [jan,feb,mar,apr,may,jun,jul,aug,sep,oct,nov,dec] %]
```

■Note Commas are used to separate the values in the example, but they are not required. A space can be used just the same.

These elements are accessed with dot notation, with the first index indicated by 0. For example, this code accesses the second element in the months list example just shown:

```
[% month.1 %]
```

Based on that earlier example, the value for [% month.1 %] is feb.

While lists or arrays are indicated by brackets, [and], hashes are indicated by braces, { and }:

```
[% months = {
    jan => 'January'
    feb => 'February'
    mar => 'March'
    apr => 'April'
  }
%]
```

Values belonging to the keys of the hash are accessed using the dot operator with hash variables. For example, the following code accesses the value for the key named mar in the previous example:

```
[% months.mar %]
```

The value contained in [% months.mar %] is March. You can also use multiple dot operators to create and retrieve arbitrarily long nested hashes.

■Note Variables declared with a leading underscore (_) character are defined as private and will not be used outside the object's methods.

Whereas the variable types just explained are static, meaning they only return values explicitly set or assigned to them, dynamic variables can be assigned to Perl subroutines and objects, which will then process and return information to the variables for use in template processing.

Working with Variables

Mathematical operations can also be performed on variables when they are being set or retrieved. This example adds the result of two dice being rolled:

```
[% GET die1 + die2 %]
```

In addition to the mathematical operators, logical operators such as and, or, and not can be used:

```
[% GET diceroll or 0 %]
```

When a variable is accessed, either implicitly or with a GET, it is printed within the output. The CALL directive enables access to variables or, more likely, subroutines and objects, without printing the results from that call:

```
[% CALL diceroll.roll %]
```

Virtual Methods

According to the perldoc for Template::Manual, "The Template Toolkit provides virtual methods for manipulating variable values." To programmers familiar with object-oriented concepts, some of these methods might be more readily referred to as *properties*. In any event, these *virtual methods*, as they are known, enable you to quickly find out information about variables and their contents.

For example, you can find out if a variable has been defined using the defined method:

```
[% IF connection.defined %]
```

and you can also determine the length of a variable:

```
[% textvar.length %]
```

Several other virtual methods are available to match, search and replace, split, and perform other functions. Refer to the perldoc for Template::Manual::VMethods for more information on these and other methods.

Directives

Directives are at the heart of working with templates. After reviewing some general information about working with directives, this section moves on to cover includes, loops, conditionals, exception handling, and blocks of Perl.

Working with Directives

You can retrieve output from directives by assigning that output to a variable within the directive:

```
[% months = PROCESS monthnames %]
```

Writing semicomplex code for processing can cause problems with readability of the template. Rather than opening and closing each line of code, you can indicate a multiple-line directive by ending the line with a semicolon, as in this example:

```
[% PROCESS header;
    IF something;
        INCLUDE file.txt;
    END
%]
```

Includes

You can include content from another template to reuse the code from that other template. The INCLUDE, INSERT, PROCESS, and WRAPPER directives can all be used to insert or process external code within the current template. The BLOCK directive can be used to localize parts of template code that you want to process but don't want to create an entirely new file for. Regardless of which option you use, the INCLUDE_PATH option determines the location that will be searched for the files to be included.

INCLUDE Directive

The INCLUDE directive causes a file to be included within the current template. You can send arguments to the INCLUDE directive as well:

```
[% INCLUDE otherfile album="5150" %]
```

The INCLUDE directive localizes variables. This means that changes to variables made inside an included file will not be seen by the file into which the included template is placed. If you plan on using an INCLUDE, I recommend reading the perldoc for Template::Manual::Directives to find out how variables are scoped when using INCLUDE.

To demonstrate this behavior, first create a file called diceroll with these contents:

```
[% dice = 5 %]
```

You'll bring the contents of that file into a template called includeexample.tt. The following listing shows the contents of the includeexample.tt file:

```
[%- dice = 11 -%
dice roll is [% dice %]
[%- INCLUDE diceroll -%]
dice roll is now [% dice %]
```

This file is then fed into tpage with this command:

```
tpage processexample.tt
```

The output is as follows:

```
dice roll is 11
dice roll is now 11
```

Notice that the value of the dice variable was not affected by the diceroll file. This behavior is in contrast to the PROCESS directive, which is described next.

PROCESS Directive

The PROCESS directive is similar to the INCLUDE directive, with the significant difference being the way PROCESS handles variables. Unlike the INCLUDE directive, changes made to variables within a file called through a PROCESS directive will be seen by the template into which the file is brought. Let's demonstrate this behavior with an example.

First, create a file called diceroll with these contents:

```
[% dice = 5 %]
```

You'll bring the contents of the `diceroll` file into a template called `processexample.tt`. Here are the `processexample.tt` file contents:

```
[% dice = 11 %]
dice roll is [% dice %]
[% PROCESS diceroll %]
dice roll is now [% dice %]
```

This file is then fed into `tpage` with the following command:

```
tpage processexample.tt
```

The output is as follows:

```
dice roll is 11


dice roll is now 5
```

Tip Notice that you don't have chomping enabled in this example. Since chomping isn't enabled, the output has extra newlines. Recall that you will either set pre- or post-chomping (or both) or use a dash to indicate that chomping should be enabled, as in the earlier example.

Examination of the output shows that the value for the dice was indeed changed by the file called in with the `PROCESS` directive.

INSERT Directive

The `INSERT` directive is used to insert the contents of a file at the current position of the template. Its syntax is similar to that of `INCLUDE`:

```
[% INSERT otherfile %]
```

Use a plus sign (+) to concatenate multiple files with `INSERT`:

```
[% INSERT file1 + file2 %]
```

WRAPPER Directive

The `WRAPPER` directive causes a template file to be wrapped around the current text. While `WRAPPER` is sometimes handy, coverage of this directive is beyond the scope of this chapter. Refer to the `perldoc` for `Template::Manual::Directives` for more information on the `WRAPPER` directive.

BLOCK Directive

The `BLOCK` directive can be used to localize parts of template code that you want to process but don't want to create an entirely new file for. The following is an example of using a `BLOCK` directive:

```
[%- BLOCK blockname -%]
    This text is inside of a block and I can send in arguments
    since they are so [% argument %]
[%- END -%]
```

The code within the BLOCK can then be called with a PROCESS or INCLUDE directive:

```
[% PROCESS blockname argument = "fun" %]
```

When this example is run through tpage, the output is as follows:

```
This text is inside of a block and I can send in arguments since they are so fun
```

Loops

As with loops in Perl, you can use loops in the template language to control the flow of processing. The template language provides FOREACH and WHILE type loops. WHILE is useful for performing an action until a condition occurs. FOREACH is useful when handling a known set of data that should be iterated through in turn. Both directives process the code within their logical block up until a corresponding [% END %] is encountered.

FOREACH Directive

The syntax for the FOREACH directive is as follows:

```
[% FOREACH something IN listofthings %]
    #Perform actions
[% END %]
```

The listofthings can be any valid list or array type variable, or it can be defined at the time of the FOREACH loop's definition, as in Listing 12-3.

Listing 12-3. *FOREACH Directive*

```
[% FOREACH number IN [ 1..5 ] -%]
        [% number %]
[% END -%]
```

When this example is processed through tpage (tpage foreachex.tt), the output is as follows:

```
1
2
3
4
5
```

There are several helpful methods for iterating through items within a FOREACH block. These methods are available through a variable called loop, which I'll discuss later in the chapter. An object called an *iterator* is used to traverse the list. Table 12-2 shows the methods available to the loop variable.

Table 12-2. *Methods Available Within a FOREACH Directive*

Directive	Description
count	The number of the current location within the list, beginning at 1
first	A Boolean to indicate if the current location is the first item in the list
index	The number of the current location within the list, beginning at 0
last	A Boolean to indicate if the current location is the last item in the list
max	The largest or maximum index number for the list
next	The next item in the list, or undef if there are no additional items
prev	The previous item in the list, or undef if the current location is already on the first item
size	The size of the list

Some of the differences between these methods are subtle but important. For example, the index and count methods both can provide the location of the iterator within the list, and max and count can both provide the size. Recall the example in Listing 12-3. I've added some code to it to print the count, index, size, and max, as shown in Listing 12-4.

Listing 12-4. *Using the loop Variable Within a FOREACH Directive*

```
[% FOREACH number IN [ 1..5 ] -%]
        Item:   [% number %]
        Count:  [% loop.count %]
        Index:  [% loop.index %]
        Max:    [% loop.max %]
        Size:   [% loop.size %]
        ----------------------
[% END -%]
```

The output from this code, when processed through tpage, is as follows:

```
        Item:   1
        Count:  1
        Index:  0
        Max:    4
        Size:   5
        ----------------------
        Item:   2
        Count:  2
        Index:  1
        Max:    4
        Size:   5
        ----------------------
        Item:   3
        Count:  3
        Index:  2
```

```
Max:    4
Size:   5
----------------------
Item:   4
Count:  4
Index:  3
Max:    4
Size:   5
----------------------
Item:   5
Count:  5
Index:  4
Max:    4
Size:   5
----------------------
```

Notice that as each item is processed, the count and index values increase, but they started from different values: 0 for index and 1 for count. Notice also that the values for max and size stayed the same, but because max begins counting from 0, it lists 4 as the maximum number of items, whereas size shows 5.

Like native Perl, FOREACH loops are useful for iterating through hashed data within the Template Toolkit as well. The example in Listing 12-5 shows a hash structure being created and then iterated through with a FOREACH directive.

Listing 12-5. *Iterating Through a Hashed Data Structure with FOREACH*

```
[%- employees = [
    {
        name => "Frank Sanbeans"
        username => "frank.sanbeans"
    } {
        name => "Sandy Sanbeans"
        username => "sandy.sanbeans"
    } ]

    domain = "example.com"
-%]
    ---===Employees===----

[% FOREACH emp IN employees -%]
    Employee Name: [% emp.name %]
    Username: [% emp.username %]
    E-Mail: [% emp.username %]@[% domain %]

[% END -%]
```

Here's the output from this example:

```
---===Employees===---

Employee Name: Frank Sanbeans
Username: frank.sanbeans
E-Mail: frank.sanbeans@example.com

Employee Name: Sandy Sanbeans
Username: sandy.sanbeans
E-Mail: sandy.sanbeans@example.com
```

You can also nest FOREACH loops. The loop special variable will be scoped correctly within the nests and when exiting from the nest into the main FOREACH loop.

WHILE Directive

The WHILE directive works like its native Perl counterpart. The syntax is similar to that of FOREACH insofar as [% END %] denotes the end of the block to be executed by the WHILE loop:

```
[%- count = 0 -%]
[% WHILE count < 10 -%]
Count is [% count %]
[% count = count + 1 -%]
[%- END -%]
```

The NEXT and LAST options are also available within a WHILE loop, and they work like their native Perl counterparts.

Tip There is a default limit of 1,000 loops within a WHILE directive, to prevent never-ending loop conditions. You can change this value by setting $Template::Directive::WHILE_MAX.

Conditionals

The Template Toolkit provides IF-ELSIF-ELSE, UNLESS, SWITCH, and CASE types of conditionals. Like FOREACH loops, conditionals are terminated with [% END %].

IF-ELSIF-ELSE and UNLESS

Using the IF-ELSIF-ELSE structure is rather simple in the template language:

```
[% IF variable = = "true" %]
    [% somethingelse = 43 %]
    If was true.
[% ELSIF variable = "false" %]
    [% somethingelse = 12 %]
    It's false.
[% ELSE %]
```

```
    The variable was neither true nor false.
[% END %]
```

Notice that within the IF and ELSIF sections, the equality test is two equals signs separated by a space:

```
= =
```

This is different from Perl-ish equality testing, which is either eq or two equals signs with no space between them:

```
==
```

The UNLESS conditional is used like its Perl counterpart, as follows:

```
[% UNLESS variable = = "true" %]
```

SWITCH and CASE

Also like Perl, SWITCH and CASE type conditionals are available, though technically SWITCH is not native in Perl, but rather is part of the switch module (though it will be standard in Perl 6). With this much commonality between Perl and the template language, you can see that if you know Perl, it should be easy to make the leap to the Template Toolkit language.

```
[% SWITCH searchengine %]
    [% CASE "google" %]
        Google was chosen.
    [% CASE "yahoo" %]
        Yahoo was chosen.
    [% CASE %]
        No choice was made
[% END %]
```

Notice that the last CASE statement contained no value for the variable. This is the default case if no others match.

Exception Handling

Exception handling and error catching is necessary when working with templates, just as it is when working with Perl. This is because templates can get quite complex, incorporating connections to databases and external files and programs. The Template Toolkit provides TRY-CATCH blocks to trap errors within template code.

The TRY directive introduces a template and other information for processing. The TRY directive continues processing until a corresponding END is encountered. If an error occurs, the code within the CATCH block is executed. Consider the example in Listing 12-6.

Listing 12-6. *TRY-CATCH Block*

```
[% TRY %]
    This code doesn't do much except maybe fail.
    [% CALL othercode %]
    [% INCLUDE sometemplatefile %]
```

```
[% CATCH %]
    Error: [% error.type %]: [% error.info %]
[% END %]
```

Along with some leading and trailing blank lines (not shown), the output from this example is as follows:

```
This code doesn't do much except maybe fail.


    Error: file: sometemplatefile: not found
```

As you can see in the preceding example, a special object called error is created within the CATCH block. This error object has two properties, type and info, both of which are printed. You can use the error type to perform more granular exception handling. Listing 12-7 shows the file type error being caught.

Listing 12-7. *Adding the Error Type to the CATCH Block*

```
[% TRY %]
    This code doesn't do much except maybe fail.
    [% CALL othercode %]
    [% INCLUDE sometemplatefile %]
[% CATCH file %]
    File Error: [% error.info %]
[% CATCH %]
    Error: [% error.type %]: [% error.info %]
[% END %]
```

The output from Listing 12-7 is as follows:

```
This code doesn't do much except maybe fail.


    File Error: sometemplatefile: not found
```

The code sample used two new items. First, the type of error was checked and caught if it was a file type (as would be reported by error.type), and a default CATCH block was also created.

One additional feature of the TRY-CATCH syntax is a FINAL block. Content and code within a FINAL block get processed regardless of what happens within the TRY-CATCH blocks. This can be helpful for printing footer or other information that's necessary for the template you're processing.

Blocks of Perl

As if all of the power of template processing with Template Toolkit shown already isn't enough, you can also execute blocks of pure Perl code within a template by defining the code within a PERL block inside of the template. The following example shows a Perl block in action:

```
[% PERL -%]
    print "Hello, this is Perl!\n";
[% END -%]
```

Running this template through `tpage` yields the following output:

```
Hello, this is Perl!
```

If you run this template through `tpage` (`tpage listing12-8.tt`, for example) and you receive no output—except maybe something flashing on the screen—then you need to enable the `EVAL_PERL` option. The quickest way to do this is by using the `--eval_perl` command-line option with `tpage` (`tpage --eval_perl listing12-8.tt`). You can also enable this option within your configuration file.

■**Note** Also available is the `RAWPERL` directive, which I don't cover in this chapter. For more information on the `RAWPERL` directive, refer to the `perldoc` for `Template::Manual::Directives`.

Plug-ins

Plug-ins provide interfaces to the world outside your template. Several standard plug-ins come with the Template Toolkit, including a plug-in for date functions, one for the CGI module, and one for the DBI module, just to name a few. You can specify and code your own plug-ins as well.

Date Plug-in

You use a plug-in by first calling it with the `USE` directive:

```
[% USE date %]
```

The date is then available throughout the template by calling the `date` variable, as follows:

```
[% USE date -%]
[% date.format %]
```

Here's the output from this template:

```
21:09:07 30-Aug-2005
```

The date plug-in uses the `strftime()` routine to format dates. This means you have incredible flexibility in formatting the date to fit your needs. The following code shows one way to output just the date with the date plug-in:

```
[% USE date(format = '%m/%d/%Y') %]
[% date.format %]
```

The output from this code is as follows:

```
08/30/2005
```

■**Note** See the `date` manual page (`man date`) for more information on the date formatting options available.

You can also change the date format and manipulate the date. See the `perldoc` for `Template::Plugin::Date` for more information.

CGI Module Plug-in

The CGI module is available as a plug-in, too. Bring the CGI module into the namespace with a USE directive:

```
[% USE q = CGI %]
```

You can then access the subroutines within the CGI module using dot notation, for example:

```
[% USE q = CGI %]
[% q.start_html %]
[% q.h1 %]Hello
[% q.end_html %]
```

The output from this template is as follows:

```
<!DOCTYPE html
        PUBLIC "-//W3C//DTD XHTML 1.0 Transitional//EN"
         "http://www.w3.org/TR/xhtml1/DTD/xhtml1-transitional.dtd">
<html xmlns="http://www.w3.org/1999/xhtml" lang="en-US"
  xml:lang="en-US"><head><title>Untitled Document</title>
</head><body>
<h1 />Hello
</body></html>
```

In addition to the standard CGI subroutines and methods, a `params()` method specific to the Template Toolkit is provided. This method enables named parameter processing within the template. For example, an HTML form parameter of `username` could be accessed as follows:

```
[% params.username %]
```

■**Tip** Be sure not to confuse the `params()` method that is specific to the toolkit with the `param` subroutine provided by the CGI module. Both can be used here, so it can get confusing. Use whichever is comfortable for you. Assuming a CGI assignment of q, as in the previous example, you could even do something like `q.param('username')`.

DBI Module Plug-in

The DBI module can be used as a plug-in as well:

```
[% USE DBI('dbi:mysql:databasename, 'username', 'password') %]
```

Queries can be performed by calling the `query` method:

```
[% DBI.query('SELECT * from tablename') %]
```

For non-SELECT statements, a do method is provided:

```
[% DBI.do('DELETE FROM tablename ') %]
```

See the perldoc for Template::Plugin::DBI for more information on the DBI module, and refer to the perldoc for Template::Manual::Plugins for information on the myriad other plug-ins available with the Template Toolkit.

Note It is difficult to cover everything you need to know about something as complex and powerful as the Template Toolkit in a single chapter of a beginner-level book such as this. I invite you to serve yourself large helpings of the perldoc for Template::Manual and its related documentation. There you'll learn about a number of subtleties to the items covered in this chapter and also some useful aspects of the Template Toolkit that I wasn't able to cover here.

Building a Web Site with Template::Toolkit

So far you've covered a lot of information on the Template Toolkit. It's now time to look at some of the aspects of building and maintaining a web site using the Template Toolkit. When maintaining a site with the Template Toolkit, a good approach is to operate at the directory level for global changes, which means using ttree. When making everyday changes to an individual page, use tpage to process that file rather than processing all of the templates again.

Considering how templating can help you is likely the first step in converting to or designing a web site for the Template Toolkit. You'll likely take advantage of headers and footers, since these elements are relatively common and static over most pages of a web site. Your needs and goals for the site will determine which additional pieces of the Template Toolkit that you want to use. These might include dynamic content or complex variables or plug-ins or other parts of the toolkit.

In this section, you'll first walk through the process of creating a site configuration file, and then you'll build the site itself.

Creating a Site Configuration File

When you create and maintain a web site using the Template Toolkit, a project configuration file is essential for keeping templates separate from output files and also to configure the behavior of the processor. You'll initially use three primary directories with the toolkit:

- A source directory to hold your template source files

- An output directory to hold the final HTML pages

- A library directory to will hold common bits of code that you may use in the project

You'll bring these in with an INCLUDE directive (and related directives), as follows:

```
mkdir webproject
cd webproject
mkdir source output lib
```

With those directories created, you can start creating your configuration file for the project. Recall from earlier in the chapter that a sample configuration file called .ttreerc was created when you first ran ttree. You'll use this file as the base for this project, so copy it into your project directory. From within the webproject directory

```
cp ~/.ttreerc ./project.cfg
```

edit the project.cfg file and add configuration options to direct ttree toward your source, output, and library directories. Note that by default, these are placed at the bottom of the sample file, but they are commented out. Either uncomment and edit those or add your own. Either way, the three lines should look like this:

```
src = /home/youruser/webproject/source
dest = /home/youruser/webproject/output
lib = /home/youruser/webproject/lib
```

You can use multiple library directories by specifying each on its own lib line in the configuration file.

Other default options in the configuration file include the following (note that if these are missing, you should add them for now and tweak the configuration later when you become more comfortable with the Template Toolkit):

```
# print summary of what's going on
verbose

# recurse into any sub-directories and process files
recurse

# regexen of things that aren't templates and should be ignored
ignore = \b(CVS|RCS)\b
ignore = ^#

# ditto for things that should be copied rather than processed.
copy = \.png$
copy = \.gif$
```

As to the first two options, verbose and recurse, I've always found that it's helpful to get more information until I'm comfortable with what's happening in the background. The recurse option tells the processor to look in subdirectories within your source tree for additional files to process. This is an extremely helpful option, especially on medium- and large-sized web sites that have multiple directories of files and images.

The ignore options set up some file types that won't be copied from the source to the destination directory. And speaking of copying, the copy option specifies files that should be copied. Two types of images are included in this example. If you have image (or other) files that should be copied from the source to the destination output directory, include them on another copy line and note the use of regular expressions.

If you'll use headers and footers, you can specify that those should be pre- and post-processed with the pre_process and post_process configuration options:

```
pre_process = header.tt
post_process = footer.tt
```

The full configuration file, `project.cfg`, follows in Listing 12-8. Place this file in the `webproject` directory.

Listing 12-8. *Sample Project Configuration File*

```
src = /home/youruser/webproject/source
dest = /home/youruser/webproject/output
lib = /home/youruser/webproject/lib

verbose
recurse

ignore = \b(CVS|RCS)\b
ignore = ^#

copy = \.png$
copy = \.gif$

pre_process = header.tt
post_process = footer.tt
```

Building the Site

Now that you've created both the directory structure and the configuration file, it's time to create a couple of web pages to be processed through the Template Toolkit. The pages you create in this section will use the configuration file shown in the previous section, along with the `pre_process` and `post_process` options pointing to `header.tt` and `footer.tt`, respectively.

Place the template files for this project in the `webproject/source` directory created earlier. Place the `header.tt` and `footer.tt` files in the `webproject/lib` directory.

The content for the `lib/header.tt` file is as follows:

```
<!DOCTYPE html
        PUBLIC "-//W3C//DTD XHTML 1.0 Transitional//EN"
         "http://www.w3.org/TR/xhtml1/DTD/xhtml1-transitional.dtd">
<html xmlns="http://www.w3.org/1999/xhtml"
        lang="en-US" xml:lang="en-US"><head>
<title>[% template.title %]</title>
</head><body>
```

Please note that the bolded line of code will cause the META variable `template.title` to be placed into the output. Each page has its own title in the web site. The value for this title is stored within each page itself. Therefore, since the header file is preprocessed, the title wouldn't be available to the header when it is being processed. This is where the META directive comes into play. As you'll see within the actual page, the `title` variable will be defined with the META directive. This does, however, mean that the `title` variable must be prefixed with the `template` special variable.

The `lib/footer.tt` file contains the following:

```
[% USE date(format = '%Y') -%]
<p>Copyright (c) [% date.format %] Steve Suehring</p>
</body></html>
```

Within the footer, the date plug-in is used. For copyright notices, only the year is necessary, so the date format is set appropriately.

Finally, the actual page is created. This page is stored in the source directory and is called index.html in this example. The source/index.html file contains the following:

```
[% META title = "Home Page" -%]
<p> Welcome to the home page </p>
```

Obviously, the page is quite simple in this example. Notice, however, that the title for the page is defined and is done so with the META directive, so that the title will be available to the preprocessed header.tt file.

With the three files created, it's time to run ttree. You should have the following directory and file layout:

```
Directory: /home/youruser/webproject
File: /home/youruser/webproject/project.cfg

Directory: /home/youruser/webproject/output

Directory: /home/youruser/webproject/source
File: /home/youruser/webproject/source/index.html

Directory: /home/youruser/webproject/lib
File: /home/youruser/webproject/lib/header.tt
File: /home/youruser/webproject/lib/footer.tt
```

From within the webproject directory, run ttree and point it toward your configuration file:

```
ttree -f project.cfg
```

Here's the output:

```
ttree 2.78 (Template Toolkit version 2.14)

      Source: /home/suehring/webproject/source
 Destination: /home/suehring/webproject/output
Include Path: [ /home/suehring/webproject/lib ]
      Ignore: [ \b(CVS|RCS)\b, ^#, \b(CVS|RCS)\b, ^# ]
        Copy: [ \.png$, \.gif$, \.png$, \.gif$ ]
      Accept: [   ]
      Suffix: [   ]

  + index.html
```

If you run into problems, ensure your paths are correct and that you've placed the files in the correct locations.

The contents of output/index.html will now be as follows:

```
<!DOCTYPE html
        PUBLIC "-//W3C//DTD XHTML 1.0 Transitional//EN"
         "http://www.w3.org/TR/xhtml1/DTD/xhtml1-transitional.dtd">
<html xmlns="http://www.w3.org/1999/xhtml"
        lang="en-US" xml:lang="en-US"><head>
<title>Home Page</title>
</head><body>

<p> Welcome to the home page </p>
<p>Copyright (c) 2005 Steve Suehring</p>
</body></html>
```

Notice that the three files have been joined, the title called in the header but defined within the page has been properly filled in, and the date has been placed correctly in the footer.

Building a second page and subsequent pages gets easier, as you now have the infrastructure in place to process the templates for the project. For example, you can create a web form using the CGI plug-in as follows:

```
[% META title = "Order Form" -%]
[% USE localcgi = CGI -%]
[% localcgi.start_form(action => 'order.cgi');
   localcgi.textfield(name => 'username'
                                    size => '25');
   localcgi.p;
   localcgi.submit(name => 'submit_user');
%]
```

The file is called order.html and is located in the source directory. Running ttree with both the index.html and order.html files in place yields this output:

```
ttree 2.78 (Template Toolkit version 2.14)

     Source: /home/suehring/webproject/source
Destination: /home/suehring/webproject/output
Include Path: [ /home/suehring/webproject/lib ]
     Ignore: [ \b(CVS|RCS)\b, ^#, \b(CVS|RCS)\b, ^# ]
       Copy: [ \.png$, \.gif$, \.png$, \.gif$ ]
     Accept: [  ]
     Suffix: [  ]

  + order.html
  - index.html                    (not modified)
```

Notice that the index.html file was not processed by ttree this time through because it had not been modified since the last run of ttree. You can change this by adding the -a option to the ttree command or by adding the all option to the configuration file for the project.

Security Considerations

For the most part, if you merely use the Template Toolkit to manage a web site by keeping common text such as headers and footers, then there is very little to worry about security-wise. However, as mentioned throughout this chapter, the Template Toolkit is quite powerful. With that power comes the ability to do some things that can lead to security problems. One such problem is unauthorized information disclosure through the template. Storing items such as database names, usernames, and passwords within template files can lead to this information being discovered by a potential attacker. If you use advanced options, such as CGI processing, through the Template Toolkit, you must take care to ensure that input data is properly sanitized. Again, if the Template Toolkit is used to merely generate these pages rather than process the input, then the risk is essentially negated.

Summary

The Template Toolkit's unrivaled power and flexibility make it an excellent choice for managing a web site of any size. In this chapter, you learned that through the definition of both static and dynamic variables, the use of looping and conditionals, and the large number of plug-ins, the Template Toolkit can also make the management of a complex site rather easy. This chapter covered several available plug-ins that really extend the usefulness of the toolkit. As you've seen, the Template Toolkit can be used for much more than simple web page generation.

If this chapter has piqued your interest in the Template Toolkit, I encourage you to read the excellent documentation available on this software. Begin with the `perldoc` for `Template::Manual`, which will point you toward even more specific documentation for the various aspects of the Template Toolkit.

## CHAPTER 13

Perl Web Sites with Mason

The Mason software program creates dynamic web sites by enabling Perl code to be inserted into HTML.[1] Programming languages such as PHP or ASP.NET operate under a similar premise. While each of these languages has its own set of advantages, neither of them are Perl. And since this book is devoted to Perl, I'll cover only dynamic web sites with Perl and Mason.

I use Mason for my own web site (http://www.braingia.org), and I've done consulting with clients where Mason has been the recommended approach for their sites. Not only is Mason easy to use, but it's also powerful. Elements such as headers and footers (the text at the top and bottom of web site pages), site maps, copyright notices, terms and conditions, contact information, and so on—sometimes referred to collectively as the "look and feel" of a site—are all relatively common on each page within a given site. Using Mason, developers can quickly create, for example, a common header and footer to be used across all pages within a site. Even though the pages are similar, however, they are not exactly the same. For example, the titles of pages usually change from page to page. Mason enables arguments to be passed into its components to handle such differences. As you'll learn in the chapter, components are central to working with Mason.

With that, it's time to jump into a quick introduction to Mason. Then you'll learn how to install Mason, followed by coverage of Mason's syntax. Finally, you'll walk through building a sample site using Mason.

Introducing Mason

As stated previously, Mason enables Perl code to be interspersed within HTML and other such web languages. Though it can operate in other modes, Mason requires mod_perl to run. The intention of the developer is to create dynamic web sites, rendered at runtime or the time of the request/response cycle. For example, here's a fully functional web page that could be served with an Apache server running mod_perl and Mason:

---

1. Other tools to embed Perl are available as well, one of which is called Embperl.
    (http://perl.apache.org/embperl).

```
<html><head><title>Song List</title></head>
% my $song = "Driven";
% my $artist = "Rush";
<body>
<h1>Steve's Music Stream</h1>
<p>The current song playing on Steve's Apache music stream is <% $song %>
by <% $artist %>.</p>
</body>
</html>
```

The output from this code when viewed in a web browser looks as shown in Figure 13-1.

Figure 13-1. *A Mason example*

As you'll learn a little later, Mason is built around an object called a *component*, which is nothing more than a file that is processed by Mason. Within that file can be a line or two of code, HTML, or something else entirely. Alternatively, a component can be a complex Perl program. A component is essentially what you make it.

At the very top of the component hierarchy is something called the *top-level component*. The top-level component is the first component called when Mason processes a request for a page. It could be a simple HTML page; a page with some Perl code on it (like that shown in the preceding example); or a component that calls other components, which in turn call other components, and so on.

Mason can do far more than was shown in the previous example. For example, you can load database queries, pass values between components, and handle pages completely dynamically with Mason—the pages don't even need to exist on the filesystem!

The rest of this chapter is devoted to showing you the basic syntax for Mason, but please be aware that there is far more to Mason than I was able to cover in this chapter. I invite you to supplement the material in this chapter with information from the Mason perldocs and the Mason web site (http://www.masonhq.com).

Installing Mason

Mason is already included with many Linux distributions, saving the need to install it from source. Debian, for example, includes Mason in the `libhtml-mason-perl` package along with other packages containing documentation and examples. Use the package search capabilities within your distribution to find out if Mason is available as a package with your distribution.

If Mason isn't available with your distribution, or if you want to compile from source for some other reason, you can download Mason from `http://www.masonhq.com`. Although they're not technically required to use Mason, you'll need Apache and `mod_perl`. You could get by without them and still use Mason, but this chapter will not cover any of those other uses. You will also need Perl to install Mason (though I suspect that if you didn't have Perl by now, you might have had trouble with the previous 12 chapters!). Some additional modules are required to install Mason, including the following:

- `Class::Container`

- `Exception::Class`

- `File::Spec` (this may already be included in your version of Perl)

- `Params::Validate`

- `Scalar::Util`

Optionally, you can also install the following:

- `Test::More`

- `Cache::Cache`

You can obtain these modules from your favorite CPAN mirror.

■**Note** `Apache::Request` and `CGI.pm` aren't technically required to compile the Mason software, but they are required if you'd like to follow along with the examples in this chapter, and you'll likely need them for programming Mason anyway. (You likely have them both already.)

Compiling Mason

Mason is downloaded as a gzipped `tar` archive and will have a filename like `HTML-Mason-N.NN.tar.gz`, where `NNN` is the version number, such as 1.28. Unzip and unarchive the file:

`tar -zxvf HTML-Mason-1.28.tar.gz`

and change into the `HTML-Mason-N.NN` directory:

`cd HTML-Mason-1.28`

Once you're inside the directory, run the Perl-style `Makefile.PL` by typing

`perl Makefile.PL`

This program will check for prerequisites and output the following:

```
Checking for Scalar::Util...ok
Checking for File::Spec...ok
Checking for CGI...ok
Checking for Cache::Cache...ok
Checking for Exception::Class...ok
Checking for Test::More...ok
Checking for Params::Validate...ok
Checking for Class::Container...ok
Checking for Apache::Request...ok
Checking if your kit is complete...
Looks good
Writing Makefile for HTML::Mason
```

If you're missing any of the prerequisites, you'll be notified and likely required to install the missing prerequisites before continuing. If you receive a notice that the make file has been written, as shown in the example, then you can continue the installation by typing the following:

```
make
```

Though obviously dependent on the available resources, the make process will go quickly. At this point, you could simply install the software, but I recommend running the tests available prior to installing the software. Doing so can save headaches later if the software mysteriously doesn't work. Run the tests by typing

```
make test
```

The tests will run, producing output similar to the following:

```
PERL_DL_NONLAZY=1 /usr/bin/perl "-MExtUtils::Command::MM" "-e" "
\$ENV{PORT}=8228; \$ENV{APACHE_DIR}=q^^; \$ENV{MASON_MAINTAINER}=0;
test_harness(0, 'blib/lib', 'blib/arch')" t/*.t
t/01-syntax...........ok
t/02-sections.........ok
t/02a-filter..........ok
t/04-misc.............ok
t/05-request..........ok
t/06-compiler.........ok
t/06a-compiler_obj....ok
t/07-interp...........ok
t/08-ah...............skipped
        all skipped: no reason given
t/09-component........ok
t/09a-comp_content....ok
t/10-cache............ok
t/10a-cache-1.0x......ok
t/11-inherit..........ok
t/12-taint............ok
t/13-errors...........ok
t/14-cgi..............ok
t/14a-fake_apache.....ok
```

```
t/15-subclass.........ok
t/16-live_cgi.........skipped
        all skipped: no reason given
t/17-print...........ok
t/18-leak............ok
t/19-subrequest.......ok
All tests successful, 2 tests skipped.
Files=23, Tests=393, 33 wallclock secs (15.66 cusr +  0.96 csys = 16.62
CPU)
```

If any of the tests fail, refer to the Mason documentation at http://www.masonhq.com. It's actually rather uncommon for tests to fail at this point, but it can happen.

If the tests were successful, as they were in the output shown in the example, you can install the software. To install the software, you will likely need to be the root user. Run the installation by typing the following:

```
make install
```

The next section guides you through the steps required to configure Mason for use with your Apache installation.

Configuring Apache and Mason

With the help of the configuration in Apache, Mason can be automatically called to interpret or process files of various extensions or for an entire directory or site. Apache directives are used to load the Mason Apache module and then to configure a handler for certain files or directories. Within the Mason-related Apache configuration you can (and likely will) use Mason-specific configuration parameters to configure and change the behavior of Mason when it processes your templates. A configuration for Apache might look like this:

```
PerlModule HTML::Mason::ApacheHandler
<FilesMatch "\.mhtml$">
 SetHandler perl-script
 PerlHandler HTML::Mason::ApacheHandler
</FilesMatch>
```

This configuration would be placed within the httpd.conf file for Apache, and files with the extension .mhtml would be processed by Mason. You could also limit this processing to the files within a given directory, as shown here:

```
PerlModule HTML::Mason::ApacheHandler
<Directory /path/to/mason/files>
<FilesMatch "\.mhtml$">
 SetHandler perl-script
 PerlHandler HTML::Mason::ApacheHandler
</FilesMatch>
</Directory>
```

In practice, you'll find that it's helpful to define certain types of files to be processed by Mason limited to a given directory or site. For example, the configurations shown might be placed in a <VirtualHost> directive within the Apache configuration file. Using this, you wouldn't have to define a special file extension for your Mason files.

Within the Mason configuration area in the Apache configuration file, you may find it necessary to set one or more additional Mason-specific configuration parameters. These parameters can be set within the Apache configuration file, when making a subrequest, or within a Mason script. There are different names for the parameters based on where they are being set. For example, a parameter would be called args_method if set within a subrequest, but it would be called MasonArgsMethod if set within the Apache configuration file. For the purposes of this section, we'll use the name of the parameter as it would appear in the Apache configuration file.

You can find a full list of configuration parameters on the Mason web site at http://www.masonhq.com/docs/manual/Params.html. Some of the parameters you may find necessary to set within the Apache configuration file include those listed in Table 13-1.

Table 13-1. *Select Configuration Parameters for Use with Mason*

Parameter	Values	Description
MasonArgsMethod	mod_perl or CGI	Used to set the way in which arguments from GETs and POSTs are unpacked. The default is mod_perl. You may need to set the value to CGI while converting the site to work with Mason.
MasonAutoSentHeaders	true or false	Used to determine whether or not Mason will automatically send HTTP headers to the client. The default is true.
MasonCompRoot	No default	Used to set the default path for the component root. The component root will be explained later.
MasonDataDir	No default	Used to set the directory that Mason uses to write temporary files for some features.
MasonUseStrict	true or false	Used to configure whether or not the Mason files should take advantage of the use strict pragma. The default is true.

When using parameters within the Apache configuration file, the PerlSetVar and PerlAddVar directives must be used. For example, to set the MasonCompRoot parameter, you would use the following line in the Apache configuration file:

```
PerlSetVar MasonCompRoot /path/to/comp_root
```

In my own configuration, I'm running Apache within a chroot and have various virtual hosts running on the server for which I have different configurations from the main Apache server process. I've therefore set both the MasonCompRoot and MasonDataDir parameters within the <VirtualHost> configuration on the server.

I'm now using Mason for serving every file that has an .html extension on the site, which I configured using the <FilesMatch> directive shown earlier. However, when I initially converted to Mason, I used a <FilesMatch> directive of .mhtml.

I've also had to bring some legacy CGI scripts over to the site. In doing so, I found that I needed to set the MasonArgsMethod to CGI, away from its default of mod_perl. I suspect (or hope) that I'll have time to port these scripts to mod_perl by the time you're reading this book.

In addition to that basic configuration, I've also tightened the security for the site by sending a "404: Not Found" error whenever someone tries to access one of the Mason-specific components that I might or might not use. I accomplish this with the help of a <LocationMatch> directive and Apache::Constants::NOT_FOUND, as directed by the perldoc for HTML::Mason::Admin.

Here is the full configuration for Mason as it appears in my httpd.conf. Your configuration may vary from this, but my hope is to pass along some practical information about a real-world implementation of Mason.

```
PerlModule HTML::Mason::ApacheHandler
<FilesMatch "\.html$">
    SetHandler perl-script
    PerlHandler HTML::Mason::ApacheHandler
        PerlSetVar MasonCompRoot /home/suehring/www
        PerlSetVar MasonDataDir /home/suehring/mason
        #sws 5/27/2005
        PerlSetVar MasonArgsMethod CGI
</FilesMatch>
<LocationMatch "(\.m(html|pl|ase)|dhandler|autohandler)$">
        SetHandler perl-script
        PerlInitHandler Apache::Constants::NOT_FOUND
</LocationMatch>
```

With the appropriate configuration for your Apache installation in place, you can restart the Apache server.

Mason Syntax

It's time to create a "Hello World" example, Mason-style. In general, I'm fed up with "Hello World" examples, though, so I'm going to create something even more annoying: a page that uses the <blink> HTML tag. I'll do this by wrapping the output inside of a <%perl> block in the page. Listing 13-1 shows the simple text for this page.

Listing 13-1. *A Mason-Style Page Using <%perl> to Print a Blinking Tag*

```
<%perl> print "<blink>This is the blinkin' example.</blink><P>\n"; </%perl>
```

The page can be saved within the directory you configured as the MasonCompRoot and viewed in a web browser. When I viewed the page, I saw blinking text. It's difficult to illustrate blinking text in a screenshot, however, so Figure 13-2 shows the text when it appears.

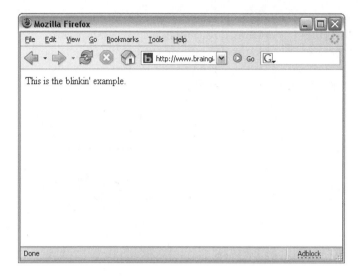

Figure 13-2. *The output from the <blink> tag example*

As with any terse example of this nature, it only serves to show that your Mason installation is working and not much else. In addition, there are multiple ways to create the output shown in Figure 13-2. I chose one of the more verbose ways to do it, since it provides a good transition into some of the less verbose methods shown later in this section.

In this section, we'll start off by examining components, and then we'll move on to look at request objects, handlers, and subrequests.

Components

As mentioned previously, central to working with Mason is the component object. The Mason Developer's Manual describes a component as "a mix of Perl and HTML" and the "basic building block and computational unit." A component can be a portion of a page that contains Mason sections, or it can be an entire page, or it can be anything in between. Components can call other components, passing information between them and the current request.

The example shown in Listing 13-1 is itself a component. A slightly more complex example is shown in Listing 13-2.

Listing 13-2. *A Slightly More Complex Mason Example*

```
% my $time = time;
The time is <% $time %>, thanks for visiting.
```

The results of this example appear in Figure 13-3.

Figure 13-3. *The output from Listing 13-2, which uses a slightly more complex Mason example to process a variable*

As you can see from Listing 13-2 and Figure 13-3, the variable $time is substituted at the time the template is processed. Using the browser's Reload function shows that the time keeps changing on every refresh, unless of course you reload more than once in a second.

In Listing 13-2, you also saw another type of syntax, a single percent sign (%). A % is used to indicate a single line of Perl code within a Masonized page. We'll cover the syntax of components in more detail in the next section, and then we'll move on to look at the arguments of components as well as return values.

Syntax

The syntax of components is fairly simple when you consider how powerful they are. Blocks of code to be processed are indicated by a few types of delimiters, as you saw in the examples in Listings 13-1 and 13-2. Items within <%perl> and </%perl> are evaluated as blocks of Perl. This syntax is usually used when multiple lines of Perl are necessary. Items within <% and %> are evaluated as single expressions. This syntax is frequently used for interpolation of variables or single statements interspersed within the text of the web page. Finally, % is used to indicate a single line of Perl code on a page. This syntax is frequently used with conditionals and loops. Consider the example in Listing 13-3.

Listing 13-3. *A Conditional Within a Mason Page*

```
% my $name = "Steve";
Welcome to the page,
% if ($name eq "Steve") {
  thank you for visiting again <% $name %>.
```

```
% } else {
 it is nice of you to visit.
% }
```

The output from this example is shown in Figure 13-4.

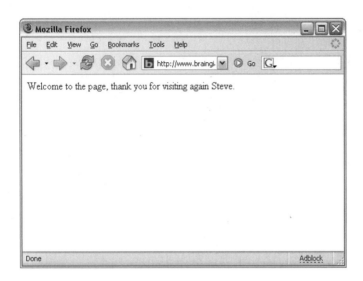

Figure 13-4. *An example using a conditional*

Since the variable was predefined as `"Steve"` in the example, the conditional in the `if()` statement matched. If the value of the `$name` variable is changed, then the `else` will take effect. Consider the modified code in Listing 13-4.

Listing 13-4. *A Slightly Modified Conditional Within a Mason Page*

```
% my $name = "sssSteve";
Welcome to the page,
% if ($name eq "Steve") {
 thank you for visiting again <% $name %>.
% } else {
 it is nice of you to visit.
% }
```

The result of this code is shown in Figure 13-5.

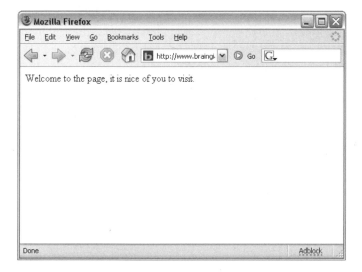

Figure 13-5. *The modified conditional code in action*

■**Tip** In practice, I use either <% and %> or a single % on each line of code when I have just a few lines to process. I find it easier to type % on each line rather than the more formal <%perl> and </%perl>, unless there's another reason for using <%perl>, an example of which you'll see later.

Four additional types of tags are used rather frequently with Mason. These types include <& and &> to indicate another component call. Consider this akin to a function call; arguments can be carried with the call. Another type is <%init> and </%init>, which indicate a block of code to be processed before the main page is processed. The <%once> and </%once> tags are used for code that should run once at component load time, such as the use pragma to import the DBI into a namespace (use DBI;). A final type of delimiter or markup for Mason is <%args> and </%args>, which process the arguments being passed into the component.

Other types of markup are available with Mason, but the seven tag types described in this section are the ones you'll likely encounter right away when getting to know Mason. Table 13-2 presents a recap of the seven frequently used Mason delimiters.

Table 13-2. *Frequently Used Mason Delimiters*

Delimiter	Purpose
<% ... %>	Evaluate statements and interpolate values inline.
%	Execute single lines of Perl, conditionals, and loops.
<& ... &>	Call another component.
<%args> ... </%args>	Process incoming arguments to a component.
<%init> ... </%init>	Process prior to the main page.
<%once> ... </%once>	Process once at component initialization.
<%perl> ... </%perl>	Execute multiple lines of Perl.

Still other tags are available for use, such as those for initialization and cleanup. Notably, the <%shared> tag is helpful when writing CGIs with Mason. Variables declared with <%shared> are initialized with every request as opposed to being initialized with each component, as you'd find with <%once>. Therefore, using <%shared> is a good approach for variable declaration within a CGI application.

For example, when a component is initialized the first time, you'll likely want to share the DBI namespace for use across the component's lifetime. However, any variables used within the CGI should live only on a per-request basis. The code would therefore look something like this:

```
<%once>
use DBI;
</%once>
<%shared>
my $variable1;
my $othervariable;
</%shared>
```

Arguments

When you call a component with Mason, it's common to pass one or more arguments. For example, you might use Mason to manage common headers and footers of web pages. The header's HTML needs to set the page title and other parameters specific to the page being built. When calling the component, you pass along arguments such as the title to the component being called.

Now that I've tried to explain this concept in writing (perhaps with limited success) twice, I'll show you an example in code that may help clarify things. The example in Listing 13-5 is pulled directly from my web site's home page, http://www.braingia.org.

Listing 13-5. *Calling a Mason Component with Arguments*

```
<& /header.mase, title=>"Braingia.org - Steve Suehring's Home Page",maintitle=>
    "Intarweb" &>
(HTML continues hereafter...)
```

From the example in Listing 13-5, you can see the opening tag for a component, <&, followed by the name of the component, in this case header.mase. Next are two arguments, title and maintitle. These arguments are then defined within the <%args> ... </%args> section of the file header.mase.

The header.mase file begins by declaring the arguments:

```
<%args>
$title
$maintitle
</%args>
```

The file continues with HTML and JavaScript, and eventually within the file the standard HTML <title> ... </title> tag is used:

```
<title><% $title %></title>
```

Somewhat later in the markup contained in header.mase, the $maintitle variable appears:

```
<%perl> unless ($maintitle eq "Intarweb") { </%perl>
<a href="http://www.braingia.org/">Braingia.org Home </a>  /
<% $maintitle %>
<%perl> } </%perl>
```

Since the lines wrapped in <%perl> and </%perl> contain only one line of code, they could have been written with a single %. However, the page source was indented for easier viewing; therefore, because the % needs to be placed at the beginning of the line, it would have broken the indenting. (Note that indenting is not represented in the code sample shown here.)

When this Masonized code is viewed in a web browser, it results in a page like the one shown in Figure 13-6. As you can see from the figure, the title and maintitle have been placed in the page.

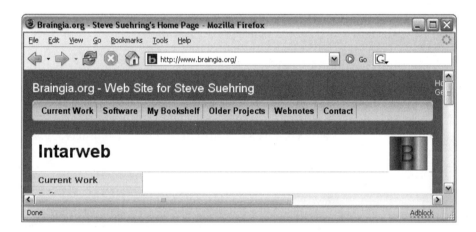

Figure 13-6. *The Mason page when viewed in a web browser*

Return Values

Mason components can also return values when called, as opposed to the normal behavior of components to return undef. The return() function makes this possible. Using a return from a component enables code reuse by enabling you to define commonly used functions inside their own components. Having a component return a value is as simple as calling Perl's standard return() function. Consider this example, which returns the temperature:

```
<%init>
my $temperature = 4;
return $temperature;
</%init>
```

Calling a component with a return value is not necessarily intuitive. Rather than calling the component with the normal <& ... &> syntax, you're required to call it with the soon-to-be-introduced $m->comp('component_name') syntax. So, for example, to obtain the temperature from the code just shown, you might save the component within a file called get_temp and then call that component from your normal Mason component:

```
% my $temp = $m->comp('get_temp');
```

At runtime, Mason will interpret this line, call the function located in the file get_temp, and place its return value into the $temp variable.

Request Objects

Two request objects are automatically provided within a Mason component: $r and $m. The $r request object is the Apache request object from mod_perl. As such, the methods available with $r when programming in a mod_perl environment are automatically sent to the component in Mason. Both $r and $m are specific to the current request being handled by Apache.

The $m object is a Mason-specific object that gives access to various Mason parameters, methods, and other components. You can control caching, read in files, and perform many advanced tasks with $m. For example, you can call other components through $m with the following syntax:

```
$m->comp(component_name, arguments)
```

When you call a component in this way, anything returned by the component is sent to the normal output stream. This is fine for cases where the component returns HTML, as in the header example shown earlier. However, when a component's output shouldn't be sent to the output stream, the scomp function is available. Using scomp to call a component results in its output being sent to a string as opposed to the stream:

```
$m->scomp(component_name, arguments)
```

The Mason method abort() aborts or stops the processing of a component. This can be helpful in cases where you want to immediately stop processing and throw an error if a certain condition is met—for example, if a user or IP address isn't authorized to view a document.

```
$m->abort()
```

For more information on the abort() method, see the perldoc for HTML::Mason::Exception::Abort. For a complete description of the Apache request object, see the perldoc for HTML::Mason::Request and refer back to Chapters 10 and 11 of this book. Additionally, Apache::Request contains pertinent information for methods and attributes available through $r.

Handlers

Handlers are used in specific cases for executing code either prior to the component being processed or when a component cannot be found. A handler essentially takes care of special cases where you might want preprocessing for a component or you might want to dynamically load a component. The two types of handlers are dhandlers and autohandlers, both of which are discussed in the sections that follow.

Dhandlers

You use *dhandlers*, or *default handlers*, to create or handle requests for resources that don't actually exist and need to be created dynamically. For example, you might create a dynamic web page at `http://www.example.com/products/item/01`. You don't, however, actually have a page at `/products/item/01`, but rather rely on a dhandler to serve the request.

When Mason receives a request for a component that doesn't exist, it searches backward through the path of the URI looking for a component with the name `dhandler`. When Mason finds it, the dhandler component is processed and passed the name of the original component being called. The exact argument passed to the dhandler depends on the location where Mason finds the dhandler.

Following the example, here's the original request, but there's no such resource:

`http://www.example.com/products/item/01`

The following searches in the immediate directory:

`http://www.example.com/products/item/dhandler`

If no dhandler is found, go up one level and try again:

`http://www.example.com/products/dhandler`

If the dhandler is found, pass the argument `'item/01'` to the dhandler and stop searching. The dhandler is passed its argument as `$m->dhandler_arg`. This means that the component `'item/01'` would be passed into the dhandler and could be loaded, say, from a database or other place dynamically at runtime.

You can cascade or pass execution to the next dhandler by calling `$m->decline`. In addition, you can use the `dhandler_name` parameter to change the name of the component from the default (`dhandler`). Within the Apache configuration, this would be called as `MasonDhandlerName` and accepts a string:

`MasonDhandlerName default_handler_doc`

You can also disable dhandlers entirely by setting `MasonDhandlerName` to an empty string:

`MasonDhandlerName ""`

Autohandlers

Autohandlers actually get processed prior to the top-level component and are commonly used to set a common header or footer as well as global variables. The autohandler searches within the directory of the current request for a component named `autohandler`, which is then processed prior to processing the top-level component from the request.

Like the dhandler, the autohandler's name can be changed from the default `autohandler` to another valid name using the `autohandler_name` parameter. In the Apache configuration, this parameter is known as `MasonAutohandlerName`.

There can be more than one autohandler. See the Mason Developer's Manual at `http://www.masonhq.com/docs/manual/Devel.html` for more information.

Subrequests and More

When you call a component, it won't normally go through the same steps as a top-level component, such as some initialization and searching for handlers. If you'd like the called component
to go through those steps, you need to make it into a *subrequest*. Creating and executing a subrequest is a two-step process: first create the subrequest itself and then call its exec method.
Subrequests are created with the make_subrequest method of $m, for example:

```
<%perl>
my $subreq = $m->make_subrequest( comp => 'component_name', args => 'arguments' );
$subreq->exec;
</%perl>
```

In addition to subrequests, there are other features of Mason that might be helpful to
you as you learn Mason and need additional functionality. See the Mason web site at http://
www.masonhq.com for more information on these other functions. The Mason site is an excellent
resource for administrators and developers wishing to learn the ins and outs of Mason.

Building a Web Site with Mason

Both the amount and extent to which you use Mason for your web site will be determined by
the goals you have and applications you wish to deploy on the site. For example, deploying
Mason across a (mostly) static site by using common headers and footers is an excellent way
to begin learning about Mason, its syntax, and its structure. Using Mason to build a full-blown
application can, obviously, get more involved and require the use of more areas of Mason. This
section gives some hands-on Masonized web site examples.

I do assume in this section that you've already set up your Mason environment with Apache.
I also assume that Mason will be processing files with the .mhtml extension. This assumption
is not based on preference so much as on just choosing something and running with it for the
examples, so if you're using .html or .anything as the standard extension for Mason, you
shouldn't feel the need to change it.

Building a Page

Likely the easiest place to begin is to simply create a web page, which I'll call myfirstmason.mhtml.
Inside that page, I'll put some poorly formed HTML, place code to initialize a variable, set
a value for that variable, and output that variable to the browser along with some other text.
Listing 13-6 presents the code for myfirstmason.mhtml.

Listing 13-6. *A First Mason Page*

```
<html><head><title>My First Mason</title></head>

% my ($sec,$min,$hour,$mday,$mon,$year,$wday,$yday,$isdst)
    = localtime(time);

<body>

<p>This is all just plain text on my web site. Thanks for visiting
```

```
today.</p>

<p>Copyright (c) <% $year+1900 %>, Steve Suehring</p>

</body>
</html>
```

Listing 13-6 is something you might actually see in a web page footer (and you can bet that it will show up again in this chapter). The current date and time are retrieved through the standard Perl localtime function. The next bit of Mason code shows up with the call to $year. Since localtime returns the number of years since 1900, it would return 105 normally, so I added 1900 to the value to come up with the result 2005, as shown in Figure 13-7.

Figure 13-7. *A first Mason example, printing a copyright notice of all things*

Creating Headers and Footers

The code in Listing 13-6 lends itself to creating a common header and footer. For example, the copyright notice will have to be displayed on every page in the site.

For this section's example, you'll use three files, two of which are new. The myfirstmason.mhtml file will be edited, and a header and footer called header.mase and footer.mase, respectively, will be created. Like the .mhtml extension, the .mase extension was chosen arbitrarily, though as you'll recall from the earlier example of my configuration, I have Apache configured to disallow any attempts to access a .mase file directly, for security reasons.

The contents of the header.mase file are as follows:

```
<html><head><title>My First Mason</title></head>

<body>
```

Notice that the Perl statement has been removed from the header. The footer.mase file contains the following code:

```
<%args>
$year
</%args>

<p>Copyright (c) <% $year+1900 %>, Steve Suehring</p>


</body>
</html>
```

Within this code, you'll notice the addition of the `<%args>` section. This is because the footer will be called with an argument of the year, which will come from the `localtime()` function. That `localtime()` function is now located in the source file, `myfirstmason.html`, which now looks like this:

```
<& header.mase &>

% my ($sec,$min,$hour,$mday,$mon,$year,$wday,$yday,$isdst) = localtime(time);

<p>This is all just plain text on my web site. Thanks for visiting
today.</p>

<& footer.mase, year => $year &>
```

Of note in this file is that the header was called into the file with the standard `<& . . . &>` tags, the Perl `localtime()` function was called, followed by the HTML for the page, finally followed by the call to the footer file. The call to the footer contained an argument of the year that corresponds to the year in the `<%args>` section of the `footer.mase` file. The results from this page are the same as those shown in Figure 13-7.

So that was version 1 of the header and footer example. It's barely been released when I want to make improvements to it. For example, it's really unnecessary to send the year as an argument to the footer. The Perl code for the `localtime()` function could have just as easily been placed directly in the footer itself. However, using `<%args>` is something you'll likely be doing a lot of when developing CGIs with Mason, so I thought it might be helpful to see it again.

Using Return Values

Another improvement I will implement is to place the `localtime()` function inside its own component with a return value. This final version of the example will use the same three files: `filesheader.mase`, `footer.mase`, and `myfirstmason.mhtml`. A new file will be added called get_year (with no extension). The contents of get_year are shown in Listing 13-7.

Listing 13-7. *The get_year Component*

```
<%init>
my ($sec,$min,$hour,$mday,$mon,$year,$wday,$yday,$isdst) = localtime(time);
return $year;
</%init>
```

Even though this function actually returns much more than just the year, the year is all I need for the copyright and is therefore all that's returned by this function. In practice, I'd likely return the entire date structure as an array.

The contents of `footer.mase` change to remove the `<%args>` section and replace it with a call to the component. The contents of `footer.mase` are now as follows:

```
% my $year = $m->comp('get_year');
<p>Copyright (c) <% $year+1900 %>, Steve Suehring</p>


</body>
</html>
```

The previous code could be written without the use of the temporary $year variable:

```
<p>Copyright (c) <% $m->comp('get_year')+1900 %>, Steve Suehring</p>


</body>
</html>
```

Finally, the `myfirstmason.html` file no longer needs to include the year argument in the call to the footer component. The contents are now as follows:

```
<& header.mase &>

<p>This is all just plain text on my web site. Thanks for visiting
today.</p>

<& footer.mase &>
```

Security Considerations with Mason

Mason doesn't, by itself, introduce any specific security considerations.

Summary

In this chapter you learned about Mason, a powerful dynamic templating system for Perl. Although Mason can run in a number of environments, the environment covered in this chapter was Apache with `mod_perl`. You explored the basic building block of Mason, the component, and you learned how to call components. You also covered the various tags available for use with Mason. You examined handlers, specifically dhandlers and autohandlers, and you learned a bit about Mason design.

Perl Basics

This appendix contains lightly edited passages from *Beginning Perl, Second Edition* by James Lee, (Apress, 2004; ISBN: 1-59059-391-X). The goal is to provide you with a refresher course on the basics of Perl. If you're completely unfamiliar with Perl, I recommend picking up a copy of *Beginning Perl* to get the most out of this book.

Our First Perl Program

Assuming that you now have a copy of Perl installed on your machine, you are ready to start using Perl. If not, go back and follow the instructions (in *Beginning Perl, Second Edition*). The next step is to write our first Perl program.

Here's what it will look like:

```
#!/usr/bin/perl -w

print "Hello, world!\ n";
```

We highly suggest that you type this example in and try to make it work, so before we go any further, a quick note on editors. Perl source code is just plain text and should be written with a plain text editor rather than a word processor. Your operating system, whether Unix or Windows, comes with a selection of text editors. You may have a favorite already, so feel free to use it. If not, may we suggest vi (http://www.vim.org), emacs (http://www.xemacs.org), and nedit (http://www.nedit.org). Windows provides WordPad and Notepad, but they lack many features of modern text editors, so they should be avoided. nedit is the most WordPad- and Notepad-like, so give it a try.

The next step is to fire up your editor of choice, type in the code shown previously, and save it into a file named helloworld.pl in the directory we just made. Then, to execute it, type

```
$ perl helloworld.pl
Hello, world!
$
```

Congratulations! You've successfully written and executed your first Perl program.

Keywords

A *keyword* is a term in Perl that has a predefined meaning. One example is the term use as we saw in the statement

```
use warnings;
```

Other types of keywords include built-in functions such as print() and control flow constructs such as if and while. We will talk about many built-in functions and control flow constructs in detail as we progress in our discussion of Perl.

It's a good idea to respect keywords and not give anything else the same name as one. For example, a little later on you'll learn that you can create and name a variable, and that calling your variable $print is perfectly allowable. The problem with this is that it leads to confusing and uninformative statements like print $print. It is always a good idea to give a variable a meaningful name, one that relates to its content in a logical manner—for example, $my_name, @telephone_numbers, %account_info, and so on, rather than $a, @b, and %c.

Statements and Statement Blocks

If functions are the verbs of Perl, then *statements* are the sentences. Instead of a period, a statement in Perl usually ends with a semicolon, as shown earlier:

```
print "Hello, world!\ n";
```

To print some more text, we can add another statement:

```
print "Hello, world!\ n";
print "Goodbye, world!\ n";
```

Escape Sequences

UTF8 gives us 65,536 characters, and ASCII gives us 256 characters, but on the average keyboard, there's only a hundred or so keys. Even using the Shift keys, there will still be some characters that you aren't going to be able to type. There will also be some things that you don't want to stick in the middle of your program, because they would make it messy or confusing. However, you'll want to refer to some of these characters in strings that you output. Perl provides us with mechanisms called *escape sequences* as an alternative way of getting to them. You've already seen the use of \ n to start a new line. Table A-1 lists the more common escape sequences.

Table A-1. *Escape Sequences*

Escape Sequence	Meaning
\ t	Tab
\ n	Start a new line (usually called *newline*)
\ r	Carriage return
\ b	Back up one character (backspace)
\ a	Alarm (rings the system bell)
\ x{ 1F18}	Unicode character

In the last example in the table, 1F18 is a hexadecimal number referring to a character in the Unicode character set, which runs from 0000-FFFF. As another example, \ x{ 2620} is the Unicode character for a skull-and-crossbones!

White Space

As mentioned previously, *white space* is the name we give to tabs, spaces, and newlines. Perl is very flexible about where you put white space in your program. You've already seen that you're free to use indentation to help show the structure of blocks. You don't need to use any white space at all, if you don't want to. If you'd prefer, your programs can all look like this:

```
print"Top level\ n";{ print"2nd level\ n";{ print"3rd level\ n";}
print"Where are we?";}
```

This is considered a bad idea. White space is another tool we have to make our programs more understandable; let's use it as such.

Types of Data

A lot of programming jargon is about familiar words in an unfamiliar context. You've already seen a string, which was a series of characters. You could also describe that string as a scalar literal constant. What does that mean?

By calling a value a scalar, you're describing the type of data it contains. If you remember your math (and even if you don't), a scalar is a plain, simple, one-dimensional value. In math, the word is used to distinguish it from a vector, which is expressed as several numbers. Velocity, for example, has a pair of coordinates (speed and direction), and so must be a vector. In Perl, a scalar is the fundamental, basic unit of data of which there are two kinds: numbers and strings.

A literal is value that never changes. The value 5 is a scalar literal—and is literally 5; it can never be 4. Perl has three types of scalar literals: integers (such as 5), floating-point numbers (like 3.14159), and strings (for example, "hello, world"). To put it another way, a literal is a constant—it never changes, as opposed to a variable, which is a piece of memory that can hold a scalar value. Variables are so named because the value stored within them can vary. For instance, $number can be assigned 5, and then later can be changed to the value 6. We will talk more about variables later in this appendix.

Numbers

There are two types of numbers that we're interested in as Perl programmers: integers and floating-point numbers. The latter we'll come to in a minute, but let's work a bit with integers right now. Integers are whole numbers with no numbers after the decimal point, such as 42, –1, or 10. The following program prints a couple of integer literals in Perl:

```
#!/usr/bin/perl -w
# number1.pl

print 25, -4;
```

```
$ perl number1.pl
25-4$
```

Well, that's what we see, but it's not exactly what we want. Fortunately, this is pretty easy to fix. First, we didn't tell Perl to separate the numbers with a space, and second, we didn't tell it to put a new line on the end. Let's change the program so it does that:

```
#!/usr/bin/perl -w
# number2.pl

print 25, " ", -4, "\ n";
```

This will do what we were thinking of:

```
$ perl number2.pl
25 -4
$
```

For the purpose of human readability, we often write large integers such as 10000000 by splitting up the number with commas: 10,000,000. This is sometimes known as *chunking*. While we might write 10 million with a comma if we wrote a check for that amount, don't use the comma to chunk in a Perl program. Instead, use the underscore: 10_000_000. Change the program to look like the following:

```
#!/usr/bin/perl -w
# number3.pl

print 25_000_000, " ", -4, "\ n";
```

Notice that those underscores don't appear in the output:

```
$ perl number3.pl
25000000 -4
$
```

As well as integers, there's another type of number: floating-point numbers. These contain everything else, such as 0.5, –0.01333, and 1.1.

Note that floating-point numbers are accurate to a certain number of digits. For instance, the number 15.39 may in fact be stored in memory as 15.3899999999999. This is accurate enough for most scientists, so it will have to be for us programmers as well.

Here is an example of printing the approximate value of pi:

```
#!/usr/bin/perl -w
# number4.pl

print "pi is approximately: ", 3.14159, "\ n";
```

Executing this program produces the following result:

```
$ perl number4.pl
pi is approximately: 3.14159
$
```

Binary, Hexadecimal, and Octal Numbers

We can express numbers as binary, hexadecimal, or octal numbers in our programs. Let's look at a program to demonstrate how we use the various number systems. Type in the following code, and save it as goodnums.pl:

```
#!/usr/bin/perl -w
# goodnums.pl

print 255,        "\ n";
print 0377,       "\ n";
print 0b11111111, "\ n";
print 0xFF,       "\ n";
```

All of these are representations of the number 255, and accordingly, we get the following output:

```
$ perl goodnums.pl
255
255
255
255
$
```

When Perl reads this program, it reads and understands numbers in any of the allowed number systems: 0 for octal, 0b for binary, and 0x for hex.

What happens, you might ask, if you specify a number in the wrong system? Well, let's try it out. Edit goodnums.pl to give a new program, badnums.pl, that looks like this:

```
#!/usr/bin/perl -w
# badnums.pl

print 255,        "\ n";
print 0378,       "\ n";
print 0b11111112, "\ n";
print 0xFG,       "\ n";
```

Since octal digits only run from 0 to 7, binary digits from 0 to 1, and hex digits from 0 to F, none of the last three lines make any sense. Let's see what Perl makes of it:

```
$ perl badnums.pl
Bareword found where operator expected at badnums.pl line 7, near "0xFG"
        (Missing operator before G?)
Illegal octal digit '8' at badnums.pl line 5, at end of line
Illegal binary digit '2' at badnums.pl line 6, at end of line
syntax error at badnums.pl line 7, near "0xFG"
Execution of badnums.pl aborted due to compilation errors.
$
```

Now, let's match those errors up with the relevant lines:

```
Illegal octal digit '8' at badnums.pl line 5, at end of line
```

And line 5 is

```
print 0378,      "\ n";
```

As you can see, Perl thought it was dealing with an octal number, but then along came an 8, which stopped making sense, so Perl quite rightly complained. The same thing happened on the next line:

```
Illegal binary digit '2' at badnums.pl line 6, at end of line
```

And line 4 is

```
print 0b11111112, "\ n";
```

The problem with the next line is even bigger:

```
Bareword found where operator expected at badnums.pl line 7, near "0xFG"
        (Missing operator before G?)
syntax error at badnums.pl line 7, near "0xFG"
```

The line starting "Bareword" is a warning (since we are using the -w option). Then it is followed by a syntax error. A bareword is a series of characters outside of a string that Perl doesn't recognize. The word could mean a number of things, and Perl is usually quite good about knowing what you mean. In this case, the bareword was G: Perl had understood 0xF, but couldn't see how the G fit in. We might have wanted an operator do something with it, but there was no operator there. In the end, Perl gave us a syntax error, which is the equivalent of it giving up and saying, "How do you expect me to understand this?"

Strings

The other type of scalar available to us is the string, and you've already seen a few examples of them. Earlier in the appendix, you met the string "Hello, world!\ n". A string is a series of characters surrounded by some sort of quotation marks. Strings can contain ASCII (or Unicode) data and escape sequences such as the \ n of our example, and there is no maximum length restriction on a string imposed by Perl. Practically speaking, there is a limit imposed by the amount of memory in your computer, but it's quite hard to hit.

Single- vs. Double-Quoted Strings

The quotation marks you choose for your string are significant. So far you've only seen double-quoted strings, like this: "Hello, world!\ n". There is another type of string—one that has been single-quoted. Predictably, they are surrounded by single quotes: ' '. The important difference is that no processing is done within single-quoted strings, except on \ \ and \ '. You'll also see later that variable names inside double-quoted strings are replaced by their contents, whereas single-quoted strings treat them as ordinary text. You call both these types of processing interpolation, and say that single-quoted strings are not interpolated.

Consider the following program, bearing in mind that \ t is the escape sequence that represents a tab.

```
#!/usr/bin/perl -w
# quotes.pl
```

```
print '\ tThis is a single-quoted string.\ n';
print "\ tThis is a double-quoted string.\ n";
```

The double-quoted string will have its escape sequences processed, and the single-quoted string will not. The output is

```
$ perl quotes.pl
\ tThis is a single quoted string.\ n    This is a double-quoted string.
$
```

What do we do if we want to have a backslash in a string? This is a common concern for Windows users, as a Windows path looks something like this: C:\ WINNT\ Profiles\. . .. In a double-quoted string, a backslash will start an escape sequence, which is not what we want it to do.

There is, of course, more than one way to do it. We can either use a single-quoted string, as shown previously, or we can escape the backslash. One principle that you'll see often in Perl, and especially when you get to regular expressions, is that you can use a backslash to turn off any special effect a character may have. This operation is called escaping or, more commonly, backwhacking.

In this case, we want to turn off the special effect a backslash has, and so we escape it:

```
#!/usr/bin/perl -w
# quotes2.pl

print "C:\ \ WINNT\ \ Profiles\ \ \ n";
print 'C:\ WINNT\ Profiles\ ', "\ n";
```

This prints the following:

```
$ perl quotes2.pl
C:\ WINNT\ Profiles\
C:\ WINNT\ Profiles\
$
```

Aha! Some of you may have gotten this message instead:

```
Can't find string terminator " ' " anywhere before EOF at quotes2.pl line 5.
```

The reason for this is that you probably left out the space character in line 5 before the second single quote. Remember that \ ' tells Perl to escape the single quote, and so it merrily heads off to look for the next quote, which of course is not there. Try this program to see how Perl treats these special cases:

```
#!/usr/bin/perl -w
# aside1.pl

print 'ex\ \  er\ \ ' , ' ci\ ' se\ '' , "\ n";
```

The output you get this time is

```
$ perl aside1.pl
ex\  er\  ci' se'
$
```

Can you see how Perl did this? Well, we simply escaped the backslashes and single quotes. It will help you to sort out what is happening if you look at each element individually. Remember, there are three arguments in this example. Don't let all the quotes confuse you.

Actually, there's an altogether sneakier way of doing it. Internally, Windows allows you to separate paths in the Unix style with a forward slash, instead of a backslash. If you're referring to directories in Perl on Windows, you may find it easier to use `C:/WINNT/Profiles/` instead. This allows you to get the variable interpolation of double-quoted strings without the "leaning toothpick syndrome" of multiple backslashes.

So much for backslashes—what about quotation marks? The trick is making sure Perl knows where the end of the string is. Naturally, there's no problem with putting single quotes inside a double-quoted string, or vice versa:

```
#!/usr/bin/perl -w
# quotes3.pl

print "It's as easy as that.\ n";
print '"Stop," he cried.', "\ n";
```

This will produce the quotation marks in the right places:

```
$ perl quotes3.pl
It's as easy as that.
"Stop," he cried.
$
```

The trick comes when we want to have double quotes inside a double-quoted string or single quotes inside a single-quoted string. As you might have guessed, though, the solution is to escape the quotes on the inside. Suppose we want to print out the following quote, including both sets of quotation marks:

```
'"Hi," said Jack. "Have you read Slashdot today?"'
```

Here's a way of doing it with a double-quoted string:

```
#!/usr/bin/perl -w
# quotes4.pl

print "'\ "Hi,\ " said Jack. \ "Have you read Slashdot today?\ "'\ n";
```

Now see if you can modify this to make it a single-quoted string—don't forget that \ n needs to go in separate double quotes to make it interpolate.

q// and qq//

It would be nice if you could select a completely different set of quotes so that there would be no ambiguity and no need to escape any quotes inside the text. The first operators we're going to meet are the quote-like operators that do this for us. They're written as q// and qq//, the first acting like a single-quoted string, and the second like a double-quoted string. Now instead of the preceding, we can write

```
#!/usr/bin/perl -w
```

```
# quotes5.pl

print qq/'"Hi," said Jack. "Have you read Slashdot today?"'\ n/;
```

Alternative Delimiters

That's all very well, of course, until we want a / in the string. Suppose we want to replace "Slashdot" with "/."—now we're back where we started, having to escape things again. Thankfully, Perl allows us to choose our own delimiters so we don't have to stick with //. Any nonalphanumeric (that is, nonalphabetic and nonnumeric) character can be used as a delimiter, provided it's the same on both sides of the text. Furthermore, you can use {}, [], (), and <> as left and right delimiters. Here are a few ways of doing the print qq/.../;, all of which have the same effect:

```
#!/usr/bin/perl -w
# quotes6.pl

print qq|'"Hi," said Jack. "Have you read /. today?"'\ n|;
print qq#'"Hi," said Jack. "Have you read /. today?"'\ n#;
print qq('"Hi," said Jack. "Have you read /. today?"'\ n);
print qq<'"Hi," said Jack. "Have you read /. today?"'\ n>;
```

You'll see more of these alternative delimiters when you start working with regular expressions.

Here-Documents

There's one final way of specifying a string: by means of a here-document. This idea was taken from the Unix shell, and it works on any platform. Effectively, it means that you can write a large amount of text within your program, and it will be treated as a string provided it is identified correctly. Here's an example:

```
#!/usr/bin/perl -w
# heredoc.pl

print <<EOF;

This is a here-document. It starts on the line after the two arrows,
and it ends when the text following the arrows is found at the beginning
of a line, like this:

EOF
```

A here-document must start with << and then a label. The label can be anything, but is traditionally EOF (end of file) or EOT (end of text). The label must immediately follow the arrows with no spaces between, unless the same number of spaces precedes the end marker. It ends when the label is found at the beginning of a line. In our case, the semicolon does not form part of the label, because it marks the end of the print() function call.

By default, a here-document works like a double-quoted string. In order for it to work like a single-quoted string, surround the label in single quotes. This will become important when variable interpolation comes into play, as you'll see later on.

Converting Between Numbers and Strings

Perl treats numbers and strings on an equal footing, and where necessary, Perl converts between strings, integers, and floating-point numbers behind the scenes. There is a special term for this: automatic conversion of scalars. This means that you don't have to worry about making the conversions yourself, like you do in other languages. If you have a string literal "0.25" and multiply it by 4, Perl treats it as a number and gives you the expected answer, 1. For example:

```
#!/usr/bin/perl -w
# autoconvert.pl

print "0.25" * 4, "\ n";
```

The asterisk (*) is the multiplication operator. All of Perl's operators, including this one, are discussed in the next section.

There is, however, one area where this automatic conversion does not take place. Octal, hex, and binary numbers in string literals or strings stored in variables don't get converted automatically.

```
#!/usr/bin/perl -w
# octhex1.pl

print "0x30\ n";
print "030\ n";
```

gives you

```
$ perl octhex1.pl
0x30
030
$
```

If you ever find yourself with a string containing a hex or octal value that you need to convert into a number, you can use the hex() or oct() functions accordingly:

```
#!/usr/bin/perl -w
# octhex2.pl

print hex("0x30"), "\ n";
print oct("030"), "\ n";
```

This will now produce the expected answers, 48 and 24. Note that for hex() or oct(), the prefix 0x or 0, respectively, is not required. If you know that what you have is definitely supposed to be a hex or octal number, then hex(30) and oct(30) will produce the preceding results. As you can see from that, the string "30" and the number 30 are treated as the same.

Furthermore, these functions will stop reading when they get to a digit that doesn't make sense in that number system:

```
#!/usr/bin/perl -w
# octhex3.pl

print hex("FFG"), "\ n";
print oct("178"), "\ n";
```

These will stop at FF and 17, respectively, and convert to 255 and 15. Perl will warn you, though, since those are illegal characters in hex and octal numbers.

What about binary numbers? Well, there's no corresponding bin() function, but there is actually a little trick here. If you have the correct prefix in place for any of the number systems (0, 0b, or 0x), you can use oct() to convert it to decimal. For example, print oct("0b11010") prints 26.

Operators

Now that you know how to specify strings and numbers, let's see what you can do with them. The majority of the things we'll be looking at here are numeric operators (operators that act on and produce numbers) like plus and minus, which take two numbers as arguments, called operands, and add or subtract them. There aren't as many string operators, but there are a lot of string functions. Perl doesn't draw a very strong distinction between functions and operators, but the main difference between the two is that operators tend to go in the middle of their arguments—for example, 2 + 2. Functions go before their arguments and have them separated by commas. Both of them take arguments, do something with them, and produce a new value; we generally say they return a value, or evaluate to a value. Let's take a look.

Numeric Operators

The numeric operators take at least one number as an argument, and evaluate to another number. Of course, because Perl automatically converts between strings and numbers, the arguments may appear as string literals or come from strings in variables. We'll group these operators into three types: arithmetic operators, bitwise operators, and logic operators.

Arithmetic Operators

The arithmetic operators are those that deal with basic mathematics like adding, subtracting, multiplying, dividing, and so on. To add two numbers together, we would write something like this:

```
#!/usr/bin/perl -w
# arithop1.pl

print 69 + 118, "\ n";
```

And, of course, we would see the answer 187. Subtracting numbers is easy too, and we can subtract at the same time:

```
#!/usr/bin/perl -w
# arithop2.pl

print "21 from 25 is: ", 25 - 21, "\ n";
print "4 + 13 - 7 is: ", 4 + 13 - 7, "\ n";

$ perl arithop2.pl
21 from 25 is: 4
4 + 13 - 7 is: 10
$
```

Our next set of operators (multiplying and dividing) is where it gets interesting. We use the * and / operators to multiply and divide, respectively.

```
#!/usr/bin/perl -w
# arithop3.pl

print "7 times 15 is ", 7 * 15, "\ n";
print "249 divided by 3 is ", 249 / 3, "\ n";
```

The fun comes when you want to multiply something and then add something, or add and then divide. Here's an example of the problem:

```
#!/usr/bin/perl -w
# arithop4.pl

print 3 + 7 * 15, "\ n";
```

This could mean one of two things: either Perl must add the 3 and the 7, and then multiply by 15, or multiply 7 and 15 first, and then add. Which does Perl do? Try it and see . . .

Perl should have given you 108, meaning it did the multiplication first. The order in which Perl performs operations is called operator precedence. Multiply and divide have a higher precedence than add and subtract, and so they get performed first. We can start to draw up a list of precedence as follows:

   * /

   + -

To force Perl to perform an operation of lower precedence first, we need to use parentheses, like so:

```
#!/usr/bin/perl -w
# arithop5.pl

print (3 + 7) * 15, "\ n";
```

Unfortunately, if you run that, you'll get a warning and 10 is printed. What happened? The problem is that print() is a function and the parentheses around 3 + 7 are treated as the only argument to print().

`print()` as an operator takes a list of arguments, performs an operation (printing them to the screen), and returns a 1 if it succeeds, or no value if it does not. Perl calculated 3 plus 7, printed the result, and then multiplied the result of the returned value (1) by 15, throwing away the final result of 15.

To get what we actually want, then, we need another set of parentheses:

```
#!/usr/bin/perl -w
# arithop6.pl

print((3 + 7) * 15, "\ n");
```

This now gives us the correct answer, 150, and we can put another entry in our list of precedence:

List operators

* /

+ -

Next we have the exponentiation operator, **, which simply raises one number to the power of another—squaring, cubing, and so on. Here's an example of some exponentiation:

```
#!/usr/bin/perl -w
# arithop7.pl

print 2**4, " ", 3**5, " ", -2**4, "\ n";
```

That's 2*2*2*2, 3*3*3*3*3, and –2*–2*–2*–2. Or is it?
The output we get is

```
$ perl arithop7.pl
16 243 -16
$
```

Hmm, the first two look OK, but the last one's a bit wrong: –2 to the fourth power should be positive. Again, it's a precedence issue. Turning a number into a negative number requires an operator, the unary minus operator. It's called "unary" because unlike the ordinary minus operator, it only takes one argument. Although unary minus has a higher precedence than multiply and divide, it has a lower precedence than exponentiation. What's actually happening, then, is `-(2**4)` instead of `(-2)**4`. Let's put these two operators in our list of precedence as well:

List operators

**

Unary minus

* /

+ -

The last arithmetic operator remainder, or modulo operator. This calculates the remainder when one number divides another. For example, 6 divides into 15 twice, with a remainder of 3, as our next program will confirm:

```
#!/usr/bin/perl -w
# arithop8.pl

print "15 divided by 6 is exactly ", 15 / 6, "\ n";
print "That's a remainder of ", 15 % 6, "\ n";

$ perl arithop8.pl
15 divided by 6 is exactly 2.5
That's a remainder of 3
$
```

The modulo operator has the same precedence as multiply and divide.

Bitwise Operators

Up to this point, the operators worked on numbers in the way we think of them. However, as we already know, computers don't see numbers the same as we do; they see them as a string of bits. These next few operators perform operations on numbers one bit at a time—that's why we call them bitwise operators. These aren't used quite so much in Perl as in other languages, but we'll see them when dealing with things like low-level file access.

First, let's have a look at the kind of numbers we're going to use in this section, just so we get used to them:

- 0 in binary is 0, but let's write it as 8 bits: 00000000.

- 51 in binary is 00110011.

- 85 in binary is 01010101.

- 170 in binary is 10101010.

- 204 in binary is 11001100.

- 255 in binary is 11111111.

Does it surprise you that 10101010 (170) is twice as much as 01010101 (85)? It shouldn't—when we multiply a number by 10 in base 10, all we do is slap a 0 on the end, so 21 becomes 210. Similarly, to multiply a number by 2 in base 2, we do exactly the same.

People think of bitwise operators as working from right to left; the rightmost bit is called the least significant bit and the leftmost is called the most significant bit.

The AND Operator

The easiest bitwise operator to fathom is called the AND operator, and is written &. This compares pairs of bits as follows:

- 1 and 1 gives 1.

- 1 and 0 gives 0.

- 0 and 1 gives 0.

- 0 and 0 gives 0.

For example, 51 & 85 looks like this:

```
51    00110011
85    01010101
---------------
17    00010001
```

Sure enough, if we ask Perl the following:

```
#!/usr/bin/perl -w
# bitop1.pl

print "51 ANDed with 85 gives us ", 51 & 85, "\ n";
```

it will tell us the answer is 17. Notice that since we're comparing one pair of bits at a time, it doesn't really matter which way around the arguments go: 51 & 85 is exactly the same as 85 & 51. Operators with this property are called associative operators. Addition (+) and multiplication (*) are also associative: 5 * 12 produces the same result as 12 * 5. Subtraction (–) and division (/) are not associative: 5 – 12 does not produce the same result as 12 – 5.

Here's another example—look at the bits, and see what you get:

```
51    00110011
170   10101010
---------------
34    00100010
```

The OR Operator

As well as checking whether the first and the second bits are 1, we can check whether one or another is 1, the OR operator in Perl is |. This is how we would calculate 204 | 85:

```
204   11001100
85    01010101
---------------
221   11011101
```

Now we produce 0s only if both the bits are 0; if either or both are 1, we produce a 1. As a quick rule of thumb, X & Y will always be smaller or equal to the smallest value of X and Y, and X | Y will be bigger than or equal to the largest value of X or Y.

The XOR Operator

What if you really want to know if one or the other, but not both, are 1? For this, you need the exclusive or (XOR) operator, written as the ^ operator:

```
204   11001100
170   10101010
---------------
102   01100110
```

The NOT Operator

Finally, you can flip the number completely, and replace all the 1s by 0s and vice versa. This is done with the NOT, or ~, operator:

```
85      01010101
170      10101010
```

Let's see, however, what happens when we try this in Perl:

```
#!/usr/bin/perl -w
# bitop2.pl

print "NOT 85 is ", ~85, "\ n";
```

Depending on the computer, the answer might be

```
$ perl bitop2.pl
NOT 85 is 4294967210
$
```

Your answer might be different, and we'll explain why in a second.

Why is it so big? Well, let's look at that number in binary to see if we can find a clue as to what's going on:

```
4294697210     11111111111111111111111110101010
```

Aha! The last part is right, but it's a lot wider than we're used to. That's because the previous examples only used 8 bits across, whereas many computers store integers as 32 bits across, so what's actually happened is this:

```
85                      00000000000000000000000001010101
4294697210              11111111111111111111111110101010
```

If you get a much bigger number, it's because your computer represents numbers internally with 64 bits instead of 32, and Perl has been configured to take advantage of this.

Truth and Falsehood

True and false are important in Perl. In Perl, false is defined as

- 0

- "0"

- "" (also known as the "empty string")

- Undefined

- Empty list (This is discussed in detail in Chapter 4 of *Beginning Perl*.)

Later, we will want to perform actions based on whether something is true or false, like if one number is bigger than another, or unless a problem has occurred, or while there is data left to examine. We will use comparison operators to evaluate whether these things are true or false so that we can make decisions based on them.

Some programming languages represent false as 0 and true as 1, and this allows us to use operators very similar to those bitwise operators we've just met to combine our comparisons, and to say "if this or this is true," "if this is not true," and so on. The idea of combining values that represent truth and falsehood is called Boolean logic, after George Boole, who invented the concept in 1847, and we call the operators that do the combining Boolean operators.

Comparing Numbers for Equality

The first simple comparison operator is ==. Two equals signs tells Perl to "return true if the two numeric arguments are equal." If they're not equal, return false. Boolean values of truth and falsehood aren't very exciting to look at, but let's see them anyway:

```
#!/usr/bin/perl -w
# bool1.pl

print "Is two equal to four? ",            2 == 4, "\ n";
print "OK, then, is six equal to six? ", 6 == 6, "\ n";
```

This will produce

```
$ perl bool1.pl
Is two equal to four?
OK, then, is six equal to six? 1
$
```

This output shows that in Perl, operators that evaluate to false evaluate to the empty string ("") and when true evaluate to 1.

The obvious counterpart to testing whether things are equal is testing whether they're not equal, and the way we do this is with the != operator. Note that there's only one = this time; we'll find out later why there had to be two before.

```
#!/usr/bin/perl -w
# bool2.pl

print "So, two isn't equal to four? ", 2 != 4, "\ n";
```

```
$ perl bool2.pl
So, two isn't equal to four? 1
$
```

There you have it, irrefutable proof that 2 is not 4. Good.

Comparing Numbers for Inequality

So much for equality; let's check if one thing is bigger than another. Just like in mathematics, we use the greater-than and less-than signs to do this: < and >.

```
#!/usr/bin/perl -w
# bool3.pl

print "Five is more than six? ",       5 > 6, "\ n";
```

```
print "Seven is less than sixteen? ", 7 < 16, "\ n";
print "Two is equal to two? ",        2 == 2, "\ n";
print "One is more than one? ",        1 >  1, "\ n";
print "Six is not equal to seven? ",  6 != 7, "\ n";
```

The results should hopefully not be very new to you:

```
$ perl bool3.pl
Five is more than six?
Seven is less than sixteen? 1
Two is equal to two? 1
One is more than one?
Six is not equal to seven? 1
$
```

Let's have a look at one last pair of comparisons. We can check greater-than-or-equal-to and less-than-or-equal-to with the >= and <= operators, respectively.

```
#!/usr/bin/perl -w
# bool4.pl

print "Seven is less than or equal to sixteen? ", 7 <= 16, "\ n";
print "Two is more than or equal to two? ",        2 >= 2,  "\ n";
```

As expected, Perl faithfully prints out

```
$ perl bool4.pl
Seven is less than or equal to sixteen? 1
Two is more than or equal to two? 1
$
```

There's also a special operator that isn't really a Boolean comparison because it doesn't give us a true-or-false value; instead it returns 0 if the two are equal, –1 if the right-hand side is_ bigger, and 1 if the left-hand side is bigger. It is denoted by <=>.

```
#!/usr/bin/perl -w
# bool5.pl

print "Compare six and nine? ",    6 <=> 9, "\ n";
print "Compare seven and seven? ", 7 <=> 7, "\ n";
print "Compare eight and four? ",  8 <=> 4, "\ n";
```

gives us

```
$ perl bool5.pl
Compare six and nine? -1
Compare seven and seven? 0
Compare eight and four? 1
$
```

The <=> operator is also known as the spaceship operator or the shuttle operator due to its shape.

We'll see this operator used when we look at sorting things, where we have to know whether something goes before, after, or in the same place as something else.

Boolean Operators

As well as being able to evaluate the truth and falsehood of some statements, we can also combine such statements. For example, we may want to do something if one number is bigger than another and another two numbers are the same. The combining is done in a very similar manner to the bitwise operators we saw earlier. We can ask if one value and another value are both true, or if one value or another value are true, and so on.

The operators even resemble the bitwise operators. To ask if both truth values are true, we would use && instead of &.

So, to test whether 6 is more than 3 and 12 is more than 4, we can write

```
6 > 3 && 12 > 4
```

To test if 9 is more than 7 or 8 is less than 6, we use the doubled form of the | operator, ||:

```
9 > 7 || 6 > 8
```

To negate the sense of a test, however, use the slightly different operator !. This has a higher precedence than the comparison operators, so use parentheses. For example, this tests whether 2 is not more than 3:

```
!(2>3)
```

while this one tests whether !2 is more than 3:

```
!2>3
```

2 is a true value. !2 is therefore a false value, which gets converted to 0 when we do a numeric comparison. We're actually testing if 0 is more than 3, which has the opposite effect to what we wanted.

Instead of those forms, &&, ||, and !, we can also use the slightly easier-to-read versions, AND, OR, and NOT. There's also XOR, for exclusive or (one or the other but not both are true), which doesn't have a symbolic form. However, you need to be careful about precedence again:

```
#!/usr/bin/perl -w
# bool6.pl

print "Test one: ", 6 > 3 && 3 > 4, "\ n";
print "Test two: ", 6 > 3 and 3 > 4, "\ n";
```

This prints, somewhat surprisingly, the following:

```
$ perl bool6.pl
Useless use of a constant in void context at bool6.pl line 5.
Test one:
Test two: 1$
```

We can tell from the presence of the warning about line 5 and from the position of the prompt that something is amiss (or least Unix users can—Windows users need to be a bit more alert since Windows automatically adds a newline character at the end of the program so the system prompt will be on the next line, but the blank line that is expected will not be there). Notice the second newline did not get printed. The trouble is, and has a lower precedence than &&. What has actually happened is this:

```
print("Test two: ", 6 > 3) and (3 > 4, "\ n");
```

Now, 6 is more than 3, so that returned 1, print() then returned 1, and the rest was irrelevant.

String Operators

After that lot, there are surprisingly few string operators. Actually, for the moment, we're only going to look at two.

The first one is the concatenation operator, which glues two strings together into one. Instead of using this:

```
print "Print ", "several ", "strings ", "here", "\ n";
```

we could use this:

```
print "Print " . "one ". "string " . "here" . "\ n";
```

As it happens, printing several strings is slightly more efficient, but there will be times you really do need to combine strings together, especially if you're putting them into variables.

What happens if we try and join a number to a string? The number is evaluated and then converted:

```
#!/usr/bin/perl -w
# string1.pl

print "Four sevens are ". 4*7 ."\ n";
```

which tells us, reassuringly, that

```
$  perl string1.pl
Four sevens are 28
$
```

The other string operator is the repetition operator, marked with an x. This repeats a string a given number of times:

```
#!/usr/bin/perl -w
# string2.pl

print "GO! " x 3, "\ n";
```

will print

```
$ perl string2.pl
GO! GO! GO!
$
```

We can, of course, use it in conjunction with concatenation. Its precedence is higher than the concatenation operator's, as we can easily see for ourselves:

```
#!/usr/bin/perl -w
# string3.pl

print "Ba" . "na" x 4 ,"\ n";
```

On running this, we'll get

```
$ perl string3.pl
Banananana
$
```

In this case, the repetition is done first ("nananana") and then it is concatenated with the "Ba". The precedence of the repetition operator is the same as the arithmetic operators, so if you're working out how many times to repeat something, you're going to need parentheses:

```
#!/usr/bin/perl -w
# string4.pl

print "Ba" . "na" x 4*3 ,"\ n";
print "Ba" . "na" x (4*3) ,"\ n";
```

Compare the preceding code with this:

```
$ perl string4.pl
Argument "nananana" isn't numeric in multiplication (*) at string4.pl line 4.
Ba0
Banananananananananananananana
$
```

Why was the first one Ba0? The first thing was the repetition, giving us "nananana". Then the multiplication—what's "nananana" times 3? When Perl converts a string to a number, it takes any spaces, an optional minus sign, and then as many digits as it can from the beginning of the string, and ignores everything else. Since there were no digits here, the number value of "nananana" was 0. Also note that if the string that is converted to a number contains no numeric characters, Perl will warn you about it, as shown previously.

That 0 was then multiplied by 3, to give 0. Finally, the 0 was turned back into a string to be concatenated onto the "Ba".

Here is an example showing how strings automatically convert to numbers by adding 0 to them:

```
#!/usr/bin/perl -w
# str2num.pl

print "12 monkeys"    + 0,  "\ n";
print "Eleven to fly" + 0,  "\ n";
print "UB40"          + 0,  "\ n";
print "-20 10"        + 0,  "\ n";
print "0x30"          + 0,  "\ n";
```

You get a warning for each line saying that the strings aren't "numeric in addition (+)," but what can be converted is as follows:

```
$ perl str2num.pl
Argument "12 monkeys" isn't numeric in addition (+) at str2num.pl line 4.
Argument "Eleven to fly" isn't numeric in addition (+) at str2num.pl line 5.
Argument "UB40" isn't numeric in addition (+) at str2num.pl line 6.
Argument "-20 10" isn't numeric in addition (+) at str2num.pl line 7.
Argument "0x30" isn't numeric in addition (+) at str2num.pl line 8.
12
0
0
-20
0
$
```

Notice how for each of these strings, when converted to numeric values, Perl complains that the string is not numeric. This happens because the string is not a simple numeric value. But also note that Perl does convert the strings to numbers (in the case of three of the strings, the value is 0).

Our first string, `"12 monkeys"`, did pretty well. Perl understood the 12, and stopped after that. The next one was not so brilliant—English words don't get converted to numbers. Our third string was also a nonstarter, as Perl only looks for a number at the beginning of the string. If there's something there that isn't a number, it's evaluated as a 0. Similarly, Perl only looks for the first number in the string. Any numbers after that are discarded. Finally, Perl doesn't convert binary, hex, or octal to decimal when it's stringifying a number, so you have to use the hex() or oct() functions to do that. On our last effort, Perl stopped at the x, returning 0. If we had an octal number, such as 030, that would be treated as the decimal number 30.

Therefore, conversion from strings to numbers can be summed up with these rules:

- A string that is purely a number is automatically converted to the number ("21.42" is converted to 21.42).

- Leading white space is ignored (" 12" is converted to 12).

- Trailing nonnumerics are discarded ("12perl" is converted to 12).

- Strings that do not start with numeric values are treated as 0 ("perl12" is converted to 0).

The last three conversions listed will produce a warning message if the -w option is used.

String Comparison

As well as comparing the value of numbers, we can compare the value of strings. This does not mean we convert a string to a number, although if you say something like `"12" > "30"`, Perl will convert to numbers for you. This means we can compare the strings alphabetically: "Bravo" comes after "Alpha" but before "Charlie", for instance.

In fact, it's more than alphabetical order; the computer is using either ASCII or Unicode internally to represent the string, and so has converted it to a series of numbers in the relevant sequence. This means, for example, "Fowl" comes before "fish", because a capital "F" has a smaller ASCII value (70) than a lowercase "f" (102).

We can find a character's value by using the ord() function, which tells us where in the (ASCII) order it comes. Let's see which comes first, a # or a *?.

```
#!/usr/bin/perl -w
# ascii.pl

print "A # has ASCII value ", ord("#"), "\ n";
print "A * has ASCII value ", ord("*"), "\ n";
```

This should say

```
$ perl ascii.pl
A # has ASCII value 35
A * has ASCII value 42
$
```

If we're only concerned with a character at a time, we can compare the return values of ord() using the < and > operators. However, when comparing entire strings, it may get a bit tedious. If the first character of each string is the same, we would move on to the next character in each string, and then the next, and so on.

Instead, there are string comparison operators that do this for us. Whereas the comparison operators for numbers are mathematical symbols, the operators for strings are abbreviations. To test whether one string is less than another, use lt. "Greater than" becomes gt, "equal to" becomes eq, and "not equal to" becomes ne. There's also ge and le for "greater than or equal to" and "less than and equal to." The three-way-comparison becomes cmp.

Here are a few examples of these:

```
#!/usr/bin/perl -w
# strcomp1.pl

print "Which came first, the chicken or the egg? ";
print "chicken" cmp "egg", "\ n";
print "Are dogs greater than cats? ";
print "dog" gt "cat", "\ n";
print "Is ^ less than + ? ";
print "^" lt "+", "\ n";
```

And here are the results:

```
$ perl strcomp1.pl
Which came first, the chicken or the egg? -1
Are dogs greater than cats? 1
Is ^ less than + ?
$
```

The last line prints nothing as a result of "^" lt "+" since this operation returns the empty string indicating false.

Be careful when comparing strings with numeric comparison operators (or numeric values with string comparison operators):

```
#!/usr/bin/perl -w
# strcomp2.pl

print "Test one: ", "four" eq "six", "\ n";
print "Test two: ", "four" == "six", "\ n";
```

This code produces

```
$ perl strcomp2.pl
Argument "six" isn't numeric in numeric eq (==) at strcmp2.pl line 5.
Argument "four" isn't numeric in numeric eq (==) at strcmp2.pl line 5.
Test one:
Test two: 1
$
```

Is the second line really claiming that "four" is equal to "six"? Yes, when treated as numbers. If you compare them as numbers, they get converted to numbers. "four" converts to 0, "six" converts to 0, and the 0s are equal, so our test returns true and we get a couple of warnings telling us that they were not numbers to begin with. The moral of this story is, compare strings with string comparison operators and compare numbers with numeric comparison operators. Otherwise, your results may not be what you anticipate.

Variables

Now it is time to talk about variables. As explained earlier, a variable is storage for your scalars. Once you've calculated 42*7, it's gone. If you want to know what it was, you must do the calculation again. Instead of being able to use the result as a halfway point in more complicated calculations, you have to spell it all out in full. That's no fun. What we need to be able to do, and what variables allow us to do, is store a scalar away and refer to it again later.

A scalar variable name starts with a dollar sign—for example, $name. Scalar variables can hold either numbers or strings, and are only limited by the size of your computer's memory. To put data into our scalar, we assign the data to it with the assignment operator =. (Incidentally, this is why numeric comparison is ==, because = was taken to mean the assignment operator.)

What we're going to do here is tell Perl that our scalar contains the string "fred". Now we can get at that data by simply using the variable's name:

```
#!/usr/bin/perl -w
# vars1.pl

$name = "fred";
print "My name is ", $name, "\ n";
```

Lo and behold, our computer announces to us that

```
$ perl vars1.pl
My name is fred
$
```

Now we have somewhere to store our data, and some way to get it back again. The next logical step is to be able to change it.

Modifying a Variable

Modifying the contents of a variable is easy; just assign something different to it. We can use the following:

```
#!/usr/bin/perl -w
# vars2.pl

$name = "fred";
print "My name is ",              $name, "\ n";
print "It's still ",             $name, "\ n";
$name = "bill";
print "Well, actually, now it's ", $name, "\ n";
$name = "fred";
print "No, really, now it's ",     $name, "\ n";
```

and watch our computer have an identity crisis:

```
$ perl vars2.pl
My name is fred
It's still fred
Well, actually, now it's bill
No, really, now it's fred
$
```

We can also do a calculation in several stages:

```
#!/usr/bin/perl -w
# vars3.pl

$a = 6 * 9;
print "Six nines are ", $a, "\ n";
$b = $a + 3;
print "Plus three is ", $b, "\ n";
$c = $b / 3;
print "All over three is ", $c, "\ n";
$d = $c + 1;
print "Add one is ", $d, "\ n";
print "\ nThose stages again: ", $a, " ", $b, " ", $c, " ", $d, "\ n";
```

This code prints

```
$ perl vars3.pl
Six nines are 54
Plus three is 57
All over three is 19
Add one is 20
Those stages again: 54 57 19 20
$
```

While this works perfectly fine, it's often easier to stick with one variable and modify its value, if you don't need to know the stages you went through at the end:

```
#!/usr/bin/perl -w
# vars4.pl
```

```
$a = 6 * 9;
print "Six nines are ", $a, "\ n";
$a = $a + 3;
print "Plus three is ", $a, "\ n";
$a = $a / 3;
print "All over three is ", $a, "\ n";
$a = $a + 1;
print "Add one is ", $a, "\ n";
```

The assignment operator = has very low precedence. This means that Perl will do the calculations on the right-hand side of it, including fetching the current value, before assigning the new value. To illustrate this, take a look at the sixth line of our example. Perl takes the current value of $a, adds 3 to it, and then stores it back in $a.

Operating and Assigning at Once

Operations, like fetching a value, modifying it, or storing it, are very common, so there's a special syntax for them. Generally

```
$a = $a <some operator> $b;
```

can be written as

```
$a <some operator>= $b;
```

For instance, we could rewrite the preceding example as follows:

```
#!/usr/bin/perl -w
# vars5.pl

$a = 6 * 9;
print "Six nines are ", $a, "\ n";
$a += 3;
print "Plus three is ", $a, "\ n";
$a /= 3;
print "All over three is ", $a, "\ n";
$a += 1;
print "Add one is ", $a, "\ n";
```

This works for **=, *=, +=, -=, /=, .=, %=, &=, |=, ^=, <<=, >>=, &&=, and ||=. These all have the same precedence as the assignment operator =.

Autoincrement and Autodecrement

There are also two more operators, ++ and --. They add and subtract one from the variable, but their precedence is a little strange. When they precede a variable, they act before everything else. If they come afterward, they act after everything else. Let's examine these in the following example:

```
#!/usr/bin/perl -w
# auto1.pl
```

```
$a = 4;
$b = 10;
print "Our variables are ", $a, " and ", $b, "\ n";
$b = $a++;
print "After incrementing, we have ", $a, " and ", $b, "\ n";
$b = ++$a * 2;
print "Now, we have ", $a, " and ", $b, "\ n";
$a = --$b + 4;
print "Finally, we have ", $a, " and ", $b, "\ n";
```

We should see the following output:

```
$ perl auto1.pl
Our variables are 4 and 10
After incrementing, we have 5 and 4
Now, we have 6 and 12
Finally, we have 15 and 11
$
```

Let's work this through a piece at a time. First we set up our variables, giving the values 4 and 10 to $a and $b, respectively:

```
$a = 4;
$b = 10;
print "Our variables are ", $a, " and ", $b, "\ n";
```

In the following line, the assignment happens before the increment—this is known as a post-increment. So $b is set to $a's current value, 4, and then $a is autoincremented, becoming 5.

```
$b = $a++;
print "After incrementing, we have ", $a, " and ", $b, "\ n";
```

In the next line, however, the incrementing takes place first—this is known as a pre-increment. $a is now 6, and $b is set to twice that, 12.

```
$b= ++$a * 2;
print "Now, we have ", $a, " and ", $b, "\ n";
```

Finally, $b is decremented first (a pre-decrement), and becomes 11. $a is set to $b plus 4, which is 15.

```
$a= --$b + 4;
print "Finally, we have ", $a, " and ", $b, "\ n";
```

The autoincrement operator actually does something interesting if the variable contains a string of only alphabetic characters, followed optionally by numeric characters. Instead of converting to a number, Perl "advances" the variable along the ranges a–z, A–Z, and 0–9. This is more easily understood from a few examples.

```
#!/usr/bin/perl -w
# auto2.pl
```

```
$a = "A9"; print ++$a, "\ n";
$a = "bz"; print ++$a, "\ n";
$a = "Zz"; print ++$a, "\ n";
$a = "z9"; print ++$a, "\ n";
$a = "9z"; print ++$a, "\ n";
```

should produce

```
$ perl auto2.pl
B0
ca
AAa
aa0
10
$
```

This shows that a 9 turns into a 0 and increments the next digit left. A z turns into an a and increments the next digit left, and if there are no more digits to the left, either an a or an A is created depending on the case of the current leftmost digit.

Multiple Assignments

We've said that = is an operator, but does that mean it returns a value? Well, actually it does, it returns whatever was assigned. This allows us to set several variables up at once. Here's a simple example of this (read it from right to left):

$d = $c = $b = $a = 1;

First we set $a to 1, and the result of this is 1. $b is set with that, the result of which is 1. And so it goes on.

Scoping

All the variables we've seen so far in our programs have been global variables. That is, they can be seen and changed from anywhere in the program. For the moment, that's not too much of a problem, since our programs are very small, and we can easily understand where things get assigned and used. However, when we start writing larger programs, this becomes a problem.

Why is this? Well, suppose one part of your program uses a variable, $counter. If another part of your program wants a counter, it can't call it $counter as well for fear of clobbering the old value. This becomes more of an issue when we get into subroutines, which are little sections of code we can temporarily call upon to accomplish something for us before returning to what we were previously doing. Currently, we'd have to make sure all the variables in our program had different names, and with a large program that's not desirable. It would be easier to restrict the life of a variable to a certain area of the program.

To achieve this, Perl provides another type of variable: lexical variables. These are constrained to the enclosing block and all blocks inside it. If they're not currently inside a block, they are constrained to the current file. To tell Perl that a variable is lexical, we say my_$variable;. This creates a brand-new lexical variable for the current block, and sets it to the undefined value. Here's an example:

```perl
#!/usr/bin/perl -w
# scope1.pl

$record = 4;
print "We're at record ", $record, "\ n";

{
    my $record;
    $record = 7;
    print "Inside the block, we're at record ", $record, "\ n";
}

print "Outside, we're still at record ", $record, "\ n";
```

This should tell you

```
$ perl scope1.pl
We're at record 4
Inside the block, we're at record 7
Outside we're still at record 4
$
```

Let's look at how this program works. First, we set our global variable $record to 4.

```perl
$record = 4;
print "We're at record ", $record, "\ n";
```

Now we enter a new block and create a new lexical variable. Important! This is completely and utterly unrelated to the global variable $record as my() creates a new lexical variable. This exists for the duration of the block only, and has the undefined value.

```perl
{
    my $record;
```

Next, the lexical variable is set to 7, and printed out. The global $record is unchanged.

```perl
$record = 7;
print "Inside the block, we're at record ", $record, "\ n";
```

Finally, the block ends, and the lexical copy ends with it. We say that it has gone out of scope. The global remains, however, and so $record has the value 4.

```perl
}

print "Outside, we're still at record ", $record, "\ n";
```

In order to make us think clearly about our programming, we will ask Perl to be strict about our variable use. The statement use strict; checks that, among other things, we've declared all our variables. We declare lexicals with the my() function. Here's what happens if we change our program to use strict format:

```perl
#!/usr/bin/perl -w
# scope2.pl

use strict;

$record = 4;
print "We're at record ", $record, "\ n";

{
    my $record;
    $record = 7;
    print "Inside the block, we're at record ", $record, "\ n";
}

print "Outside, we're still at record ", $record, "\ n";
```

Now, the global $record is not declared. So sure enough, Perl complains about it, generating this output:

```
$ perl scope2.pl
Global symbol "$record" requires explicit package name at scope2.pl line 6.
Global symbol "$record" requires explicit package name at scope2.pl line 7.
Global symbol "$record" requires explicit package name at scope2.pl line 15.
Execution of scope2.pl aborted due to compilation errors.
$
```

We'll see exactly what this means in later chapters (in *Beginning Perl, Second Edition*), but for now it suffices to declare $record as a my() variable:

```perl
#!/usr/bin/perl -w
# scope3.pl

use strict;

my $record;
$record = 4;
print "We're at record ", $record, "\ n";

{
    my $record;
    $record = 7;
    print "Inside the block, we're at record ", $record, "\ n";
}

print "Outside, we're still at record ", $record, "\ n";
```

Now Perl is happy, and we get the same output as before. You should almost always start your programs with a use strict. Of course, nobody's going to force you to do so, but it will help you avoid a lot of mistakes, and it will certainly give other people who have to look at your code more confidence in it.

Variable Names

We've not really examined yet what the rules are regarding what we can call our variables. We know that scalar variables have to start with a dollar sign, but what next? The next character must be a letter (uppercase or lowercase) or an underscore, and after that, any combination of numbers, letters, and underscores is permissible.

Note that Perl's variable names, like the rest of Perl, are case-sensitive, so $user is different from $User, and both are different from $USER.

The following are legal variable names: $I_am_a_long_variable_name, $simple, $box56, $__hidden, and $B1.

The following are not legal variable names: $10c (doesn't start with letter or underscore), $mail-alias (- is not allowed), $your name (spaces are not allowed).

The Special Variable $_

There are certain variables, called special variables, that Perl provides internally that you either are not allowed to or do not want to overwrite. One that is allowed by the preceding rules is $_, a very special variable indeed. $_ is the default variable that a lot of functions read from, write to, and operate upon if no other variable is given. We'll see plenty of examples of it throughout the book. For a complete list of all the special variables that Perl uses and what they do, type **perldoc perlvar** at the command line.

Variable Interpolation

We said earlier that double-quoted strings interpolate variables. What does this mean? Well, if you mention a variable, say $name, in the middle of a double-quoted string, you get the value of the variable, rather than the actual characters. As an example, see what Perl does to this:

```
#!/usr/bin/perl -w
# varint1.pl
use strict;

my $name = "fred";
print "My name is $name\ n";
```

This produces

```
$ perl varint1.pl
My name is fred
$
```

Perl interpolates the value of $name into the string. Note that this doesn't happen with single-quoted strings, just like escape sequence interpolation:

```
#!/usr/bin/perl -w
# varint2.pl

use strict;
```

```
my $name = "fred";
print 'My name is $name\ n';
```

Here we get

```
$ perl varint2.pl
My name is $name\ n$
```

Notice that the system prompt is printed at the end of that line because \ n is not a newline character within the single quotes. This doesn't just happen in things we print, it happens every time we construct a string:

```
#!/usr/bin/perl -w
# varint3.pl

use strict;

my $name = "fred";
my $salutation = "Dear $name,";
print $salutation, "\ n";
```

This gives us

```
$ perl varint3.pl
Dear fred,
$
```

This has exactly the same effect as

```
my $salutation = "Dear " . $name . ",";
```

but is more concise and easier to understand.

If you need to place text immediately after the variable, you can use curly braces to delimit the name of the variable. Take this example:

```
#!/usr/bin/perl -w
# varint4.pl

use strict;

my $times = 8;
print "This is the $timesth time.\ n";
```

This is syntactically incorrect, because Perl looks for a variable $timesth, which hasn't been declared. In this case, we have to change the last line by wrapping the variable name in curly braces to this:

```
print "This is the ${ times} th time.\ n";
```

Now we get the right result:

```
$ perl varint4.pl
This is the 8th time.
$
```

The if Statement

In programming, we often need to test a condition, and if that condition is true, take some action. This can be performed using an `if` statement, which has the general syntax

```
if ( condition ) {
    statements
}
```

Don't type this in and try to make it run—it is meant to be a general structure of the construct.

An important note: those curly braces around the body (the statements) are required. You must use them, even if the body is one line of code.

For instance, let's say we want to divide by a number unless that number is 0. We can first check to see if the number is not 0, and if it is not, perform the division.

```
if ($number != 0) {
    $result = 100 / $number;
}
```

Let's create a program to use the `if` statement. It will prompt the user to enter a number. If the number is not 0, then 100 is divided by that number and the result is stored in `$result`. If the number is 0, the result will remain the default value of 0:

```
#!/usr/bin/perl -w
# if.pl

use strict;

print "please enter a number: ";
chomp(my $number = <STDIN>);
my $result = 0;
if ($number != 0) {
    $result = 100 / $number;
}

print "the result is: $result\ n";
```

Recall that the statement

```
chomp(my $number = <STDIN>);
```

is shorthand for the two statements that read from standard input and then remove the newline:

```
my $number = <STDIN>;
chomp $number;
```

Now let's execute the program, once with a nonzero value and once with zero:

```
$ perl if.pl
please enter a number: 8
the result is: 12.5
$ perl if.pl
please enter a number: 0
the result is: 0
$
```

Operators Revisited

The if statement and all the other control structures we're going to visit in this section test to see if a condition is true or false. They do this using the Boolean logic mentioned earlier, together with Perl's ideas of true and false. To remind you of these:

- An empty string, "", is false.

- The number 0 and the string "0" are both false.

- An empty list, (), is false.

- The undefined value is false.

- Everything else is true.

However, you need to be careful for a few traps here. A string containing invisible characters, like spaces or newlines, is true. A string that isn't "0" is true, even if its numerical value is 0, so "0.0" for instance, is true.

Larry Wall has said that programming Perl is an empirical science—you learn things about it by trying them out. Is (()) a true value? You can look it up in books and the online documentation, or you can spend a few seconds writing a program like this:

```
#!/usr/bin/perl -w
# emptylist.pl

use strict;

if ( (()) ) {
    print "Yes, it is.\ n";
}
```

This way you get the answer straight away, with the minimum of fuss. (If you're interested, it isn't a true value.) We've also seen that conditional operators can test things out, returning 1 if the test was successful and an empty string if it was not. Let's see more of the things we can test.

Comparing Numbers

We can test whether one number is bigger, smaller, or the same as another. Assuming we have two numbers stored in the variables $x and $y, Table A-2 shows the operators we can use for this.

Table A-2. *Numeric Comparison Operators*

Operator	Description
$x > $y	$x is greater than $y.
$x < $y	$x is less than $y.
$x >= $y	$x is greater than or equal to $y.
$x <= $y	$x is less than or equal to $y.
$x == $y	$x has the same numeric value as $y.
$x != $y	$x does not have the same numeric value as $y.

Don't forget that the numeric comparison needs a doubled equals sign (==) so that Perl doesn't think you're trying to set $x to the value of $y.

Also remember that Perl converts $x and $y to numbers in the usual way. It reads numbers or decimal points from the left for as long as possible, ignoring initial spaces, and then drops the rest of the string. If no numbers were found, the value is set to 0.

Let's see an example—a very simple guessing game. The computer has a number, and the user has to guess what it is. If the user doesn't guess correctly, the computer gives a hint. As we learn more about Perl, we'll add the opportunity to give more than one try, and to pick a different number each game.

```perl
#!/usr/bin/perl -w
# guessnum1.pl

use strict;

my $target = 12;
print "Guess my number!\ n";
print "Enter your guess: ";
my $guess = <STDIN>;

if ($target == $guess) {
   print "That's it! You guessed correctly!\ n";
   exit;
}
if ($guess > $target) {
   print "Your number is more than my number\ n";
   exit;
}
if ($guess < $target){
   print "Your number is less than my number\ n";
   exit;
}
```

Let's give it a few tries:

```
$ perl guessnum1.pl
Guess my number!
Enter your guess: 3
Your number is less than my number
$ perl guessnum1.pl
Guess my number!
Enter your guess: 15
Your number is more than my number
$ perl guessnum1.pl
Guess my number!
Enter your guess: 12
That's it! You guessed correctly!
$
```

The first thing we do in this program is set up our secret number. OK, at the moment it's not very secret, since it's right there in the source code, but we can improve on this later. After this, we get a number from the user:

```
my $guess = <STDIN>;
```

Then we do three sorts of comparisons with the numeric operators we've just seen. We use the basic pattern of the if statement again: if (condition) { action }.

```
if ($target == $guess) {
    print "That's it! You guessed correctly!\ n";
    exit;
}
```

Since only one of the tests can be true—the user's number can't be both smaller than our number and the same as it—we may as well stop work after a test was successful. The exit() function tells Perl to stop the program completely.

Comparing Strings

When we're comparing strings, we use a different set of operators to do the comparisons as listed in Table A-3.

Table A-3. *String Comparison Operators*

Operator	Description
$x gt $y	$x is string greater than $y.
$x lt $y	$x is string less than $y.
$x ge $y	$x is string greater than or equal to $y.
$x le $y	$x is string less than or equal to $y.
$x eq $y	$x is the same as $y.
$x ne $y	$x is not the same as $y.

Here's a very simple way of testing if a user knows a password. (Note: don't use a good password in this program since the user can just read the source code to find it!)

```perl
#!/usr/bin/perl -w
# password.pl

use strict;

my $password = "foxtrot";
print "Enter the password: ";
my $guess = <STDIN>;
chomp $guess;
if ($password eq $guess) {
    print "Pass, friend.\ n";
}
if ($password ne $guess) {
    die "Go away, imposter!\ n";
}
```

Here's our security system in action:

```
$ perl password.pl
Enter the password: abracadabra
Go away, imposter!
$ perl password.pl
Enter the password: foxtrot
Pass, friend.
$
```

This program starts by asking the user for input:

```perl
my $guess = <STDIN>;
```

Just a warning: this is a horrendously bad way of asking for a password, since it's echoed to the screen, and everyone looking at the user's computer would be able to read it. Even though you won't be using a program like this, if you ever do need to get a password from the user, the Perl FAQ provides a better method in perlfaq8. Type **perldoc -q password** to find it.

```perl
chomp $guess;
```

This statement chomps the newline off of $guess. We must never forget to remove the newline from the end of the user's data. We didn't need to do this for numeric comparison, because Perl would remove that for us anyway during conversion to a number. Otherwise, even if the user had entered the right password, Perl would have tried to compare "foxtrot" with "foxtrot\ n" and it could never be the same.

```perl
if ($password ne $guess) {
    die "Go away, imposter!\ n";
}
```

Then if the password we have isn't the same as the user's input, we send out a rude message and terminate the program.

Other Tests

What other tests can we perform? We can test if a variable is defined (it must contain something other than the undefined value) using defined().

```
#!/usr/bin/perl -w
# defined.pl

use strict;

my ($a, $b);
$b = 10;

if (defined $a) {
    print "\ $a has a value.\ n";
}
if (defined $b) {
    print "\ $b has a value.\ n";
}
```

Not surprisingly, the result we get is this:

```
$ perl defined.pl
$b has a value.
$
```

You can use this to avoid the warnings you get when you try and use a variable that doesn't have a value. If we'd tried to say if ($a == $b), Perl would have said

```
Use of uninitialized value in numeric eq (==)
```

So we have our basic comparisons. Don't forget that some functions will return a true value if they were successful and false if they were not. You will often want to check whether the return value of an operation (particularly one that relates to the operating system) is true or not.

Logical Operators

We also saw earlier that we can join together several tests into one by the use of the logical operators. Table A-4 provides a summary of those.

Table A-4. *Logical Operators*

Operator	Description
$x and $y	True if both $x and $y are true$x && $y
$x or $y	True if either of $x or $y, or both are true$x || $y
not $x	True if $x is not true! $x

The operators AND, OR, and NOT are usually used instead of &&, ||, and ! mainly due to their readability. The operator NOT means not, after all. Don't forget there is a difference in precedence between the two—AND, OR, and NOT all have lower precedence than their symbolic representations.

Multiple Choice: if . . . else

Consider these two if statements:

```
if ($password eq $guess) {
   print "Pass, friend.\ n";
}
if ($password ne $guess) {
   die "Go away, imposter!\ n";
}
```

We know that if the first test condition is true, then the second one will not be—we're asking exactly opposite questions: Are these the same? Are they not the same? In which case, it seems wasteful to do two tests. It'd be much nicer to be able to say, "If the strings are the same, do this. Otherwise, do that." And in fact we can do exactly that, although the keyword is not "otherwise" but else:

```
if ($password eq $guess) {
   print "Pass, friend.\ n";
} else {
   die "Go away, imposter!\ n";
}
```

That's

```
if ( condition ) {  action }  else {  alternative action }
```

Like the if statement, those curly braces are required in the else part.

Even More Choices: if . . . elsif . . . else

Some things in life aren't clear-cut. In some cases, we'll want to test more than one condition. When looking at several related possibilities, we'll want to ask questions such as, "Is this true? If this isn't, then is that true? If that's not true, how about the other?" Note that this is distinct from asking three independent questions; whether we ask the second depends on whether or not the first was true. In Perl, we could very easily write something like this:

```
if ( condition1 ) {
   action1
} else {
   if ( condition2 ) {
      action2
   } else {
      if ( condition3 ) {
         action3
      } else {
```

```
        action4
    }
  }
}
```

You might agree that this looks pretty messy. To make it nicer, we can combine the else and the next if into a single word, elsif. Here's what the preceding would look like when rephrased in this way:

```
if ( condition1) {
   action1
} elsif ( condition2 ) {
   action2
} elsif ( condition3 ) {
   action3
} else {
   action4
}
```

Much neater! We don't have an awful cascade of closing curly braces at the end, and it's easier to see what we're testing, and when we're testing it.

Let's look at an example. Most of us will not go outside if it's raining, but we'll always go out for a walk in the snow. We will not go outside if it's less than 18 degrees Celsius. Otherwise, we'll probably go out unless we've got too much work to do. Do we want to go for a walk?

```
#!/usr/bin/perl -w
# walking.pl

use strict;

print "What's the weather like outside? ";
chomp(my $weather = <STDIN>);
print "How hot is it, in degrees? ";
chomp(my $temperature = <STDIN>);
print "And how many emails left to reply to? ";
chomp(my $work = <STDIN>);

if ($weather eq "snowing") {
    print "It's snowing, let's go!\ n";
} elsif ($weather eq "raining") {
    print "No way, sorry, it's raining so I'm staying in.\ n";
} elsif ($temperature  < 18) {
    print "Too cold for me!\ n";
} elsif ($work > 30) {
    print "Sorry - just too busy.\ n";
} else {
    print "Well, why not?\ n";
}
```

Let's say it's 201 degrees, we have 27 e-mails to reply to, and it's cloudy out there:

```
$ perl walking.pl
What's the weather like outside? cloudy
How hot is it, in degrees? 20
And how many e-mails left to reply to? 27
Well, why not?
$
```

Looks like we can fit a walk in after all.

The point of this rather silly little program is that once it has gathered the information it needs, it runs through a series of tests, each of which could cause it to finish. First, we check to see if it's snowing:

```
if ($weather eq "snowing") {
   print "It's snowing, let's go!\ n";
```

If so, then we print our message and—this is the important part—do no more tests. If not, then we move on to the next test:

```
} elsif ($weather eq "raining") {
   print "No way, sorry, it's raining so I'm staying in.\ n";
```

Again, if this is true, we stop testing; otherwise, we move on. Finally, if none of the tests are true, we get to the else:

```
} else {
   print "Well, why not?\ n";
}
```

Please remember that this is very different to what would happen if we used four separate if statements. The tests overlap, so it is possible for more than one condition to be true at once. For example, if it was snowing and we had over 30 e-mails to reply to, we'd get two conflicting answers. elsif tests should be read as "Well, how about if . . . ?"

Another example of using an if/elsif/else is the program we saw earlier, guessnum1.pl. The decision we made in that program was implemented with three if statements:

```
if ($target == $guess) {
   print "That's it! You guessed correctly!\ n";
   exit;
}
if ($guess > $target) {
   print "Your number is more than my number\ n";
   exit;
}
if ($guess < $target){
   print "Your number is less than my number\ n";
   exit;
}
```

Notice that in each if statement we execute the exit() function since, if the condition is true, there is no reason to check any of the following conditions. Instead of using the exit() function in each of the if blocks, this would be better written with an if/elsif/else as shown in guessnum2.pl:

```perl
#!/usr/bin/perl -w
# guessnum2.pl

use strict;

my $target = 12;
print "Guess my number!\ n";
print "Enter your guess: ";
my $guess = <STDIN>;

if ($target == $guess) {
    print "That's it! You guessed correctly!\ n";
} elsif ($guess > $target) {
    print "Your number is more than my number\ n";
} elsif ($guess < $target) {
    print "Your number is less than my number\ n";
}
```

The unless Statement

There's another way of saying if (not $a). As always in Perl, there's more than one way to do it. Some people prefer to think, "If this is not true, then { ... }," but other people think "Unless this is true, then { ... }." Perl caters to both sets of thought patterns, and we could just as easily have written this:

```perl
unless ($a) {
    print "\ $a is not true\ n";
}
```

The psychology is different, but the effect is the same. We'll see later how Perl provides a few alternatives for these control structures to help them more effectively fit the way you think.

Expression Modifiers

When we're talking in English, it's quite normal for us to say

- If this is not true, then this happens, or

- Unless this is true, this happens.

Similarly, it's also quite natural to reverse the two phrases, saying

- This happens if this is not true, or

- This happens unless this is true.

In Perl-speak, we can take this `if` statement:

```
if ($number == 0) {
    die "can't divide by 0";
}
```

and rewrite it using expression modifiers as follows:

```
die "can't divide by 0" if $number == 0;
```

Notice how the syntax here is slightly different; it's action if condition. There is no need for parentheses around the condition, and there are no curly braces around the action. Indeed, the indentation isn't part of the syntax, so we could even put the whole statement on one line. Only a single statement will be covered by the condition. This form of the `if` statement is called an expression modifier.

We can turn `unless` into an expression modifier too, so, instead of this:

```
if (not $name) {
    die "\ $name has a false value";
}
```

you may find it more natural to write this:

```
die "\ $name has a false value" unless $name;
```

Using Short-Circuited Evaluation

There is yet another way to do something if a condition is true. By using the fact that Perl stops processing a logical operator when it knows the answer, we can create a sort of unless conditional:

```
$name or die "\ $name has a false value";
```

How does this work? Well, it's reliant on the fact that Perl uses short-circuited, or lazy, evaluation to give a logical operator its value. If we have the statement X or Y, then if X is true, it doesn't matter what Y is, so Perl doesn't look at it. If X isn't true, Perl has to look at Y to see whether or not that's true. So if $name has a true value, then the die() function will not be executed. Instead, it will do nothing and continue on executing the next statement.

This form of conditional is most often used when checking that something we did succeeded or returned a true value. We will see it often when we're handling files.

To create a positive if conditional this way, use AND instead of OR. For example, to add one to a counter if a test is successful, you may write

```
$success and $counter++;
```

If you'll recall, and statements are reliant on both substatements being true. So, if $success is not true, Perl won't bother evaluating $counter++ and upping its value by 1. If $success was true, then it would.

Looping Constructs

Now we know how to do everything once. What about if we need to repeat an operation or series of operations? Of course, there are constructs available to do this in Perl, too.

In programming, there are various types of loops. Some loop forever and are called infinite loops, while most, in contrast, are finite loops. We say that a program "gets into" or "enters" a loop, and then "exits" or "falls out" when finished. Infinite loops may not sound very useful, but they certainly can be—particularly because most languages, Perl included, provide you with a way by which you can exit the loop. They will also be useful for situations when you just want the program to continue running until the user stops it manually, the computer powers down, or the heat death of the universe occurs, whichever is sooner.

There's also a difference between definite loops and indefinite loops. In a definite loop, you know how many times the block will be repeated in advance. An indefinite loop will check a condition in each iteration to determine whether or not it should do another.

There's also a difference between an indefinite loop that checks before the iteration and one that checks afterward. The latter will always go through at least one iteration, in order to get to the check, whereas the former checks first and so may not go through any iterations at all.

Perl supports ways of expressing all of these types of loops. First, let's examine the while loop.

The while Loop

Let's start with the indefinite loops. These check a condition, then do an action, and then go back and check the condition again. The first one is the while loop. As you might be able to work out from the name, this loop keeps doing something while a condition is true. The syntax of while is much like the syntax of if:

```
while ( condition ) {  action }
```

Once again, those curly braces are required. Here's a very simple while loop:

```
#!/usr/bin/perl -w
# while1.pl

use strict;

my $countdown = 5;

while ($countdown > 0) {
    print "Counting down: $countdown\ n";
    $countdown--;
}
```

And here's what it produces:

```
$ perl while1.pl
Counting down: 5
Counting down: 4
Counting down: 3
```

```
Counting down: 2
Counting down: 1
$
```

Let's see a flow chart for this program. While there's still a value greater than 0 in the $counter variable, we do these two statements:

```
print "Counting down: $countdown\ n";
$countdown--;
```

Perl goes through the loop a first time when $countdown is 5—the condition is met, so a message gets printed, and $countdown gets decreased to 4. Then, as the flowchart implies, back we go to the top of the loop. We test again: $countdown is still more than 0, so off we go again. Eventually, $countdown is 1, we print our message, $countdown is decreased, and it's now 0. This time around, the test fails, and we exit the loop.

while (<STDIN>)

Recall that we talked about using <STDIN> to read from standard input (normally the keyboard). This statement reads the next line of standard input, up to and including the newline character:

```
$line_in = <STDIN>;
```

We can put this assignment within a while loop that will read from standard input until end of file (in Unix a ^D or Ctrl+D; in Windows a ^Z<Enter>). This loop reads a line at a time into $line_in and then prints the line read in:

```
while ($line_in = <STDIN>) {
    print $line_in;
}
```

This behavior, reading from standard input until end of file, is so common that if <STDIN> is by itself within the while loop parentheses (and only within the while loop parentheses), then the line of standard input is magically assigned to the special variable $_. This loop reads each line into $_, and then the line is printed:

```
while (<STDIN>) {
    print $_;
}
```

This is so common that print() defaults to printing $_:

```
while (<STDIN>) {
    print;
}
```

Let's look at an example of using this magic variable $_. This program will loop through standard input one line at a time until end of file, and for each line it will print a message followed by the line entered:

```
#!/usr/bin/perl -w
# while2.pl
```

```
use strict;

while (<STDIN>) {
    print "You entered: ";
    print;
}
```

Following is an example of running this program in Unix:

```
$ perl while2.pl
hello
You entered: hello
world
You entered: world
good
You entered: good
bye
You entered: bye
^D
$
```

The $_ variable is a useful variable—it is the default argument for many different functions. An example is the chomp() function. The statement

```
chomp $_;
```

could have been written as

```
chomp;
```

Many Perl programmers find it convenient and readable to write a loop like this one:

```
while ($line = <STDIN>) {
    chomp $line;
    ...
}
```

using the default nature of $_:

```
while (<STDIN>) {
    chomp;
    ...
}
```

Whether or not you write code to take advantage of the magic nature of $_ is a choice for you to make, but we suggest you practice with it enough to be able to read code that others have written where $_ is used.

Infinite Loops

The important but obvious point is that what we're testing gets changed inside the loop. If our condition is always going to give a true result, we have ourselves an infinite loop. Let's just remove the second of those two statements:

```perl
#!/usr/bin/perl -w
# while3.pl

use strict;

my $countdown = 5;

while ($countdown > 0) {
    print "Counting down: $countdown\ n";
}
```

$countdown never changes. It's always going to be 5, and 5 is, we hope, always going to be more than 0. So this program will keep printing its message until you interrupt it by holding down Ctrl+C. Hopefully, you can see why you need to ensure that what you do in your loop affects your condition.

Should we actually want an infinite loop, there's a fairly standard way to do it. Just put a true value—typically 1—as the condition:

```perl
while (1) {
    print "Bored yet?\ n";
}
```

The converse, of course, is to say while (0) in the loop's declaration, but nothing will ever happen because this condition is tested before any of the commands in the loop are executed. A bit silly, really.

Looping Until

The opposite of if is unless, and the opposite of while is until. It's exactly the same as while (not condition) { ... }. Using the condition in the program while1.pl shown previously

```perl
while ($countdown > 0) {
```

its logical negation would be

```perl
until ($countdown <= 0) {
```

Therefore, we can write while1.pl as

```perl
#!/usr/bin/perl -w
# until.pl

use strict;

my $countdown = 5;
```

```
until ($countdown <= 0) {
    print "Counting down: $countdown\ n";
    $countdown--;
}
```

And here's what it produces:

```
$ perl until.pl
Counting down: 5
Counting down: 4
Counting down: 3
Counting down: 2
Counting down: 1
$
```

The for Loop

Perl has a for loop, similar to the one found in C/C++/Java. Its syntax is

```
for (init_expr; test_expr; step_expr) {
    action
}
```

The init_expr is done first and once. Then the test_expr is tested to be true or false. If true, the action is executed, and the step_expr is executed. Then the test_expr is tested to be true or false, etc.

The most common use of a for loop is as an alternative way of writing a while loop that might resemble this one:

```
$i = 1;
while ($i <= 5) {
    # do something important
    $i++;
}
```

This can be written in a for loop as follows:

```
for ($i = 1; $i <= 5; $i++) {
    # do something important
}
```

The foreach Loop

Perl has another loop called the foreach loop. It is used to loop through lists and arrays. Arrays are discussed in detail in *Beginning Perl*, but since we have seen examples of a list, we can look at the foreach loop processing a list of numbers:

```
#!/usr/bin/perl -w
# foreach.pl

use strict;
```

```
my $number;

foreach $number (1 .. 10) {
    print "the number is: $number\ n";
}
```

The foreach loop executes the body of the loop (the print() function in this example) for each number in the list. $number is called the loop control variable, and it takes on the values in the list, one at a time. Recall that (1 .. 10) is shorthand for (1, 2, 3, 4, 5, 6, 7, 8, 9, 10). This code produces this result:

```
$ perl foreach.pl
the number is: 1
the number is: 2
the number is: 3
the number is: 4
the number is: 5
the number is: 6
the number is: 7
the number is: 8
the number is: 9
the number is: 10
$
```

A note about the keywords for and foreach: they are synonyms for each other. In other words, we can write

```
foreach ($i = 1; $i <= 10; $i++)_ {  .. }
```

and

```
for $number (1..10) {  .. }
```

foreach is rarely used in place of for, but for is often used instead of foreach. In the spirit of minimal confusion, we will spell out foreach when we have a foreach loop.

do .. while and do .. until

When we were categorizing our lists, we divided indefinite loops into those that execute at least once and those that may execute zero times. The while loop we've seen so far tests the condition first, and so if the condition isn't true the first time around, the "body" of the loop never gets executed. There are two other ways to write our loop to ensure that the body is always executed at least once:

```
do {  action }  while ( condition );
do {  action }  until ( condition );
```

Now we do the test after the block. This is equivalent to moving the diamond in our flow-chart from the top to the bottom. Here is an example:

```
#!/usr/bin/perl -w
# dowhiledountil.pl
```

```perl
use strict;

my $i = 1;

print "starting do...while:\ n";
do {
    print "    the value of \ $i: $i\ n";
    $i++;
} while ($i < 6);

$i = 1;

print "starting do...until\ n";
do {
    print "    the value of \ $i: $i\ n";
    $i++;
} until ($i >= 6);
```

Executing this program produces the following:

```
$ perl dowhiledountil.pl
starting do...while:
    the value of $i: 1
    the value of $i: 2
    the value of $i: 3
    the value of $i: 4
    the value of $i: 5
starting do...until
    the value of $i: 1
    the value of $i: 2
    the value of $i: 3
    the value of $i: 4
    the value of $i: 5
$
```

The importance of the do..while and do..until loop is that the body of the loop is always executed at least once.

Expression Modifying

As before, you can use while as a statement modifier. Following the pattern for if, here's what you'd do with while:

```perl
while ( condition ) {  statement }
```

becomes

```perl
statement while condition;
```

Similarly,

```perl
until ( condition ) {  statement }
```

becomes

```
statement until condition;
```

Therefore, this loop:

```
while (<STDIN>) {
    print "You entered: $_";
}
```

can be written as

```
print "You entered: $_" while <STDIN>;
```

Loop Control Constructs

Perl provides constructs to allow us to control the flow of our loops. They allow us to break out of a loop, go to the next iteration of the loop, or re-execute the loop. We'll start with breaking out of a loop.

Breaking Out

last, in the body of a loop, will make Perl immediately exit, or "break out of" that loop. The remaining statements in the loop are not executed, and you end up right at the end. Here is an example of a program that breaks out of the loop when the user enters the text **done**:

```
#!/usr/bin/perl -w
# last1.pl

use strict;

while (<STDIN>) {
    if ($_ eq "done\ n") {
        last;
    }
    print "You entered: $_";
}

print "All done!\ n";

$ perl last1.pl
Songs
You entered: Songs
from
You entered: from
the
You entered: the
Wood
You entered: Wood
```

done
All done!
$

You can use a last in any looping construct (while, until, for, and foreach). However, the last does not work with the do { } while or do { } until loops.

Note that last1.pl could have been written using an expression modifier. It can be argued that this code is a bit more readable:

```perl
#!/usr/bin/perl -w
# last2.pl

use strict;

while (<STDIN>) {
    last if $_ eq "done\ n";
    print "You entered: $_";
}

print "All done!\ n";
```

Going On to the Next

If you want to skip the rest of the processing of the body, but don't want to exit the loop, you can use next to immediately go execute the next iteration of the loop by testing the expression. Here is an example of a program that reads input from the user, and if the line of input is not blank, the line is printed. It the line is blank, then we immediately go back to read the next line:

```perl
#!/usr/bin/perl -w
# next1.pl

use strict;

print "Please enter some text:\ n";
while (<STDIN>) {
    if ($_ eq "\ n") {
        next;
    }
    chomp;
    print "You entered: [$_]\ n";
}
```

Here is an example of running this program in Windows:

```
$ perl next1.pl
Please enter some text:
testing
You entered: [testing]
one
You entered: [one]
```

two three
You entered: [two three]
^Z<enter>
$

Notice that when the user entered a blank line, then the program immediately read the next line of input.

This program could have be written with an expression modifier:

```
#!/usr/bin/perl -w
# next2.pl

use strict;

print "Please enter some text:\ n";
while (<STDIN>) {
    next if $_ eq "\ n";
    chomp;
    print "You entered: [$_]\ n";
}
```

Reexecuting the Loop

On rare occasions, you'll want to go back to the top of the loop, but without testing the condition (in the case of a for or while loop) or getting the next element in the list (as in a for or while loop). If you feel you need to do this, the keyword to use is redo. This is illustrated in this example:

```
#!/usr/bin/perl -w
# redo.pl

use strict;

my $number = 10;

while (<STDIN>) {
    chomp;
    print "You entered: $_\ n";
    if ($_ == $number) {
        $_++;
        redo;
    }
    print "Going to read the next number now...\ n";
}
```

If the user enters the value 10, then the input is incremented to 11 and we jump to the beginning of the block, at which point the value will be chomped (which has no effect on the value since it does not end in newline), and then the value 11 is reported. Executing this program in Windows would look like the following:

```
$ perl redo.pl
5
You entered: 5
Going to read the next number now...
20
You entered: 20
Going to read the next number now...
10
You entered: 10
You entered: 11
Going to read the next number now...
^Z<enter>
$
```

Loop Labels

By default, last, next, and redo operate on the innermost looping construct only. For instance, in this code:

```perl
#!/usr/bin/perl -w
# looplabel1.pl

use strict;

my $i = 1;

while ($i <= 5) {
    my $j = 1;
    while ($j <= 5) {
        last if $j == 3;
        print "$i ** $j = ", $i ** $j, "\ n";
        $j++;
    }
    $i++;
}
```

the last statement within the innermost loop construct (while ($j <= 5)) will last out of the innermost looping construct only. Therefore, each time $j reaches 3 within the inner loop, we last out of the inner loop, increment $i, and go back up to test the expression for the outer while loop. This generates the following output:

```
$ perl looplabel1.pl
1 ** 1 = 1
2 ** 1 = 2
2 ** 2 = 4
3 ** 1 = 3
3 ** 2 = 9
4 ** 1 = 4
4 ** 2 = 16
```

```
5 ** 1 = 5
5 ** 2 = 25
$
```

To make the last statement last out of the outer looping construct, we must label the outer looping construct with a loop label. A loop label is a variable that the programmer creates (it is recommended that you use all uppercase names), followed by a colon, preceding the looping construct. This is illustrated in looplabel2.pl:

```perl
#!/usr/bin/perl -w
# looplabel2.pl

use strict;

my $i = 1;

OUTER: while ($i <= 5) {
    my $j = 1;
    while ($j <= 5) {
        last OUTER if $j == 3;
        print "$i ** $j = ", $i ** $j, "\ n";
        $j++;
    }
    $i++;
}
```

Now, when the last statement is executed, the code jumps out of the outer loop named OUTER:

```
$ perl looplabel2.pl
1 ** 1 = 1
2 ** 1 = 2
$
```

goto

As a matter of fact, you can put a label before any statement whatsoever. If you want to really mess around with the structure of your programs, you can use goto LABEL to jump anywhere in your program. Whatever you do, don't do this. This is not to be used. Don't go that way.

We're telling you about it for the simple reason that if you see it in anyone else's Perl, you can laugh heartily at them. goto with a label is to be avoided like the plague.

Why? Because not only does it turn the clock back 30 years (the structured programming movement started with the publication of a paper called "Use of goto considered harmful"), but it tends to make your programs amazingly hard to follow. The flow of control can shoot off in any direction at any time, into any part of the file—maybe into a different file. You can even find yourself jumping into the middle of loops, which really doesn't bear thinking about. Don't use it unless you really, really, really understand why you shouldn't. And even then, don't use it. Larry Wall has never used goto with a label in Perl, and he created Perl.

Don't. (He's watching.—Ed.)

Summary

This appendix contains lightly edited excerpts from *Beginning Perl, Second Edition* by James Lee (Apress, 2004; ISBN: 1-59059-391-X), the goal being to give you a refresher on some of the basics of Perl. There are still many aspects of Perl you should cover, including many more detailed within *Beginning Perl* that were used in this book. For example, Chapter 4 contains coverage of lists and arrays, Chapter 5 works with hashes, and Chapter 6 describes subroutines and functions. Not to mention the nine other chapters of introductory material on Perl. *Beginning Perl* is a great companion to this book; if you still need assistance with Perl, I recommend picking up a copy of *Beginning Perl*.

Index

forums.apress.com

JOIN THE APRESS FORUMS AND BE PART OF OUR COMMUNITY. You'll find discussions that cover topics of interest to IT professionals, programmers, and enthusiasts just like you. If you post a query to one of our forums, you can expect that some of the best minds in the business—especially Apress authors, who all write with *The Expert's Voice*™—will chime in to help you. Why not aim to become one of our most valuable participants (MVPs) and win cool stuff? Here's a sampling of what you'll find:

DATABASES
Data drives everything.

Share information, exchange ideas, and discuss any database programming or administration issues.

INTERNET TECHNOLOGIES AND NETWORKING
Try living without plumbing (and eventually IPv6).

Talk about networking topics including protocols, design, administration, wireless, wired, storage, backup, certifications, trends, and new technologies.

JAVA
We've come a long way from the old Oak tree.

Hang out and discuss Java in whatever flavor you choose: J2SE, J2EE, J2ME, Jakarta, and so on.

MAC OS X
All about the Zen of OS X.

OS X is both the present and the future for Mac apps. Make suggestions, offer up ideas, or boast about your new hardware.

OPEN SOURCE
Source code is good; understanding (open) source is better.

Discuss open source technologies and related topics such as PHP, MySQL, Linux, Perl, Apache, Python, and more.

PROGRAMMING/BUSINESS
Unfortunately, it is.

Talk about the Apress line of books that cover software methodology, best practices, and how programmers interact with the "suits."

WEB DEVELOPMENT/DESIGN
Ugly doesn't cut it anymore, and CGI is absurd.

Help is in sight for your site. Find design solutions for your projects and get ideas for building an interactive Web site.

SECURITY
Lots of bad guys out there—the good guys need help.

Discuss computer and network security issues here. Just don't let anyone else know the answers!

TECHNOLOGY IN ACTION
Cool things. Fun things.

It's after hours. It's time to play. Whether you're into LEGO® MINDSTORMS™ or turning an old PC into a DVR, this is where technology turns into fun.

WINDOWS
No defenestration here.

Ask questions about all aspects of Windows programming, get help on Microsoft technologies covered in Apress books, or provide feedback on any Apress Windows book.

HOW TO PARTICIPATE:
Go to the Apress Forums site at **http://forums.apress.com/**.
Click the New User link.